Introduction to Sensation/Perception

120596

DONALD McBURNEY
University of Pittsburgh

VIRGINIA COLLINGS
University of Pittsburgh

Prentice-Hall, Inc., Englewood Cliffs, New Jersey 07632

Library of Congress Cataloging in Publication Data

McBurney, Donald, Date
    Introduction to sensation/perception.

    (The Prentice-Hall series in experimental psychology)
    Bibliography: p.
    Includes index.
    1. Perception. 2. Senses and sensation.
I. Collings, Virginia, Date joint author. II. Title.
BF311.M126   152.1   76-28549
ISBN   0-13-496000-9

The Prentice-Hall Series in Experimental Psychology

James J. Jenkins, editor

Printed in the United States of America

10 9 8 7 6 5 4 3 2 1

Prentice-Hall International, Inc., *London*
Prentice-Hall of Australia Pty. Limited, *Sydney*
Prentice-Hall of Canada, Ltd., *Toronto*
Prentice-Hall of India Private Limited, *New Delhi*
Prentice-Hall of Japan, Inc., *Tokyo*
Prentice-Hall of Southeast Asia Pte. Ltd., *Singapore*
Whitehall Books Limited, *Wellington, New Zeland*

Contents

3   SENSORY CODING, 34

4   ENERGY RELATIONSHIPS, 77

5   ADAPTATION, 91

6   INTERACTIONS BETWEEN STIMULI, 104

Acknowledgements

Although it is futile to attempt to acknowledge all of the people who have made a project of this sort possible, we would like to name some of them. McBurney was fortunate to be a graduate student at Brown at a time when Carl Pfaffmann, Trygg Engen, Harold Schlosberg, and Lorrin Riggs were all on the faculty. At Tennessee, William Verplanck's influence was benevolent. At Pittsburgh, besides educating each other, we have learned much from Frank Colavita, Robert Bilger, Bruce Goldstein, and Richard Rosinski. All of these and others have had their influence on this book in various ways. For example, it may have been a discussion with J. C. Stevens that gave us the idea for the organization of the book. We cannot remember. H. W. Leibowitz and Irvin Rock both read virtually the entire manuscript and made many helpful suggestions, most of which we followed. The editorial and production staff at Prentice-Hall have been most helpful and supportive.

We would like to thank all of the authors and publishers who gave us permission to reproduce material. Finally, we gratefully acknowledge the support and encouragement of our spouses, which did not include typing the manuscript, drawing graphs, or reading proofs, for which they are grateful.

D. H. M.
V. B. C.

Introduction

THE STUDY OF PERCEPTION

The purpose of this chapter is to give you an overview of the topic of perception—why you might want to study it and what you can expect when you do. The first reason for studying perception is that it is *intrinsically interesting.* Most people have wondered what causes the sounds heard when you cup your hand or a seashell over your ear, why your orange juice tastes sour after eating Sugar-O's cereal, or why you cannot tickle yourself. If you cannot remember asking these or similar questions, perhaps you have forgotten how curious you were (and children are) about the physical world around you. In answering these and many other questions we think are interesting in their own right, we will often use everyday phenomena to illustrate perceptual principles. We are familiar enough with college students to know that they sometimes suspect their professors of taking an interesting subject and making it dry and dull. On the other hand, the professor's aim is probably to discover what principle lies behind a certain phenomenon and relate it to a larger body of knowledge. In this book we will try to strike a balance between fact, theory, and example.

The second reason for studying perception is historical. Most courses using this book will be taught in psychology departments. But perception is a highly interdisciplinary area, with people trained in physics, chemistry, and physiology all contributing to our knowledge of perception. To many people it seems curious that people called psychologists study the chemistry of the retina or the physics of the ear. But back when psychology was the science of the mind, it seemed important for psychologists to study how the "contents" of the mind got there. The senses were obviously the most important route, if not the only one. This explains why most of those philosophers, physicists, and physiologists whom psychologists claim as their intellectual forebears come from the tradition of perception. It also explains why, when Wundt founded the first psychological laboratory, it was a perception laboratory. When behaviorism took over, it was still necessary to study how certain physical events became stimuli for organisms and why others did not. More modern variations of behaviorism, such as the information processing and the cognitive approaches to psychology, find perception equally fundamental. Today perception forms a relatively smaller part of psychology than it did 75 or even 25 years ago because other areas of psychology have developed in the meantime.

A third reason for studying perception is more philosophical. One basic question of philosophy can be stated simply and naively: how do we know what is real, or how do we gain knowledge about the nature of the world? Without attempting to answer this question systematically we want to demonstrate the importance of a theory of perception in gaining knowledge about the world. This point is well made by the following incident.

In 1796 Maskelyne, the astronomer at Greenwich Observatory, fired his assistant Kinnebrook because of a consistent difference of eight-tenths of a second in their measurements of stellar transits. The method in use at that time required a difficult comparison of information from the eye and the ear. The observer watched the star through a telescope and simultaneously listened to the beat of a clock. The task was to estimate, to a tenth of a second, when the star crossed a line in the telescope. Bessel noticed the report of the incident in the observatory journal. He realized that if the difference between two observers were consistent, it would be possible to eliminate the observer as a source of error by comparing different observers with one another (Boring, 1957). Bessel's resulting "personal equation" is the earliest example of a principle first clearly grasped some time later by the physicist Ernst Mach (1838–1916), namely, that the perceptions of the scientist constitute the subject matter of every science (Mach, 1959). Today, of course, there are more accurate methods of measuring the transit of stars. However, it is still true that what the scientist deals with are his perceptions, that is, *his* response to a pointer on a dial or the color of an indicator dye, rather than the phenomenon itself. The point becomes more obvious when we examine the various ways in which we can *know* something. For example, we may know the temperature of Venus by interpreting radio signals transmitted to earth from a space probe. It is equally true, however, that we know that the ocean contains sodium chloride because it tastes salty and upon evaporation there is a hard residue with a white color and cubical shape that becomes a liquid when it is heated until a dial reads 801°C. Thus, the study of perception should ideally make us aware of the difference between an observer's subjective interpretation of a phenomenon and the phenomenon itself.

It would be desirable to define perception at the outset rather than assume, as we have done so far, that "everybody knows what it is." The difficulty is that no definition of perception is either self-evident or commonly accepted simply because psychology has not yet settled on a uniform language. It is probably impossible and certainly fruitless to define perceptual behavior as if it were distinct from, say, cognitive, emotional, or some other supposed category of behavior. For this reason we will define the field of perception, and the subject matter of this book, as *the study of the processes by which an organism responds to features of the environment with regularities in its behavior.* These processes display several characteristics that typify the behavior that we study in perception.

(1) Perception is *selective.* Although there is an enormous number of environmental cues to which an organism might respond, only a few of these trigger a response at a given time. We see one small region of the electromagnetic spectrum as light but are insensitive to the rest of it without radios or other accessory receptor devices.

(2) Perception is *appropriate* to the environment. The moth is sensitive to the sounds emitted by his predator the bat and the bat in turn uses nonvisual cues to hunt his nocturnal prey.

(3) Perception is *objective.* Except for a relatively small fraction of behavior which we term "perceptual illusions," we respond to the world as it "really is" to a surprising degree. By "really is" we mean that how we see or feel some object by and large corresponds to what a ruler or a balance tells us about it. The commonplace fact that even a four-year-old child can draw lines on a paper to which an adult will respond "house" indicates the extent to which we respond to stimuli as objects.

(4) Perception is controlled by *patterns* in the environment. We respond to distributions of energy rather than the total amount of energy; to shapes, arrays, and sequences of light and sound rather than patches of light or pure tones. Frequently, the precise nature of the pattern to which an animal responds can be specified only by example, as the difficulties that have been encountered in attempting to develop methods for computer recognition of handwriting dramatically illustrate. It is quite easy for one person to read the handwriting of another but it has proved extremely difficult so far to specify what features of the writing the computer should attend to.

(5) Perception is *active.* Animals are seldom totally inactive and spend considerable time in exploring, manipulating, and structuring their environment. When the environment does not provide enough stimulation, people see animals in cloud formations or inkblots, and hear footsteps in dark houses. When people are deprived of patterned

stimuli they begin to respond as if patterns were there. As it is sometimes difficult to separate hallucinations from real events, so is the distinction sometimes made between the environmental pattern and the animal's tendency to respond to that pattern arbitrary. Cats chase mice, but if no mice are available, a ball will do just as well.

The reader may have observed that these characteristics are true of behavior in general and not limited to the field of perception. This simply points up the inadvisability of trying to define perception exclusive of the rest of psychology. Another sort of definition of perception is provided by the outline and contents of the rest of this book.

2
Psychophysics

Every discipline develops specialized techniques to deal with its own particular problems of measurement. In the field of perception these concerns are the subject matter of psychophysics, a specialty that was both named and founded by Gustav Fechner (1801-1887). Fechner was a most interesting person. He was educated in medicine; later he turned to physics and philosophy but he inadvertently became the founder of experimental psychology by trying to prove his philosophical position of panpsychism. His aim was to prove the existence of a relationship between the physical and the mental world by means of a mathematical equation. Not many people are interested in his philosophy anymore, but the basic psychophysical methods we use are those he invented. Many students seem to find this the least interesting part of a perception course; however, we must understand these methods in order to know how perceptual experiments are conducted.

What questions are the psychophysical methods designed to help answer? They fall into several categories: (1) What is the least amount of a certain stimulus energy that can be perceived? This is commonly referred to as the absolute sensitivity of a particular receptor and is of obvious importance in understanding sensory systems. An experimenter might be interested in the effects of listening to loud music on auditory sensitivity. (2) What is the smallest difference that can be perceived between two stimuli? This is the question of differential sensitivity, exemplified by the problem one faces when trying to read an eye chart. (3) When do two stimuli appear the same? When we study the effects of backgrounds of different light intensities on the brightness of targets, we ask ourselves this question. (4) What is the relationship between the intensity of the stimulus and the perception of that intensity? Practically, we may want to find which sound intensity will sound twice as loud as another, or discover the light that will appear twice as bright as a given one.

As we proceed through the various psychophysical methods, keep in mind that they were all designed to answer specific questions of the above sort. Like any set of tools, they are principally of interest for what they do. Many sensory psychologists are very interested in them as any craftsman will be concerned for his tools. A certain number will design and build and many will sharpen them but few find them the source of esthetic pleasure.

ABSOLUTE SENSITIVITY

When a number of intensities of a stimulus are presented to an organism one finds that the intensity of the stimulus to which it almost always responds is much higher than the one to which it almost never responds. The various methods for measuring the absolute threshold (RL, from Ger. *Reiz Limen*, stimulus threshold) are rules for presenting stimuli so as to discover the value of the stimulus that will evoke a response a certain percentage of the time.

The *method of limits* is perhaps the most obvious method. The experimenter increases the stimulus intensity either in discrete steps of constant size or at a constant rate until the subject says *yes*. The threshold is considered to be halfway between the last *no* and the first *yes*. The starting place for each series is varied from one series to the next to preclude the possibility that the subject will respond on the basis of number of presentations, or time, rather than the stimulus itself. This procedure is repeated until enough determinations have been made to take an average (see Figure 2-1). Although the meth-

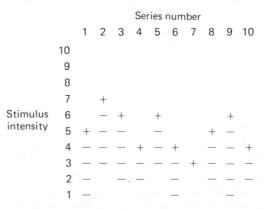

Figure 2-1 Typical threshold data obtained by the method of limits. Only ascending series were employed. The threshold for the series can be obtained by taking the mean of the stimulus intensities at which the first *yes* occurred and subtracting ½ of a stimulus step. In the case of these data, the threshold is 4.5.

Absolute Thresholds for the Various Senses

When we think that each sense organ is a living tissue that must grow, be nourished, and survive the insults to which we subject ourselves, it is amazing that they work at all, let alone last as long as they do. But that is only the beginning. Certain of the senses are as sensitive as they could possibly be from a practical point of view. If our eye were much more sensitive in the infrared range we would be able to see the heat produced by our bodies in the dark (Békésy, 1957). If our ears were more sensitive we would be able to detect the individual molecules of air bouncing off the eardrum (Békésy, 1957). If they were more sensitive to low frequencies we would hear the vibrations of our bodies. As it is we hear the noises produced by the muscles of the arm and hand when we stick a finger in our ear. In the meantime these sense organs must be able to handle energy up to more than a trillion times threshold for brief periods without damage. The skin is particularly amazing in this regard because we use it all the time to handle heavy and rough objects and expect it to discriminate a wool from a double knit suit in the dark. The sense of smell in humans rivals the sensitivity of the best man-made devices. The following table gives some representative thresholds for the various senses and examples.

Some approximate detection thresholds (modified after Galanter, 1962)

VISION	A candle flame seen from 50 kilometers on a clear, dark night (100 quanta to the eye, or 10 quanta absorbed by the rods)
AUDITION	The tick of a watch from 6 meters in very quiet conditions (.0002 dynes/cm^2).
TASTE	*One gram of table salt in 500 liters of water (.0001M).
SMELL	**One drop of perfume diffused throughout a three room apartment, or 1×10^{-12} (.000,000,000,001) Moles/liter of ethyl mercaptan
TOUCH	†The wing of a bee falling on your cheek from a height of 1 cm. (10 mg force)

*McBurney and Pfaffmann, 1963.
**Mozell, 1971.
†Weinstein, 1968.

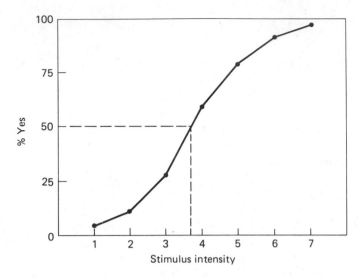

Figure 2-2 Typical threshold data obtained by the method of constant stimuli. The curve crosses the 50% *yes* point at a stimulus intensity of 3.7, which is thus considered the threshold for these data.

od of limits seems simple, it has some inherent problems. First, the subject readily learns the rule the experimenter uses for changing the intensity. He may find it hard to say *no* when he has learned that a stimulus is presented on every trial. On the other hand, if he is uncertain, he may say *no* and wait until the next trial when the stimulus will be stronger. In an attempt to balance out these tendencies, which are called the errors of "anticipation" and "habituation," respectively, some experimenters alternate a descending series with the ascending series. However, because the stronger stimulus may adapt the receptor and raise the threshold, the descending series is not often employed.

In the *method of constant stimuli,* the experimenter chooses a number of stimuli in equal steps covering the range from almost never seen to almost always seen. Each stimulus is presented an equal number of times in irregular order. The threshold is determined by connecting the data points or drawing a smooth curve through them on a graph that plots percent *yes*'s as a function of stimulus intensity. The point at which the curve crosses the 50% *yes* point (or some other arbitrary percentage) is determined by interpolation and called threshold. (Figure 2-2 illustrates this method.)

The *method of adjustment* (or the method of average error) is sometimes used to determine the absolute threshold, although it is used most for other problems. The stimulus is adjusted until it can barely be seen. Either the experimenter or the subject may control the adjustment but it is the subject's task to say when the stimulus is just visible. The stimulus is adjusted from a point above threshold on one trial and below on the next. The advantages of the method are that it seems natural to the subject and yields a value of threshold on every trial. The problems are that the subject's motor abilities are confounded with his sensory capacities and the method is limited to stimuli that are continuously variable such as a light or a tone.

Adaptive Methods

With the methods of limits and constant stimuli a great deal of time is wasted in presenting stimuli to which the subject almost always, or almost never, responds. A number of methods have been designed to allow the experimenter to spend as much time as possible near the threshold. They are called adaptive because the value of the stimulus that is presented on a given trial is determined by the subject's response on the preceding trial, or the preceding few trials, according to formal rules.

With the *staircase method* (Cornsweet, 1962) the experimenter increases the stimulus intensity in equal steps following each *no* response and decreases the intensity after each *yes*. The mean value of all stimuli presented after the first reversal is taken as the threshold. This method is similar to the method of limits and suffers from one of its defects: the subject can easily learn the rules that the experimenter is following. Therefore, Cornsweet recommends running two concurrent staircase series with a given trial, either alternately or randomly, belonging to one of the two series (see Figure 2-3). In this *double staircase method,* the value of the stimulus presented on a given trial is determined by the response on the last trial that belonged to the same series. This makes it difficult for the subject to generate a stable threshold by guessing or by any rule that does not include attending to the stimulus.

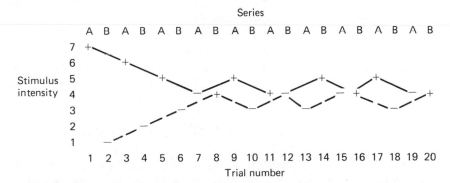

Figure 2-3 Typical threshold data from the double staircase method. The odd trials belonged to the A series and the even to the B. The first reversal for the A series occurred on trial 7 and for the B series on Trial 8. All stimulus intensities presented after those first reversals (i.e., trials 9–20) were averaged to obtain the threshold, which is 4.0.

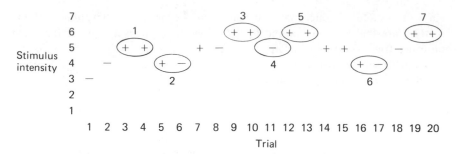

Figure 2-4 Typical data from the Up-Down-Transformed-Response method programmed to track the stimulus giving a 71% probability of response. Those responses that lead to a decision to reverse direction (from increasing intensity to decreasing, or vice versa) are circled and considered as a unit. In order to minimize the influence of the choice of starting point, the first reversal is not counted. An even number of reversals (usually six) yields a reliable estimate of the threshold—in this case, 5.2.

The *tracking method* is useful for stimuli that can be both presented and varied continuously, such as tones and lights. The subject closes a switch when he can hear the tone and opens it when he cannot. A motor drives the intensity down when the switch is closed and drives it up when the switch is open. The value of the stimulus is continuously recorded on a chart. The paper moves at a constant rate and the threshold is recorded over time. In the von Békésy audiometer, the frequency of the tone increases with time and so the subject traces his own audiogram. Because the stimulus is presented continuously, the method is useful only where adaptation is negligible at threshold, as in audition, or where it is the process of interest.

The *up-down-transformed response* (UDTR) method (Wetherill and Levitt, 1965) is similar to the staircase method, except that it is adapted for estimating the stimulus value that will produce some probability of response other than 50%. By decreasing the stimulus intensity after two consecutive *yes*'s and increasing the intensity after any *no*, the stimulus giving a 71% probability of response will be tracked. The "peaks" and "valleys" of the stimulus intensities used are averaged to obtain the desired value (see Figure 2-4). Other rules will allow the experimenter to estimate other probabilities. For example, moving down after every *yes* and up after two *no*'s will track the 29% point.

SIGNAL DETECTION THEORY

So far we have assumed that at any instant there is a stimulus intensity that will be just perceptible, or just above threshold, and that lower intensities of the stimulus will be imperceptible. This *classical* approach assumes that the threshold is an all-or-none cutoff on the continuum of stimulus intensity and that stimuli below threshold have no effect on the sense organ. The fact that a subject sometimes says *yes* to a particular stimulus and sometimes says *no* implies that the threshold changes over time. Therefore, it is necessary to present a variety of stimulus intensities to determine the average location of the threshold. If the subject says *yes* when the stimulus is below the instantaneous location of the threshold, classical theory explains it as guessing. A different approach is that of *Signal Detection Theory* (e.g., Green and Swets, 1966), a method based on decision theory.

The basic ideas of signal detection theory can be illustrated by a practical example. Suppose you were a sonar operator listening for the occurrence of a certain signal. The signal is very weak and there is some background noise present also. Sometimes you will not hear the signal when it is present, and you will sometimes swear that the signal was present when it was not. You will therefore try to form some impression of the likelihood of the signal's occurring. If it is very likely to occur you will probably report that you hear it more often than if you think it is not likely to occur. You will also try to differentiate among the kinds of things you hear, or think you hear. Some of the times when the signal occurs it will sound exactly like no signal was presented. On the other hand, there will be times when the background noise sounds exactly like the signal that you are listening for. Worse yet, there is no way of telling whether it actually was the signal or the noise except by what it sounds like. This may be a little hard to believe, but it is the common experience of one who must pick weak signals out of noise. In fact, signal detection theory was developed to account for the behavior of people in just this sort of situation.

Next, you would decide how important it was to identify each occurrence of the signal. If the signal indicated the presence of any enemy submarine, you would be very interested in detecting all of them. However, it would not be enough to say *yes* to every conceivable signal. Your captain has to account to his superior for the torpedoes fired, so he would not be happy about shooting up every whale or school of fish in the area. There are two possible states of the world—submarine present or not present. You have two possible responses, *yes* or *no*. This allows for four possibilities, each one of which is worth something to you. You can say *yes* when the sub is there and get a hit. You may say *no* when it is there and miss it. The other two possibilities are to say *yes* when there is no sub and waste a torpedo, and to say *no* when no sub is in fact there. The hit and the correct rejection have a positive value for you and the other two, the miss and the false alarm have negative value. If your captain is out to set the record for number of kills, you will err on the side of saying *yes* too often. If he is more interested in saving torpedoes you will be more conservative. It is most important to realize that you cannot conserve torpedoes without missing a few subs and you cannot hit all the subs without destroying a few whales.

Now, if we assume that our listening is divided into a number of trials, we have described the basic signal detection situation. Trials on which no signal is presented are called noise trials. The ones that contain the signal are *signal trials.* The subject, of course, does not know which are which; he only hears something we will call an event, which can be produced by either a signal or by noise alone. The events produced by noise are identical in kind to those produced by the signal. However, certain characteristics are more likely to appear when the signal is presented and certain others are more likely to be produced by the noise. It is the subject's job to decide on the *likelihood* that the event he heard was produced by a signal. Based on this estimate of likelihood, and the *costs* and *payoffs* involved in the various possible *outcomes,* he sets his *criterion* for saying *yes* or *no* to particular events.

The foregoing discussion will serve to introduce the reader to the basic ideas of Signal Detection Theory in an intuitive way. A somewhat more rigorous discussion follows.

Signal Detection Theory dispenses with the concept of threshold and assumes that there is a continuum of events, *e,* any of which can occur in trials that do not contain the stimulus (*noise alone*) as well as in trials in which the stimulus is presented (*signal + noise*). The subject knows only that a particular event, e_k, has occurred but he does not know whether it was produced by noise alone or by signal plus noise. The probability density of event e_k, given that noise alone was presented, is shown by the height of the curve labeled *N,* at that particular point in Figure 2-5. Similarly, the distribution of events produced by signal plus noise is shown by the curve labeled *S + N.* It can be seen that, on the average, signal plus noise gives rise to an event of greater magnitude on the continuum than does noise alone.

The *likelihood ratio,* $1_{(e_k)}$ is the probability of event e_k, given the occurrence of a signal, divided by the probability of the event, given noise alone.

$$1_{ek} = \frac{p(e_k \mid S + N)}{p(e_k \mid N)}$$

Equation 2-1

In the example shown in Figure 2-5, the likelihood ratio is *1* at the point representing event e_k. The likelihood ratio is less than *1* to the left of this point and greater than *1* to the right of this point. The subject can base his decision in part on the likelihood ratio. The larger the likelihood ratio, the greater is the probability that a signal would produce that event, relative to the probability that noise would produce the same event.

The subject must know one more thing before he can decide whether to say *yes* or *no.* That is the relative probabilities of signal and noise in the first place. Remember that the likelihood ratio is the ratio of the probability of a

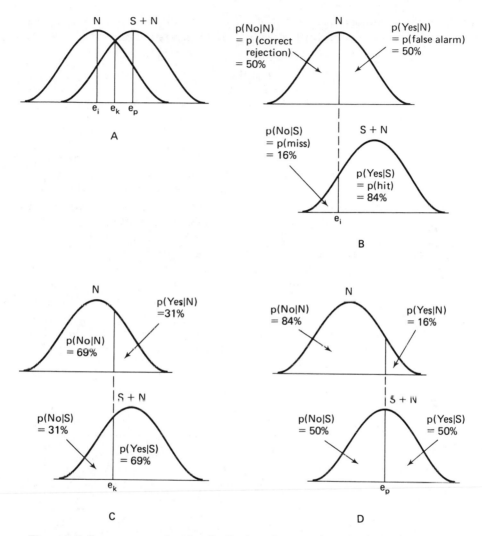

Figure 2-5 Curves representing the distribution of events given signal or noise according to Signal Detection Theory. Figure 2-5a shows the probability-density distribution of the various events given noise, indicated by N, and signal plus noise, indicated by $S + N$. The abscissa represents the event, e.g., e_i, e_k, e_p. The probability of the various outcomes of presenting signal or noise are seen by referring to the two sections of each curve.

certain event, given signal, to the probability of the same event, given noise. These are known as *conditional* probabilities. What we want to know is the probability of a certain event *and* signal relative to the probability of the event *and* noise. These are known as *joint* probabilities and they are obtained by multiplying the conditional probability of the event by the *prior* probability of the signal (the probability of signal in the first place) relative to noise.

$$\frac{p(e_k \cdot S + N)}{p(e_k \cdot N)} = \frac{p(e_k \mid S + N)}{p(e_k \mid N)} \cdot \frac{p(s)}{p(n)}$$

Equation 2-2

What the subject should do is adopt a criterion β, based on the joint probability of signal and the event relative to the joint probability of noise and the event. The value he should adopt is ordinarily *1*; that is, he should say *yes* whenever it is at least an even bet that the event he observed was produced by a signal. If signal and noise are equally likely, then the joint probability of signal is the same as the conditional probability, namely the value of the likelihood ratio. Ordinarily it is possible to think of the likelihood ratio as being related to the event continuum in such a way that events farther to the right have higher likelihood ratios and events to the left have lower likelihood ratios. The subject can adopt a high or low criterion but he would always have to say *yes* to some events that were produced by noise alone. In this situation, there are two possible states of the world (signal or noise) and two possible response alternatives (*yes* or *no*) for the subject. A convenient summary of the situation is provided below.

RESPONSE

		Yes	No
	Signal	p(Yes | S) hit	p(No | S) miss
STIMULUS			
	Noise	p(Yes |N) false alarm	p(No | N) correct rejection

The upper left- and the lower right-hand cells of the table constitute the correct responses and the other two, the incorrect responses. The proportion of the area under each curve that falls above or below the criterion is equal to the probabilities of each of the four possible outcomes when events are presented and the subject must make a decision. This is illustrated by Figure 2-5a. For clarity the two curves are separated and redrawn three times to show what happens to the probabilities of the various outcomes for each of three different criteria. Consider Figure 2-5b. This represents a criterion set at a likelihood ratio of about .6, which corresponds to event e_i. A criterion set at event e_i will divide the noise curve into two equal sections, so the probabilities of correct rejection and false alarm are both equal to 50%. Looking next at the signal curve, the probability of a miss is 16% and the probability of a hit is 84%. A criterion of .6 is a lax criterion and produces many false alarms along with many hits.

Now consider Figure 2-5c. Here the criterion is set at a likelihood ratio of *1*, corresponding to event e_k. This criterion produces a hit rate of 69% and a false alarm rate of 31%. Here the hit rate is lower than it was in Figure 2-5b but the false alarm rate is also lower. Finally, consider Figure 2-5d. Here the criterion is set at 1.6, corresponding to event e_p. The hit rate is now 50% and the false alarm rate is 16%. You will notice that the subject can be strict (adopt a high criterion) or lax (adopt a low criterion) but the best he can do is to trade one sort of error for another. There is no way he can get any hits without also getting some false alarms. Similarly there is no way he can make correct rejections without also making some misses. The best he can do, in fact, is to adopt a likelihood criterion of *1*. Here he is correct on 69% of the signal trials and also on 69% of the noise trials for an average of 69%.

The performance of the subject when he adopts various criteria can be summarized on a graph known as the *Receiver Operating Characteristic,* or ROC curve illustrated in Figure 2-6. The ordinate shows the probability of a hit and the abscissa the probability of a false alarm. The curve in this figure has been constructed from Figure 2-5 by visualizing what happens to the areas under the four sections of the two curves with a change in criterion.

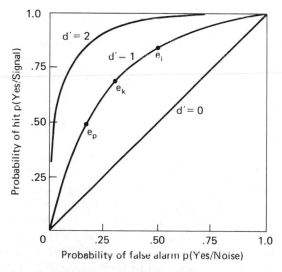

Figure 2-6 Receiver Operating Characteristic, or ROC, curve. The points generated by criteria set at e_i, e_k, and e_p in Figure 2-5 are indicated.

Criteria that are more strict produce points on the lower end of the ROC curve. Criteria that are more lax produce points on the upper end of the ROC curve. The value of the likelihood ratio that the subject adopts as his criterion is equal to the slope of the ROC curve at that point.

The diagonal line shows what the subject's performance would be if he closed his eyes. This is the same as saying that the $S + N$ distribution has the same mean and variance as the N distribution. His hit rate would equal his false alarm rate no matter how conservative or how lax he were. The likelihood ratio would be *1* for every event on the sensory continuum and the slope of the diagonal is, of course, *1* at every point. The curve in the upper left-hand corner shows the ROC curve that would be generated by a stronger stimulus. In such a case, the mean difference between the $S + N$ and N distributions is greater and thus there is less overlap between them. This difference is called d' which is defined as *the difference between the means of the two distributions divided by their (common) standard deviations.* The ROC curves in Figure 2-6 have a d' of 0, 1, and 2, going from the diagonal to the upper left-hand quadrant.

There are two ways the experimenter can manipulate the subject's criterion. The first is to change the probability of signal relative to noise. It will be obvious that the subject will tend to say *yes* more often when the probability of signal is higher. The criterion he should adopt can be predicted from Equation 2-2.

The second way of manipulating the subject's criterion is by altering the values associated with each of the four outcomes. If, for example, the value of a hit is great and the value (cost) of a false alarm is small, the subject will adopt a lower criterion to maximize the *expected value* of his decisions.

Advantages of Signal Detection Theory

The point of this rather involved discussion is that SDT allows one to do something that the classical approach does not, namely, to separate the subject's sensitivity (d') from his criterion (β). It is possible with SDT to compare the sensitivities of a subject who has a strict criterion with one who has a lax criterion even though their percent yesses are very different. It is also possible to compare measures of sensitivity from experiments that employ different psychophysical methods.

Although SDT is a theory of decision making and not a psychophysical method as such, the theory has a number of implications for how a "threshold" experiment should be conducted. First, it is necessary to measure the response probability to noise alone as carefully as the response to the signal, because the sensitivity measure depends as much on the one as on the other. The second implication is that, because the measure of sensitivity is essentially probabilistic, a rather large number of trials must be conducted. Then the standard error of the hit and false alarm proportions will be small enough so that the d' estimate remains stable. Because the number of trials required with the *yes–no* procedure is usually in the hundreds, a single stimulus intensity is generally used for a series of trials.

PROCEDURES COMPATIBLE WITH SDT

The *yes–no procedure* involves the presentation of a single stimulus intensity that has been previously determined to be *neither* almost always *nor* almost never seen; i.e., in the mid-range. A large number of signal trials are randomly interspersed with an equal number of blank (noise) trials.

In order to determine the shape of the ROC curve using the yes–no procedure, it is necessary to manipulate the subject's criterion so that d' may be measured at a number of points on the curve. A more efficient method is possible using the *rating scale procedure,* in which the subject estimates his certainty about the presence or absence of the signal on a given trial. For example, he might say 1 if he were certain that the signal had not been presented, 5 if he were certain it had been presented, and 3 if he were totally uncertain. Each number can be considered to correspond to a different likelihood-ratio criterion concerning the occurrence of the signal. By giving a single number the subject indicates which of the five simultaneously held criteria were exceeded by the event. An event that gives rise to a response of 5, total certainty that the signal occurred, may be assumed to have exceeded the criteria for all the other responses. It is possible, therefore, to construct an ROC curve by using all trials on which a response of 2, 3, 4 or 5 was given, because all of these were produced by events that exceeded the criterion for a response of 2. All of the trials that produced a 3, 4 or 5 may be used to get the point for those events that exceeded the criterion for a 3 and so forth. Because the subject must always say 1, 2, 3, 4 or 5, this point will fall at 1.0 on both axes. It is possible to determine the shape of the whole ROC curve by means of the rating scale procedure in the same number of trials it takes to obtain a single point in the yes–no procedure.

In the *forced choice procedure* there are several (usually two or four) intervals (either space or time) in which the signal may occur on a given trial. Unless a subject has a strong position or interval preference, the task may be considered to involve a comparison(s) of likelihood ratios; i.e., that the event occurring in one interval was produced by a signal over and against the likelihood ratio(s) produced by the event(s) occurring in the other interval(s). The subject chooses the interval with the greatest likelihood ratio. The d' can be obtained from a table relating percent correct to d'. The forced choice procedure is often preferred when the experimenter is interested primarily in the subject's sensitivity rather than his criterion. It is easier for the subject to choose the interval that was most likely to have contained the signal than to maintain a constant criterion over a great many trials as is required by the yes–no method. Any change in the subject's criterion during a yes-no experiment lowers the obtained value of d'.

The forced choice procedure is a very adaptable one. The staircase method and UDTR can be used with forced choice. The adaptive methods, when used with forced choice, allow for efficient collection of data that are expressible in terms of d'.

DIFFERENTIAL SENSITIVITY

The so-called absolute threshold concerns the lower limit of sensitivity to a stimulus. Another important limit of sensitivity is that of sensitivity to changes in a stimulus, the difference threshold (DL, from Ger. *Differenz Limen,* difference threshold). The methods that we use for measuring DLs are basically the same as those for the RL with addition of a standard that is presented along with the variable stimulus on each trial. Any method that asks the subject to discriminate between two stimuli is useable, although sometimes the variability of the responses about the RL or about a point of subjective equality is considered to constitute a DL. The "DL" based on measures of variability is operationally quite different from the traditional definition of DL which is based on discriminability. The DL will be illustrated by some data collected by the method of constant stimuli for lifted weights.

The abscissa in Figure 2-7 shows the values of the comparison stimuli in equal steps above and below the standard. The ordinate gives the percentage of times the variable stimulus is called heavier than the standard. The weight cor-

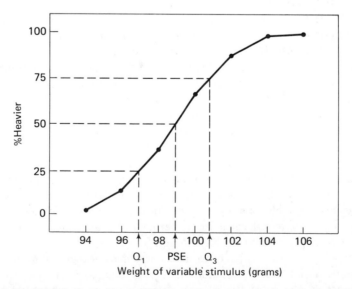

Figure 2-7 Typical data from the method of constant stimuli for the difference threshold. The standard stimulus is 100 grams, the PSE is 99 grams, the time-order error is 1.0 grams, and the DL is 1.8 grams. These data are fictitious.

Using the same materials as in the experiment demonstrating the UDTR method (p. 22), we will illustrate just how efficient the rating scale method is. Take the standard weight and one that has four additional paperclips in it (2% heavier). Blindfold the subject and on each trial present either the standard or the variable stimulus in a random fashion. The subject is to rate the stimulus as the heavier or the lighter one in the following way. He will say '5' if he is certain that it is the heavier one and '1' if he is certain it is the lighter one. He will say '4' if he is moderately certain it is the heavier and '2' if he is moderately certain it is the lighter. He should say '3' if he is totally uncertain. Present the heavier one (the signal) 100 times and the lighter one (the noise) 100 times. Do not tell your subject whether he is right or wrong. From your data sheet make up a table such as the following.

Rating*	5	4	3	2	1
a. Number of calls	40	40	40	40	40
b. Number of calls to heavier stimulus	33	26	20	14	7
c. Probability of this rating, given signal (b/100)	.33	.26	.20	.14	.07
d. Probability of this rating or a higher rating, given signal (Cumulate c, left to right, i.e.: $\Sigma Pc_5 + Pc_4 \ldots Pc_1$	.33	.59	.79	.93	1.00
e. Number of calls to lighter stimulus	7	14	20	26	33
f. Probability of this rating, given noise (e/100)	.07	.14	.20	.26	.33
g. Probability of this rating or higher, given noise (Cumulate f, left to right)	.07	.21	.41	.67	1.00

*These data are fictitious and idealized assuming 100 noise trials and 100 signal trials. In this example $d' = 1$.

Row d gives the hit probabilities for each criterion and row g, the false alarm probabilities. Plot the value of the hit against the false alarm for each of the criteria. Draw a smooth curve through the data points. The likelihood ratio that generated each point can be obtained by taking the slope of the line at that point. The d' for each point can be obtained by converting the probability of hit and false alarms into z-scores. The z associated with the false alarm probability is subtracted from the z of the hit rate to give the value of d'. This process can be done graphically, in which case the z-score for each pair of hit and false alarm probabilities is plotted and a straight line is fit to the points. Then a single value of d' can be computed that represents the whole curve (given certain assumptions.)

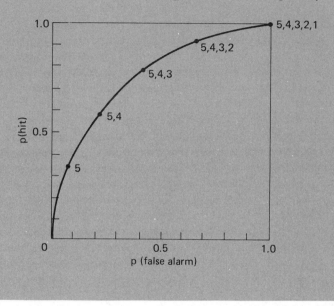

responding to the point at which the curve crosses 50% on the ordinate is the *point of subjective equality* (PSE). One measure of DL is the difference between the PSE and the stimulus that is called heavier 75% of the time. 75% is chosen because it represents half the distance between chance and 100% in a two-alternative forced choice task. Typically, the DL for increases and decreases are averaged together to give a single value of the DL

$$DL = \frac{Q_3 - Q_1}{2}$$

where Q_3 and Q_1 are the first and third quartile, the 25th and 75th percentile, respectively. The difference between the PSE and the standard is known as the *time-order error* or TOE (TOE = PSE - Std) from an earlier theory concerning its mechanism. The PSE always falls below the standard (i.e., a negative time-order error) in experiments employing an intensity dimension. The shape of the percent-correct curve is sigmoid; i.e., S shaped. This curve is often called the psychometric function because of a presumed relationship between discriminability and intensity. Transforming percent heavier to z-scores, or plotting percent heavier on normal probability paper (see Figure 2–8) will produce a straight line, implying that the responses are related to a process that is normally distributed about the PSE. One may fit a straight line to the function either by eye or by least squares and interpolate to find Q_1, Q_3 and PSE (Q_2).

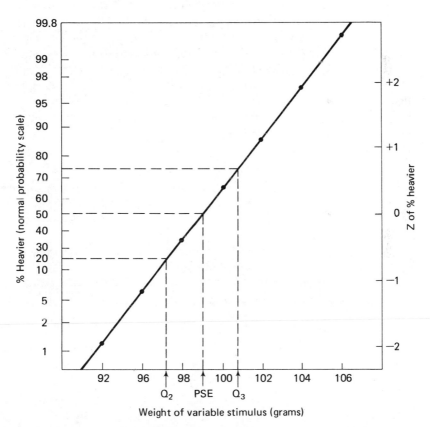

Figure 2–8 Identical data for DL plotted on normal-probability coordinates. Notice that the ordinate is not plotted in constant units of percent but that the scale is compressed near the middle and stretched out at the extremes. If you do not have access to normal-probability graph paper, you can achieve the same result by looking up in a table of the normal curve the z-score that corresponds to the percent heavier for any given weight. Then plot the z-score on the ordinate as has been done on the right-hand side of the figure. The data should approximate a straight line. We have fudged here and chosen data that fall on the straight line exactly. It is this plot of the data that is ordinarily used to determine the PSE and the DL because it is easier to fit a straight line accurately than an ogive (S-shaped curve).

Now that we are able to obtain pure measures of sensitivity by using the insights of Signal Detection Theory, we should use methods that are compatible with the theory unless we are interested only in ballpark estimates. In that case, the method of limits is useful. The yes–no method is the most straightforward application of SDT but it has two drawbacks. First, because the estimates of d' and β must be based on many presentations of a single stimulus intensity, the experimenter must be fairly certain that his choice is neither too hard nor too easy to detect because he must keep it for the duration of the experiment. Second, he should present an equal number of signal and noise trials, usually a minimum of 100 each. The rating scale method is useful when the experimenter wants to know the shape of the ROC curve but many trials are still required. If you are interested only in sensitivity, as is the case in most sensory experiments, then you may use any of the forced choice procedures. By using forced choice, you encourage the subject to maintain a criterion that is free of bias. The forced choice methods are more efficient for estimating d' than the yes–no method.

An ideal method is the UDTR. For absolute sensitivity, present the subject with a two-alternative forced choice between a signal and noise and by varying the stimulus intensity you can track the 71% correct point. The d' of this point will be .78. For differential sensitivity, present the subject with a standard and a variable stimulus and you will have an estimate of the same d'. You can also find the 29% point with the same d', but this will represent decreases from the standard stimulus.

SCALING

The detail with which we have considered the various methods of measuring sensitivity reflects the great deal of attention that this problem has received in psychology. A large number of problems may be addressed by measuring the effect of a particular manipulation on the lower limit of sensitivity. These methods are also adaptable to measuring DLs and equivalencies between stimuli. There are many occasions, however, on which one would like to know not only that a response has occurred or that a stimulus is equal or not equal to another, but how large the response is.

There have been two major approaches to scaling; the first, taken by Fechner, is based on the assumption that it is not possible directly to measure

The purpose of this experiment is to demonstrate the use of the UDTR method for the difference threshold with apparatus that could be obtained easily and/or could be done in class as a demonstration.

Materials. Two containers such as a pair of 250 ml beakers or soup cans, two boxes (200) of paperclips, a scale that weighs in grams, a random order for presenting the standard or the variable stimulus first. Weigh the containers. Add enough paperclips to each one until they both weigh 152 grams. One of these will be the standard weight and the other the variable one. Since they will have slight visual differences, you will need to make sure the subject does not see them. You can arrange a blindfold, but keep in mind that it is very difficult, if not impossible, to blindfold a subject well enough that he cannot peek if he wants to. It would be better to have him place his arm through a hole in a large box or around a barrier to pick up the cans. The reason for using the paperclips is the following. You will be changing the weight of the variable stimulus depending on the subject's response on the previous trial. This can be done easily by adding one paperclip to the can or taking it away to increase or decrease the weight of the can. One paperclip weighs about .76 g so it therefore adds 0.5% to the standard of 152 grams.

Procedure. Have the blindfolded subject rest his arm comfortably on a table. The experimenter will place the two cans, one at a time, on the table within his grasp. Ask him to lift each one once and tell you which one he thinks is heavier.

Begin at some point that seems reasonable to you. You might lift the two a few times with different numbers of paperclips added to the variable in order to get an estimate of where to start. Then follow the UDTR procedure as follows. You add a paperclip after any incorrect trial. If he gets a trial correct, you leave the number of paperclips the same for the next trial. Then, if he gets the next trial correct, take a paperclip away. Continue in this way until you have reversed direction seven times. The first reversal is not analyzed in order to minimize the effect of choosing too heavy or too light a stimulus for your starting point. The value of the stimuli used on those trials at which a reversal occurred are taken and averaged to obtain the estimate of the 71% correct point. The sequence of trials might look like that in Figure 2–4. Seventy-one percent is not the traditional percent chosen for the determination of the DL but it is perfectly good. You can look it up in a table of d' and find that it has a d' of .78.

If you wished to find the DL for decreases as well as increases you would prepare a third container like the first two. You would follow the first tracking procedure until you obtained half of your reversals and then do the lower sequence. Then finish the upper sequence (ABBA). The rule for the lower DL would be like the one for the upper, except that when the subject is correct twice in a row (calls the standard heavier) you will *add* a paperclip to the variable stimulus. You will take away a paperclip after every incorrect response. This would allow you to estimate the time order error and to have an average DL based on both increases and decreases from the standard.

a sensation. Fechner believed he could build a scale of sensation *indirectly* by taking two assumptions, one empirical generalization, and a little mathematics. The empirical generalization was what we call *Weber's law,* that the difference threshold (ΔS) is a constant proportion of the standard stimulus

$$\Delta S = k S$$

If we start at a given stimulus value, say 100 units, and find that ΔS is 10 units, then $k = 1$. Adding the value of ΔS to the first S we get a new standard S, 110. If k is, in fact, constant then the new ΔS is 11. Proceeding in this manner we find that we mark off distances in a geometric progression on the abscissa, i.e., each S is a constant proportion of the one below (see Figure 2–9).

The first assumption Fechner made was that ΔS was a unit of sensation, the just noticeable difference (*jnd*). This assumption, as we shall see later, is highly debatable but it enabled Fechner to put units on the sensation side of his equation, the ordinate in Figure 2–9. The second assumption, also debatable, was that the *jnd*'s could be added up to produce a scale of sensation.

It is apparent that the *jnd* units increase linearly as the stimulus increases geometrically. If the reader is familiar with logarithms, he will recall that geometric increases in a series of numbers will produce linear increments in the logarithms. Thus, taking the logarithm of the stimulus scale, we get the function

$$R = k \log S$$

finding that the response increases with the log of the stimulus. This is *Fechner's law*. We have illustrated it graphically, although we could use calculus as Fechner did and arrive at the same equation. There are several points to be made about Fechner's law. It has been a matter of controversy ever since it was proposed in 1860, the most important objection being that the *jnd* is not a proper unit of sensation. However, it withstood those objections and the alternative laws as long as most people agreed with Fechner that it was not possible to measure sensation directly. It is fair to say that Fechner's law is now primarily of historical importance in perception, although methods based on it are being used fruitfully in other areas of psychology (e.g., Gulliksen, 1968). Theoretical consideration aside, the fact is that cumulating *jnd*'s is a very tedious procedure, and therefore few scales of sensation were ever actually constructed using Fechner's techniques.

Direct scaling. This method has recently gained general acceptance largely as the result of the work of S. S. Stevens (1906–1973). Workers in

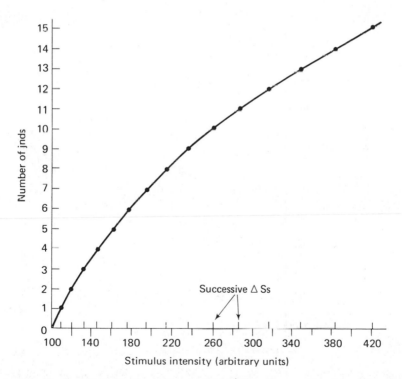

Figure 2-9 Illustration of the cumulation of DLs (ΔS) to form a scale of sensation according to Fechner. The differences between marks are the successive ΔSs. In order to construct the ordinate (Fechner's scale of sensation) the successive ΔSs are considered to correspond to units of sensation, *jnd*'s. By plotting them together, we have the function in the graph.

psychoacoustics had long realized that the decibel scale for sound intensity, which is a logarithmic scale (10 decibels = 1 log unit of energy), did not describe loudness well, as Fechner's law suggests that it should. Fechner's law says that increasing a stimulus by equal ratios will produce equal increments in a sensation. It is obvious that the difference in loudness between a whisper and normal conversation is less than the difference between normal conversation and a subway train. However, the amount of energy in a whisper and in a conversation stand in the same ratio to each other as the energy in conversation to that in a subway train do (Figure 2-10).

Stevens concluded that the proper approach was to ask the subject directly to estimate the apparent intensity of the stimulus (Stevens, 1957). The most common of his methods, known as magnitude estimation, requires the subject

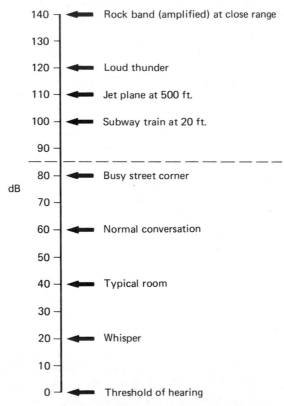

Figure 2-10 The decibel scale. The intensities of various common sounds plotted on the scale indicate that the energy in rock music is 100 trillion times threshold (or more than 100,000 times the intensity at which permanent hearing loss begins to be produced by prolonged exposure)! This level, indicated by the dashed line at 85 dB, is often surpassed by many industrial jobs.

to assign a number to indicate how loud the stimulus seems. The method appears deceptively simple, but there are some general rules for doing a good magnitude estimation experiment. The essence of the technique is that there is no upper or lower limit on the numbers the subject may use. A stimulus may or may not be presented as a standard to which the experimenter assigns an arbitrary number, or modulus, such as 10.

Such experiments done on a very large number of sensory continua have consistently given results that may be described by a power function of the form

$$R = kS^n$$

Equation 2–3

This is *Stevens' law.* Taking the logarithm of this function we obtain:

$$\log R = \log k + n \log S$$

Equation 2–4

This equation says that the logarithm of the response is linearly related to n times the logarithm of the stimulus plus a constant, $\log k$. Recall that equal log steps between two pairs of numbers represent equal ratios between the numbers. Stevens' law says that equal stimulus ratios produce equal sensation *ratios,* in contrast to Fechner's law which says that equal stimulus ratios produce equal sensation *differences.* Data that conform to Stevens' law will produce a straight line when the log of the response is plotted against the log of the stimulus. The slope of the function is given by the value of n, which is characteristic for a given sensory continuum. Figure 2–11 shows some typical functions. n varies between .33 for visual intensity to 2.5 for electrical shock. Changes in modulus affect the value of k but do not affect n, the slope.

Note that Stevens' "law" is strictly an empirical generalization. Stevens assumes only that the subject is able to respond directly to the magnitude of a sensation with the magnitude of a number. Even the reliance on numbers as the dependent variable is not inherent in Stevens' law. Take two continua that have been scaled by magnitude estimation, say, loudness (R_1) and brightness (R_2) to give the following scales:

$$R_1 = S_1{}^n$$

and

$$R_2 = S_2{}^m$$

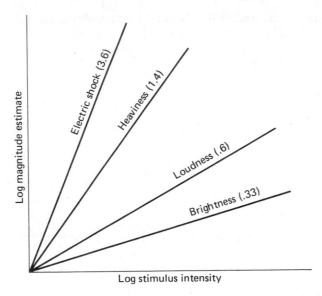

Figure 2-11 Some representative power functions. The log of the magnitude estimate is plotted as a function of the log of the stimulus intensity. The number next to each line is the value of n, the slope of the power function. The slope is obtained simply by plotting magnitude estimates in the figure and then fitting a straight line to the points. The slope is the rise divided by the run; the change in the ordinate divided by the change in the abscissa over any portion of the line. Power functions having slopes less than one are negatively accelerating (concave downward) when plotted in linear (ordinary) coordinates. Those with slopes greater than one are concave upward. Therefore those senses with slopes less than one, e.g. brightness, compress the stimulus continuum and those with slopes greater than one, such as electric shock, expand it. Remember that the dynamic range (the range of intensities to which the receptor responds) is very large for brightness and loudness and that for electric shock is quite small.

When the intensity of the light is adjusted to produce a sensation equal in intensity to that produced by the sound, then:

$$S_1{}^n = S_2{}^m$$

Taking the logarithm of this equation:

$$n \log S_1 = m \log S_2$$

Dividing by n,

$$\log S_1 = \frac{m}{n} \log S_2$$

Equation 2-5

Demonstration of Magnitude Estimation
Using the Apparent Size of Circles

This is a simple demonstration of magnitude estimation that can be carried out in class with minimal equipment.

Materials. On sheets of unlined paper of standard size (21.6 × 27.9 cm) draw circles with the following radii: .8, 1.0, 1.3, 1.6, 2.0, 2.5, 3.2, 4.0, 5.0, 6.3, 8.0 cm. These happen to be in even logarithmic intervals of radius, ten intervals to a logarithmic step. This means that the radius of each circle is the same multiple ($\simeq$ 1.26 times) of the one before and the eleventh stimulus is ten times the first. Because area is related to radius in the following way, $A = \pi r^2$ the range of areas is two log steps (10:1) but the intervals are still logarithmic. In general, you should always choose your stimuli equal logarithmic intervals apart in a perceptual experiment. We have chosen eleven stimuli but any number above six will do. If you have fewer than seven stimuli, the subject may begin to identify individual stimuli and then he might rely on his memory rather than his perception in making his rating. Now randomize your stimuli and identify each with the letters A through K. Only be sure that the one labelled "A" is one of the middle stimuli so that the subject will not start out at an extreme. The best procedure would be for each subject to see the stimuli in a different random order. A class demonstration will, of course, have to skip this nicety.

Procedure. Give each subject a piece of paper with 11 spaces indicated for writing his responses. Read the following instructions to the subjects. "This is an experiment in judging the apparent size of circles. Your job is to assign a number to each one to indicate how *large it appears to you*. You may use any number you wish to indicate the apparent size of the circle, there is no upper or lower limit to the numbers you may use. If one circle appears ten times as large as some other stimulus give it a number ten times as large; if it appears one third as large, give it a number one third as large, and so forth. There are no right or wrong answers, we want to see how large the circles appear to you. Any questions?" Pass the sheets of paper around the class in such a way that each subject sees the circles one at a time in the same order. Collect the data from as many people as you want to analyze; ten is enough. Later, prepare a table, showing the responses of the subjects to each stimulus. Next to each number write the logarithm of the response to each stimulus. Two decimal places is enough for this purpose. Find the mean of the logs of the responses to each stimulus.

Now you are ready to make your graph. Label the X-axis with the log of the radius of each circle (you can use the log of area instead but you will obtain a different slope). Label the Y-axis with the log of the response. Plot the mean log response against the log radius for each circle. With a straight edge, draw a line that best fits the data points by eye. This involves trying to minimize the vertical distance of all the data points from the line you draw. This may sound like a crude procedure but is really pretty accurate. You can do a least-squares fit if you know how and feel like it, but you will be surprised how closely it approximates your "*eyeball*" fit. Now you are ready to find the slope of the line. Slope is defined as the ratio of rise to run, or the ratio of distance along the Y-axis to distance along the X-axis represented by your line. You can also find the Y intercept. Now you can write the equation for apparent size of a circle (assuming that the data fit a straight line!): $\text{Log R} = n \text{ Log S} + \log k$. Or $R = kS^n$. n is your slope and $\log k$ is the Y intercept.

Equation 2–5 says that the relationship between intensities of a sound that will appear subjectively equal to the intensities of a light will be represented by a straight line with a slope of m/n where both coordinates are logarithmic. This *cross modal* matching has been done successfully many times and shows that the method is not dependent on the ability to use numbers, which is of course learned. It also suggests that magnitude estimation is a special case of matching one dimension to another.

A curvature is often seen near threshold in data collected by direct matching procedures, indicating a departure from the power function. It is often possible to correct the curvature by subtracting a constant from the stimulus $R = k(S - S_0)^n$. Because the value of S_0 that will straighten most functions is approximately the same as the absolute threshold, the S_0 correction is sometimes called a threshold correction. A correction applied to the response side will also straighten many functions:

$$(R + a) = kS^n$$

Equation 2–6

This correction implies an intrinsic noise that adds to loudness if the value of a is positive or a physiological masking that reduces loudness if the value of a is negative (Marks and Stevens, 1968a). It is not possible to choose between the $(R + a)$ and the $(S - S_0)$ correction with the degree of experimental resolution now possible. Both types of correction may be warranted in certain cases.

Category scales.   A commonly used scale is the category scale, also called the rating or partition scale. The defining characteristic of this scale is that the experimenter instructs the subject to use a limited range of numbers, such as 1 through 7, to rate the stimulus. Examples of the two extreme stimuli are presented to the subject as anchors. Although the apparent simplicity of partition scales appeals to both subject and experimenter, the fact is that this type of scale produces results that are different from both Fechnerian scales and magnitude scales of many continua. Stevens separates sensory continua into metathetic and prothetic on several criteria. One may think of the metathetic continua as qualitative (pitch, tone, shape) and the prothetic as intensive (loudness, brightness, and size), although the distinction is made operationally. One of the criteria for distinguishing them is the fact that the relationship between category and magnitude scales is nonlinear for prothetic dimensions. The reason the two methods yield different results is not entirely clear but the category scale instructions seem to bias the subject toward attending to discriminability of the stimuli rather than apparent magnitude.

Evaluation of scaling methods.   There is little doubt that Stevens' power function better describes sensory magnitude than does Fechner's logarithmic function. More important than the exact nature of the function, however, is the question of whether to use direct or indirect methods. Stevens argues that the *jnd* is not a proper unit of sensation on which to build a scale. A tone that is 5 *jnd*'s above threshold simply does not sound half as loud as one 10 *jnd*'s from threshold.

The power law has, among other advantages, that of face validity as well as cross-modal validity. It is derived from empirical evidence, which by now has overwhelmingly verified the function. The Fechnerian function is a theoretical one that stands on assumptions that are either demonstrably false (subjective equality of ΔSs) or questionable (Weber's law).

EFFECTS OF CONTEXT

The response to a particular stimulus depends not only on its intensity but on a great many other factors including the other stimuli presented along with or before the stimulus of interest. The Volkswagen ad says, "It makes your house look bigger." According to Helson (1964) the neutral point or adaptation level (AL) of a dimension is a weighted average of (the logarithms of) all stimuli present (X_i) plus the effects of standards (C) and past experiences,

Differential Sensitivity and Slopes of the
Magnitude Functions in Various Senses

The ability to discriminate differences in intensity varies widely among the various senses, as the following table shows. (From Teghtsoonian, 1971)

	Weber fraction	Slope of magnitude function
Electric shock	.013	2.5
Saturation, red	.019	1.7
Heaviness	.020	1.4
Finger span	.022	1.3
Length	.029	1.0
Vibration, 60 Hz	.036	.95
Loudness	.048	.6
Brightness	.079	.33
Taste, NaCl	.083	.41

The Weber fraction (the ratio of the difference threshold to the intensity of the standard stimulus) varies from 1.3% for electric shock to 8.3% for taste. In fact the differences in Weber fractions among dimensions are greater than this because only prothetic (intensive) dimensions are included in the table. If we consider metathetic (qualitative) dimensions, we find that the Weber fraction for pitch is 0.3% (Stevens, 1948), approximately four times better than any of the values listed for the prothetic dimensions in the table. Part of the differences can be attributed to the different tasks that the various senses are designed to perform. The ear is primarily a frequency analyzer and it is not surprising that the Weber fraction is smaller for pitch than for loudness. The senses of taste and smell have large Weber fractions, but intensity discrimination of taste and smell does not seem to be as important to an organism as quality and pleasantness. Teghtsoonian (1971) noticed that there is an inverse relationship between the ability of a given sense to discriminate intensity, as revealed by the Weber fraction, and the slope of the magnitude function. Notice that those dimensions which have large Weber fractions tend to have small slope values and vice versa. He proposed that all senses may have the same range of sensory magnitude regardless of the range of physical stimulus to which they respond. Thus a dimension such as brightness, where the range of stimuli is very large, would have a small slope. Electric shock, which has a small dynamic range of stimuli would have a large slope. He proposed that the Weber fraction is related to the slope because the Weber fraction represents a constant proportional change in sensory magnitude across all senses. Thus dimensions with wide dynamic ranges must spread their discriminability over a greater range of stimuli, hence larger Weber fractions. This is reminiscent of Fechner's theory but does not necessarily argue that he was right in thinking that one could build a scale of sensation based on the difference threshold. The relation of the Weber fraction to the slope of the magnitude scale is somewhat controversial, but is nonetheless interesting.

or residual stimuli (R):

$$\log \text{AL} = \frac{\left(\frac{k_1 \Sigma \log \text{X}_i}{n}\right) + k_2 \log \text{C}}{k_1 + k_2} + \log k_3$$

Equation 2-7

When a subject is asked to rate a set of weights as heavy or light, the ratings will be influenced by the range and distribution of stimuli, the presence or absence of standards, and past experience. The formula above predicts the neutral point (AL), and an equation has been derived (Helson, 1959) to predict the ratings of any stimulus in the series. The theory has been used to describe a very wide range of phenomena, from the original prediction of color constancy to such social attributes as generosity. It should be noted that the farther we get from the data that the theory was devised to describe, the farther we get from adaptation as generally defined (see Chapter 5). Stevens argues that many of the effects predicted by AL theory can be accounted for by (1) modulus changes (a small rock would not be confused with a large grain of sand), (2) the non-linear relationship between category scales, on which Helson relies, and the more valid magnitude scales (Stevens, 1958).

3

Sensory Coding

The understanding of the mechanisms by which an animal is selectively sensitive to different types of stimulus energy is the task of sensory coding. Part of the selectivity is attributable to specialized structures that bring the stimulus to bear on the receptor proper. Thus the eye gathers light and focuses it on the photosensitive rods and cones of the retina, and the ear gathers the vibrations of the air and brings them to bear on the hair cells of the basilar membrane of the cochlea. We will devote considerable attention to these accessory structures because they set limits to our sensitivity and their design is responsible for a number of interesting phenomena. But the basic problem of sensory coding is how the stimulus quality is transformed into the responses of the individual neurons that transmit the sensory information to the brain.

Johannes Müller's (1801–1858) answer was that each nerve carried a single type of information to the brain. His doctrine of *specific nerve energies* accounts for the fact that no matter whether the optic nerve is stimulated by light, pressure, or electricity, the sensation evoked is visual. However, the situation is not nearly this simple! There are about one million optic nerve fibers that must transmit all the data to the rest of the brain—the multitude of shapes, hues, brightnesses, locations, and so forth, which we are able to discriminate. The simple form of the doctrine of specific nerve energies would require a different neuron for every discriminable stimulus. However, when one records the electrical activity of individual neurons one typically finds that any one neuron responds to more than one, and frequently many, qualities of stimulation.

This situation, which was not known to Johannes Müller, will be our starting point.

Before we can proceed to study this problem, it is necessary to mention briefly some principles of sensory neural function. Sensory neurons exist in considerable variety, but it is possible to describe the typical sensory neuron which has the following specific characteristics (Davis, 1961). Cell bodies of sensory neurons generally lie in ganglia near their point of entry into the central nervous system. Thus, in the case of the sciatic nerve which innervates the big toe, a single neuron extends about 1 meter to the spinal cord. There are exceptions to this, in the eye, ear and nose, where the cell bodies of the first-order neuron lie in the receptor itself. In fact, the retina of the eye is actually part of the brain and the optic "nerve" is a tract of the brain rather than a true nerve.

There are specialized receptor cells before the first-order neuron in some senses (vision, audition, taste) that stimulate the neuron across a synapse, whereas in others (touch) the neuron may be directly stimulated by certain stimuli. The dendritic end of the neuron responds to the graded input of the stimulus, whether directly or across a synapse, with a graded generator potential. When the potential reaches the threshold of the neuron, an all-or-none response occurs that is propagated along the axon and results in a graded release of a chemical transmitter at its termination on the next neuron (the synapse). The effect of the release of the transmitter substance at the synapse is to produce an excitatory or inhibitory potential in the next neuron, the excitatory or inhibitory post-synaptic potential (EPSP or IPSP). An axon may terminate on another pre-synaptic axon and produce pre-synaptic inhibition.

Some preliminary considerations are fundamental to an understanding of sensory coding. We must begin with the question of sensory qualities. The approach of earlier investigators was to take sensory quality as the given and to look for the stimulus that produced it, the physiological mechanism that transduced it, and the neuron that conveyed the information to the cortex. The problems with this "primary quality" approach are well illustrated in color vision where a great many different colors can be distinguished and named. Some of these, red, yellow, green, and blue, appear to be "psychological primaries" and others such as orange or greenish blue appear to be a mixture of the primaries. However, it is possible to create the percept of a primary color by mixing two suitably chosen stimuli that by themselves evoke non-primaries. In fact, pure red, which is psychologically primary, is not a spectral hue, but must be produced by mixtures of spectral wavelengths.

Any three suitably chosen wavelengths will serve as "mixture primaries," which can be mixed to produce any hue. It happens that there exist three types of cones in the eye that transduce color but they are not maximally sensitive to the same wavelengths that produce the psychological primaries. In the neural pathway to the cortex there are not three but two kinds of wavelength-sensitive

	Accessory Structure	Receptor Cell	Synapse	Neuron			CNS
Environment				Dendrite	Axon and Cell Body	Synapse	
Energy	Focus, alter, amplify	Receptor potential (graded)	Chemical transmitter	Post-synaptic potential (graded)	All-or-none response	Chemical transmitter (graded)	Further processing
HEARING	ear, including cochlea	hair cell (in cochlea)	(in cochlea)	(in cochlea)	8th nerve	in medulla	dorsal cochlear nucleus of medulla
VISION	cornea and lens	rods and cones	(in retina)	(in retina)	bipolar cell (in retina), *no all-or none response*	in retina	(in retina) the retina is actually part of the CNS.
SKIN	pacinian corpuscle	neuron is receptor	none	within corpuscle	ex, sciatic nerve	in spinal cord	spinal cord
	none	neuron is receptor	none	free nerve ending	ex, sciatic nerve	in spinal cord	spinal cord
SMELL	none	olfactory receptor cell	none	none	olfactory	in olfactory bulb	olfactory bulb
TASTE	none	taste cell	in taste bud	in taste bud	ex, chorda tympani	in medulla	solitary nucleus of medulla

Heuristic table shows the features of typical sensory neuron and the variations among the sensory systems. The first row gives the function of each of the structures. Most of the sensory systems have an accessory structure that serves to bring the energy from the environment to bear on the receptor cell. Then there is a synapse between the receptor cell and the first-order neuron. The all-or-none action potential first appears in the first-order neuron; all other responses up to this point are graded potentials. The all-or-none action potential is an adaptation for transmitting information over long distances.

Notice that all of the structures are not present in each sensory system. Note also that in the visual system the retina actually constitutes part of the central nervous system. The bipolar cell, the first neuron in the visual pathway, surprisingly does not show the all-or-none response. Actually its very short length renders this an unimportant property. (It is somewhat arbitrary whether the bipolar cell is considered the first-order neuron in the visual system. Sometimes the rods and cones are considered neural elements.)

The skin senses differ among themselves in the presence or absence of an accessory structure. The sense of smell has a specialized receptor cell which is part of the olfactory neuron, therefore eliminating the synapse before the CNS. The olfactory nerve is unusually short and it projects to the cortex via the olfactory bulb. All other sensory systems project via the thalamus, which is located deep in the brain. The auditory system is the only "typical" one as far as this table is concerned. It should be noted that the axon of sensory neurons may be very long; as long as 1 meter in the case of the sciatic nerve. The cell bodies of most sensory neurons lie in ganglia close to but outside the central nervous system. Unlike the impression sometimes gained from the picture of the "typical" neuron shown in introductory psychology textbooks, the location of the cell body is unrelated to the origination of the all-or-none action potential. [Modified after Davis, H. Some principles of sensory receptor action. *Physiol. Rev.,* 1961, *41,* 391–416.]

neurons that respond with an increase in firing rate to some wavelengths and a decrease in firing to another. Thus there are two types of opponent process cells in the neural pathway. It is necessary to state whether one is talking about primary stimuli, sensations, receptors, or neurons, and in vision these are all different. In taste, the primary sensation of sour does correspond with the physical dimension of acidity, but not perfectly. In audition, pitch is mostly based on frequency but is also dependent on the amplitude of the signal. Moreover, in audition we talk about volume and density which are really interactions of the primary stimulus dimensions of amplitude and frequency rather than independent dimensions of the stimulus. For these reasons the term primary quality is avoided by researchers in vision, audition, and the cutaneous senses. The belief in primary sensations led to the futile search for receptors that transduce them: receptors in the skin that subserve warmth, cold, touch, and pain, as well as tickle, itch, pinching pain, burning pain, and so on. The modern approach does not begin with the question of psychological primaries but asks what kind of receptor and neural mechanisms will account for the sensory capacities of an organism.

The fact that there are not enough individual neurons to account for each discriminable quality, intensity, location, size, and shape requires that each neuron be able to convey information about more than one aspect of the stimulus. There are several ways to accomplish this. First, a neuron may respond at different rates to indicate some aspect of the stimulus. This is the way that stimulus *intensity* is commonly encoded, as one might expect, although in some sensory systems there are neurons that respond over a relatively narrow range of intensities.

Second, if we take individual neurons in the auditory nerve we find, by recording their electrical activity, that any one neuron will respond to many frequencies if the intensity of the stimulus is great enough. Reducing the intensity, we find that the neuron responds to a narrower range of frequencies. By finding the threshold of the neuron at a number of frequencies we obtain the tuning curve for the neuron, as shown in Figure 3-1. We can see that the neuron will be stimulated by any frequency from 300 to 7000 Hz (cycles per second) if the intensity is great enough. However, it is maximally sensitive to 7000 Hz. Its sensitivity to other frequencies falls between these extremes.

Many sensory neurons show this broad tuning curve. One may take two positions concerning their interpretation. The first is that of neural specificity: the function of the neuron is simply to signal its best frequency, and when it responds to other frequencies it is contributing "noise" to the system. This approach would predicate a neuron for every discriminable stimulus. This is conceivable for some senses like taste and audition, but not for vision. The second position is known as pattern theory or more accurately, across-fiber pattern theory (Pfaffmann, 1959). According to pattern theory, information about quality is conveyed by the relative activity in two or more neurons. Neural activity for taste is illustrated in Figure 3-2. Fibers A and B respond to both sucrose and sodium chloride. However, Fiber A is more responsive to sucrose at all concentrations, and Fiber B is more responsive to sodium chloride at all concentrations. If we look at either fiber alone, all we can say is that it is responding either to sucrose or sodium chloride. However, if Fiber A is responding more than Fiber B then it must be sucrose, and vice versa. In this two-fiber

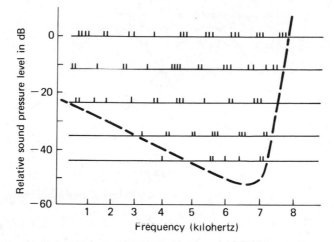

Figure 3-1 Tuning curve of a single auditory neuron. The spikes are responses of the neuron to brief tone pips of varying combinations of frequency and intensity. The dashed line represents the loci of those combinations of intensity and frequency that yield a threshold response. [From Tasaki, I. Nerve impulses in individual auditory nerve fibers of guinea pig. *J. Neurophysiol.*, 1954, *17*, 97–122.]

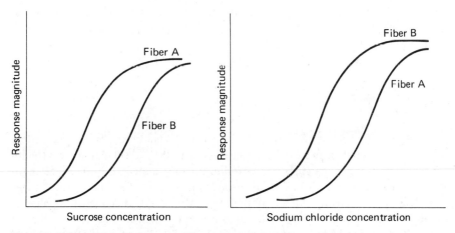

Figure 3-2 Illustration of the across-fiber pattern theory for taste.

theory, the ratio of firing in the two fiber populations could be used to encode all qualities of a stimulus.

Figure 3-3 shows a hypothetical system for discriminating, say, color or pitch. Fiber A is most sensitive to frequency P_1 and Fiber B to frequency P_2. However, the ratio of these response magnitudes is different at all frequencies and could be used to discriminate the entire range of frequencies. The across-fiber pattern theory has at least two advantages over the specificity theory. First, all fibers contribute information whenever they respond and second,

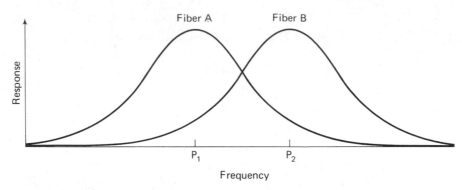

Figure 3-3 Illustration of a hypothetical system for discriminating quality based on across-fiber pattern theory.

fewer fiber types are necessary. Besides frequency of firing, there are many coding mechanisms for which there is at least some evidence (Perkel and Bullock, 1968). These include the latency of the first impulse, variability of response rate including bursting, and other aspects of the temporal pattern. These other types of codes have not received as much attention as the frequency code because of the technical difficulties involved in "cracking" them. They are important, however, in coding some qualities including spatial location and will be discussed where pertinent.

COLOR

The Stimulus for Vision

The term *light* is used to describe electromagnetic energy in the visible range of wavelengths, those approximately from 400 to 700 nanometers (nanometer [nm] = 10^{-9} meters, or one millionth of a meter). Shorter wavelength electromagnetic energy is known as ultraviolet, X-rays, and gamma rays. Longer wavelength energy is known as infrared and radio waves. It is due to the physics of the eye and the chemistry of the photoreceptor pigments in the eye that we see only wavelengths between 400 and 700 nm. We do sense infrared energy as heat, but the other wavelengths are imperceptible without the aid of devices such as the radio. Ultraviolet energy is destructive to living tissue and thus the yellow pigment in the lens of the eye is adaptive in filtering out ultraviolet energy. Persons who have had their lenses removed because of cataracts are actually able to see ultraviolet energy as light. Interestingly, they experience no new color sensation but see ultraviolet as the same color that people with normal vision experience as violet.

Light can also be thought of as consisting of individual packets of energy known as *photons* or *quanta* of light. This helps us understand some of the energy relationships concerning light; for example, the minimum number of quanta necessary for vision will be discussed in a later section.

Measurement of Light

A basic distinction in the measurement of light derives from difference between incident light (that light falling on an object) and reflected light (light reflected from the object). Incident light is referred to as *illuminance* whereas reflected light is termed *luminance*. Consider a projector casting light on a screen. The illuminance, or light falling on the screen, depends partly on the intensity of the lamp in the projector (one common measure of intensity of a light source is candlepower) and partly on the distance of the projector from the screen. As the projector is moved farther from the screen the height and width of the image both increase in direct proportion to the distance. Because area equals height times width, the illuminance of the screen decreases with the square of the distance of the projector from the screen. This relationship is known as the inverse square law and holds for any (point) source of radiant energy including sound energy.

The luminance, or light reflected from the screen, also depends on two factors. The first is the illuminance and the second is the reflectance, or the proportion of light falling on the surface that is reflected from it. White surfaces typically have reflectances of 80% and black around 10%.

Brightness is a psychological term related to luminance. For this reason, it is not proper to use the terms interchangeably because brightness depends on more than luminance; for example the luminance of the surround and the state of dark adaptation of the eye affect the perception of brightness. Notice that luminance, and also brightness, are independent of the distance of the eye from the object. Going back to the projector example, although the illuminance of the screen depends on the distance of the projector from the screen, the luminance and the brightness of the screen are independent of the distance of the eye from the screen (see Figure 3-4).

Color Space

The visible spectrum of electromagnetic energy gives rise to the experience of a number of colors. The dimensions of these sensations are conveniently described by the color solid (Figure 3-5). They are *brightness* along the vertical axis, *saturation* in distance from the vertical axis (radius), and *hue* or location, on a line following the widest point of the solid (circumference). The brightness dimension extends from black at the bottom to white at the top of the color solid. Saturation refers to the purity of the sensation as opposed to grayness. Hue is primarily dependent on wavelength; it is closest to the everyday use of the term "color" meaning red rather than green, for example.

The color solid and a two-dimensional slice through it at its widest point,

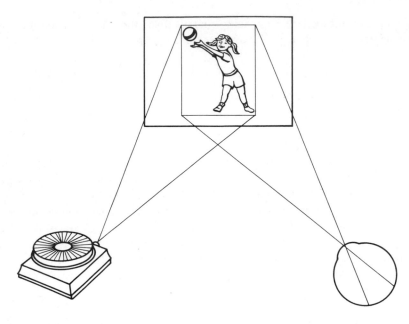

Term	Is a function of	Comment
(Source) Intensity	Nature of source (e.g., tungsten filament), power (e.g., watts)	
Illuminance (e.g., footcandles)	Source intensity, distance of screen from projector (follows inverse square law)	Refers to incident light
Reflectance (albedo)	Properties of the surface	Is a ratio of reflected to incident light
Luminance (e.g., footlamberts)	Illuminance and reflectance (does *not* depend on distance of eye from surface)	Refers to reflected light
Brightness	Luminance, surround, adaptation, etc.	is a *psychological* term all other are *physical*

Figure 3-4 Terms used in the measurement of light.

the color circle, will illustrate several points about color. The fact that the widest part of the solid is not found at the same location on the brightness axis for the various hues illustrates that the most saturated yellow is brighter than the most saturated blue that can be produced.

The reason for bending the spectrum (with the addition of some non-spectral hues) around to form a color circle (Figure 3-6) is to account for the

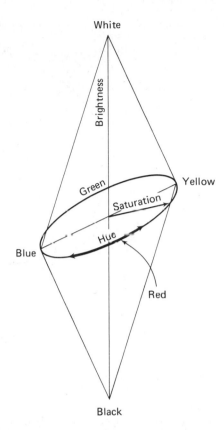

Figure 3-5 The color solid.

facts of color mixing. Color mixing may be demonstrated with a color wheel, a device in which discs of colored papers are fitted together and rotated very fast in order to produce mixtures. Or two slide projectors may be fitted with color filters that pass only certain wavelengths. The different wavelength lights can then be projected on a screen and mixed in various combinations.

Any pair of wavelengths that lie opposite one another on the color circle are known as *complementary*. When complementary colors are mixed the result will contain only the two hues of the components or gray. No new hues will appear. For example, blue and yellow when mixed will look like a bluish yellow or a yellowish blue or gray. New hues can appear only when noncomplementary hues are mixed. It should be noted that although a mixture of blue and yellow may look gray to the eye, the components can still be separated by a prism into the original blue and yellow. However, once a mixture of wavelengths matches another mixture or a pure wavelength, there is no way for the eye to tell them apart. They are identical as far as the visual system is concerned. For this reason we say that vision is synthetic rather than analytic, as is taste or audition. Examples of complementary pairs of colors are yellow and blue, red

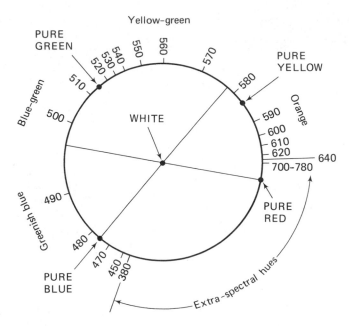

Figure 3–6 The color circle. Note that pure blue and yellow are not exactly complementary. Red is complementary to blue-green.

and blue-green, and orange and green-blue. Two noncomplementaries can be used to mix any hue that falls between them on the circle, but with reduced saturation. For example, mixing red and green results in yellow; blue and green mixed give blue-green. This mixing occurs after the lights are absorbed by the eye. There is no interaction between wavelengths themselves mixed in this way.

This information about additive mixtures may seem inconsistent with what you remember about mixing paints to produce different colors. You have probably mixed yellow and blue pigments when you needed green, for example. The reason that pigments look the way they do depends on the way they absorb and reflect different wavelengths of light. Blue pigment, for example, looks blue because it absorbs most of the wavelengths except those around the blue region of the spectrum, which includes some green. Yellow pigment would absorb most wavelengths except those around the yellow part of the spectrum including some green. When you mix blue and yellow pigments together, you see the green wavelengths, the only ones reflected by both pigments. Pigment mixtures in which colors eliminate each other are therefore called subtractive, as opposed to the additive mixtures we mentioned before. Since subtractive mixtures are not of psychological interest, we will not consider them further.

The color circle also helps to explain *afterimages*. When the eye is adapted to a given wavelength, and immediately thereafter one views a white surface, the complementary color will be perceived. Thus, if you stare at a yellow field for some time and then look at a white surface, you will see a blue afterimage. If on the other hand, you stare at yellow and then look at a blue field, it will appear a more saturated blue.

Notice that although the order of the spectrum is preserved in the color wheel, the relative distance between wavelengths is not preserved. Hue changes very rapidly in the green-yellow region but very slowly in the blue region. Notice also that "pure" red is a non-spectral hue and thus must be produced by mixing wavelengths; the longest wavelength red that can be produced by a single wavelength is rather orange. Purple is also a non-spectral color.

The relationships shown on the color circle may be stated with more precision by means of a chromaticity diagram. This system capitalizes on the fact that any three suitably chosen wavelengths mixed together will match any sample color. (In some cases, the first two are mixed together and then the third is added to the to-be-matched sample.) In a typical color matching experiment, the subject looks at a circular field split in half. The standard, or to-be-matched half, is set by the experimenter at a certain wavelength. The subject adjusts the amount of each of the three wavelengths to be mixed on the other half of the field. The three "primaries" used by the subjects in the chromaticity diagram of Figure 3-7 were 460 nm, 530 nm, and 650 nm. The subject manipulates the amount of each primary added to the mixture through the use of filters which can be set with manual controls. The subject, by trial and error, works out a match between the two halves of the field so that not only hue but also brightness and saturation appear identical.

The choice of the three primaries is reasonably arbitrary as long as the wavelengths are spaced far enough apart and no two are complementaries. Since the proportions, c_1, c_2, c_3 of the three primaries, P_1, P_2, P_3, always add

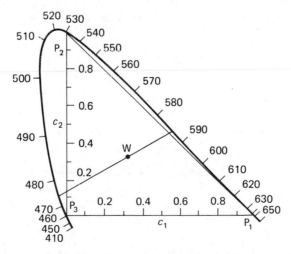

Figure 3-7 A chromaticity diagram. Those hues on either end of a line that passes through W (white) will be complementary. [From Graham, C. H. (ed.) *Vision and visual perception.* New York: Wiley, 1965.]

to 1.0, it is necessary to show only two of the three values in a two-dimensional figure. Thus, when c_1 and c_2 are 0.0, c_3 of P_3 will be one. In addition, the sum of the three coordinates (1.0) will always fall within the triangle. The diagram is intended to describe matches (metamers) between mixed wavelengths and will not necessarily correspond to the observer's concept of color mixing. The locus of spectral hues (i.e., those mixtures that match various pure wavelengths) is shown by the line along two sides of the triangle formed by the coordinates. At each of the corners of the triangle, two of the proportions become zero and the third is 1.0, thus locating the three primaries on the diagram.

Note that the spectrum falls outside the diagram except for the three primaries, at which points it touches the diagram. This illustrates that in order to match the spectral wavelength of 500 nm, one needs 0.75 of P_2, and 0.40 of P_3 but must add .15 of P_1 to the sample to be matched (500 nm.). This can be thought of as subtracting from the mixture so that the mixture of P_2 and P_3 will then match the mixture of 500 and P_1. Figure 3-8 shows the trichromatic coordinates for the spectral hues. This figure is constructed from the matches made by subjects using the primaries derived from the previous diagram. Where the value of one of the coordinates is negative, that primary must be added to the sample to be matched in order that the other two when mixed will match the sample.

What we have said so far about color simply provides a system of describing colors and summarizes some of the facts of color mixing. The means by which hue is encoded in the perceptual process is another question.

Anatomy of the Eye

Each part of the eye is a specialized structure, and together they make up an optical instrument whose sensitivity in some respects approaches theoretical

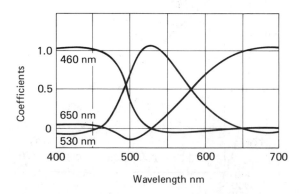

Figure 3-8 The trichromatic coordinates of the spectral hues. This figure shows what proportions of each primary would need to be added together to look the same as the wavelength shown along the abscissa. [From Graham, C. H. (ed.), *Vision and visual perception.* New York: Wiley, 1965.]

limits and which enables us to function well under a wide range of illumination. The structure of the eye is shown in Figure 3-9. The image of an object is formed by the cornea and lens and is imaged upon the retina. Muscles attached to the sides of the lens contract in order to thicken the lens and achieve a clear focus when the stimulus is near and relax when it is far away, a process called accommodation. As a person ages, the lens stiffens and its curvature cannot be changed as much. Thus one needs glasses to supplement the accommodative ability of the eye. Both the cornea and the lens derive their nutriment from the fluids or humors which fill the chambers of the eye. Blood vessels in either of these structures would interfere with their optical properties.

The retina (Figure 3-10) is composed of several types of cells in layers.

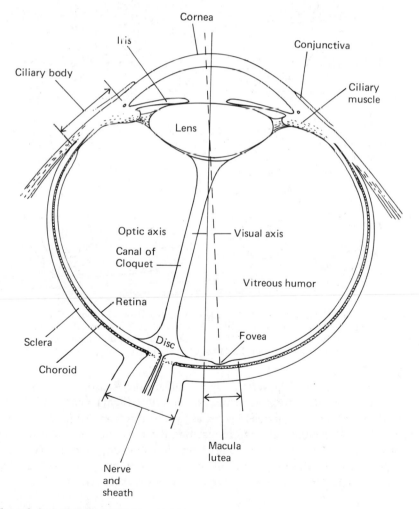

Figure 3-9 A diagram of the human eye.

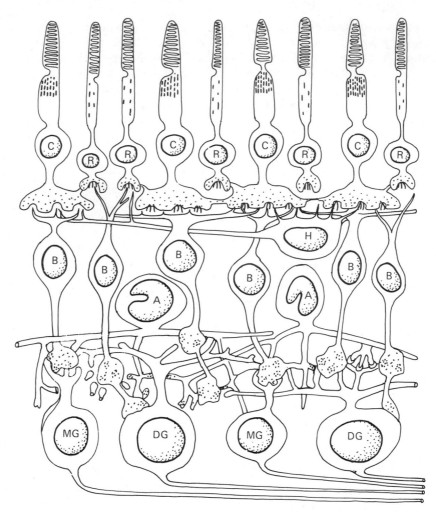

Figure 3-10 The retina. The direction of light would be from bottom (front of the eye) to top. R, rod; C, cone; B, bipolar cell; H, horizontal cell; A, amacrine cell; G, ganglion cell. [From Dowling, J. W. and Boycott, B. B. Organization of the primate retina . . . . *Proceedings of Royal Society*. (London), Ser. B., 1966, *166*, 80–111.]

The retina is considered "inverted" since, unlike other sensory systems, neural structures overlie the receptors. Thus, the stimulus (light) must pass through the ganglion cell and bipolar cell layers, as well as interconnecting cells such as amacrine and horizontal cells, before reaching the rods and cones which are the receptors proper. The excitation begins in the rods and cones and travels through the bipolar cells to the ganglion cells—in the opposite direction from the light stimulation. The ganglion cells are the cell bodies of the neurons whose axons make up the optic nerve. Since the optic nerve is actually part of the central nervous system rather than being peripheral like most sensory nerves, it would more precisely be called a tract.

According to *duplicity theory,* the rods and cones differ in a number of ways, actually yielding two different receptor systems in the eye. The cones, found mostly in the fovea, function under daylight conditions and are completely responsible for color vision. The rods, distributed throughout the retina outside the fovea are much more sensitive to light than the cones and therefore are active during night vision. You may have noticed that you can see a faint star at night only by looking a little to one side of it. Doing this causes the image to fall on the rods rather than on the cones in the fovea.

There are approximately 120 million rods and about 6 million cones in the retina. The fovea is well supplied with bipolar and ganglion cells and thus almost each cone has a "private line" to a fiber of the optic nerve. This relationship is important for visual acuity (see Chapter 4). Outside the fovea there are many fewer bipolar and ganglion cells than rods, and therefore many rods contribute excitation to each ganglion cell. For this reason, visual acuity suffers in the rod-filled periphery of the retina. However, this convergence of rods on ganglion cells is the basis of the greater absolute sensitivity of rod vision. Discussions of spatial summation and of the different photopigments of rods and cones will follow later.

The horizontal cells of the retina provide lateral connections among the receptors, whereas the amacrine cells connect bipolar cells. The importance of these connections to visual function will be discussed in Chapter 7.

The pupil of the eye reacts to the amount of light falling on the retina by expanding and contracting in such a way as to keep the amount of light approximately constant. This feedback mechanism operates within a certain fairly narrow range of illumination (about 16 to one) but the enormously greater variation in retinal illumination (about a billion to one) demands an intermediate mechanism to allow the eye to function over the whole range of illumination. This mechanism of adaptation is discussed in Chapter 5.

Color Theory

Any theory of color must account for a great many facts, including those of color mixture, chromatic adaptation, afterimages, simultaneous contrast, and color blindness as well as color appearances. For many years two positions have dominated color theory. The trichromatic theory, also known as the Young-Helmholtz theory in honor of the men who proposed it (Young, 1773-1829) and developed it in detail (Helmholtz, 1821-1894), capitalizes on the facts of color mixture. It proposes three receptors for color; red, green and blue-violet, which in combination account for all color experiences. The other theory, proposed by Hering (1834-1918), is known as opponent process theory. Hering

"Spots before the eyes." Perhaps you have noticed small dots or wavy lines in front of your eyes when you were gazing at some bright surface such as the sky. These lines are due to impurities floating in the fluids (humors) in the chambers of the eye. These floating bits of tissue cast shadows on the retina and we see them as hovering in space. They generally move when you move your eye since they are more or less fixed in the humor.

"Purkinje tree." When the doctor examines your eye with an ophthalmoscope, he shines a light onto your retina and sees the blood vessels and other structures in your eye. You can look at the blood vessels in your own retina. In a dark room, shine a small flashlight into your eye from above and to the side of your head. You will see what looks like a tree with many branches. These blood vessels are normally not visible even though they are in front of your retina. Since the image of the blood vessels always falls in the same place on the retina, the receptors cease responding to them and you are unaware of them. However, when you shine the light into your eye at a different angle, you cause the image to fall on different receptors and thus you can see the "tree."

"Purkinje shift." If you look at two flowers, one blue and one red, first in daylight and then at dusk, you will notice that under low illumination (1) both appear faded but (2) the blue seems brighter than the red. Likewise, a piece of green paper and a piece of red paper, matched for brightness in good light, will not be matched in dimmer light. The green paper will appear brighter than the red. This is called the "Purkinje shift" after the man who discovered that long-wavelength colors such as red appear duller or darker under low illumination than shorter wavelengths.

The basis of this phenomenon is the shift from high-illumination vision (cones) to low-illumination vision (rods). The rods are relatively more sensitive to light in the blue region than are the cones, thus the apparently greater brightness of the green in dim light.

These relationships are shown in the spectral sensitivity curves below. When one goes from bright light to dim light and the eye changes from cone vision to rod vision, the maximum sensitivity of the eye shifts from red to blue-green; i.e., toward the shorter wavelengths. However, since the rods do not mediate color vision, the blues and greens, although brighter, will appear faded or whitish in color.

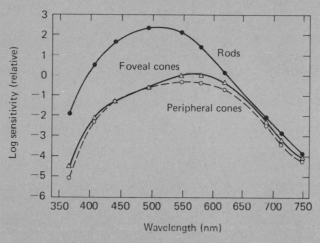

Sensitivity of the eye to various wavelengths of light. The ordinate shows the logarithm of sensitivity (the reciprocal of threshold). The curve connecting the circles shows the sensitivity of the rods and the other two are for cones. Note that the rods are more than two logarithmic units (100 times) more sensitive at their maximum and that the rods and cones have their point of maximum sensitivity in different regions of the spectrum. This accounts for the Purkinje shift. [From Wald, G. Human vision and the spectrum. *Science*, 1945, *101*, 653–58.]

Blindspot. There are no receptors (rods or cones) present at the point where the optic nerve leaves the retina. Therefore, when the image of an object falls on this spot, nothing is seen. This is called the "blindspot." You can demonstrate its presence for yourself by looking at the figure below. Close your left eye and fixate your right eye on the face on the left. Move the book back and forth from your right eye. At between 30 and 40 cm from your eye, the rabbit should disappear. The rabbit is now falling on the blindspot of your right eye.

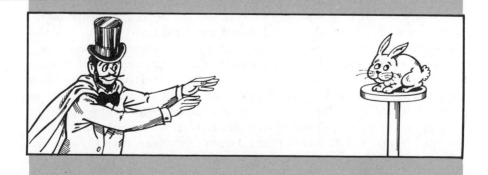

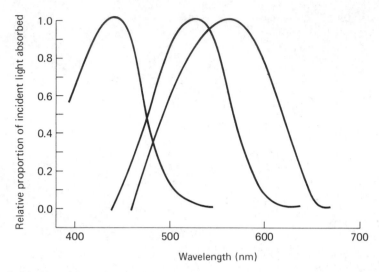

Figure 3-11 Absorption spectra of the three types of cones found in the human retina. [From Wald, G., and Brown, P. K. Human color vision and color blindness, *Cold Spring Harbor Symposia on Quantitative Biology,* 1965, *30,* 345–59.]

conceived of three pairs of mechanisms, red-green, yellow-blue, and black-white. One type of activity would produce red and an opposite activity would produce green.

Today, we think in terms of increases or decreases in neural firing rates. Current theory places more weight on the phenomena of adaptation, contrast, afterimages, and color appearances. For example, since it is impossible to see a mixture of red and green in the same patch of light, these sensations are explained as the result of opposite and incompatible activity in the same system.

There is recent evidence that the initial coding at the receptor level is trichromatic but from the bipolar layer to at least the lateral geniculate body of the thalamus the coding is by opponent processes. It has proved very difficult to extract and identify cone pigments as opposed to rod pigments. Marks, Dobelle and MacNichol (1964) and Brown and Wald (1964) in nearly simultaneous papers reported the results of microspectrophotometry of single mammalian cones. By ingenious procedures these investigators were able to measure the absorption spectra of one cone at a time from (excised) retinas. They found only three types of cones. Figure 3-11 schematizes the maximum absorption of the three types: 447, 540, and 579 nm (MacNichol, 1964). These are in the blue-violet, green, and yellow regions respectively. It will be noticed that these are not the same primaries as in Figure 3-7, but remember that many combinations of primaries will satisfy a three-primary color system.

When we proceed from the receptors to more central structures, the picture changes. Svaetichin (1956) and MacNichol and Svaetichin (1958) found graded potentials in the fish retina that are attributed to the cell layer lying

TETRACHROMATIC VISION

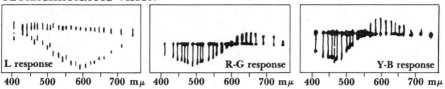

Figure 3-12 Graded response of retinal cells. [Reprinted with permission from Svaetichin, G., and MacNichol, E. F., Jr. Retinal mechanisms for chromatic and achromatic vision, *Annals of the New York Academy of Sciences,* 1958, *74,* 385–404.]

between the cones and the ganglion cell. There were three basic types of response as wavelength was varied as shown in Figure 3-12. The first was the L-type that was of the same sign for all wavelengths. The two other types, the Red-Green and Yellow-Blue, gave hyperpolarization in one end of the spectrum and depolarization in the other, with the location of the maxima determining the type of neuron. This is evidence for an opponent-process mechanism operating very close to the receptor in color vision.

Wagner, MacNichol and Wolbarsht (1960) found a similar situation with the spike activity of the ganglion cell in the goldfish. They found that stimulation at one range of wavelengths produced an increase in activity (on-response) but at another range of wavelengths the ganglion cell responded when the light was turned off (off-response). At the lateral geniculate nucleus of the thalamus, the fourth-order neurons, many of the cells respond in an opponent manner with the maximum either in the red-green or blue-yellow for the excitation or inhibition effect; the (other) nonopponent cells respond to all wavelengths with excitation or inhibition (DeValois, 1965). How the three types of cones are hooked up to the three types of opponent ganglion cells (via bipolar and other cells) to give an opponent-process mechanism is shown in Figure 3-13.

Color Blindness

The discovery of cone pigments led to a better understanding of the visual problem commonly called color blindness. "Color defective" is perhaps a better term since most of these persons are not blind to color but cannot perceive certain parts of the color spectrum. Most color defective persons are male, since this condition is inherited by means of the X chromosome; the male has only one X chromosome while the female has two. Therefore, the female must receive two defective chromosomes to show the trait while the male needs only one. About 10% of all men are color-defective, while only 1% of women are.

The color defective are divided into groups—trichromats, dichromats, and monochromats—depending upon whether they need three, two, or one primary color to match all colors of the spectrum. The person who has normal color vision is a trichromat also, but there are some people who are called anomalous trichromats because they match a yellow by mixing different propor-

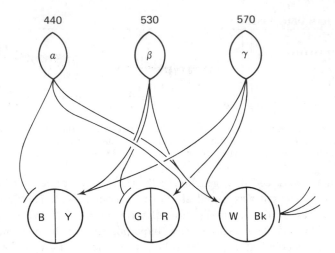

Figure 3-13 Schematic diagram of the relations between the three types of cones and the opponent-process neural mechanisms. The numbers above the cones are the wavelength of their maximum sensitivity. The circles represent the three opponent-process mechanisms; blue-yellow, green-red, and white-black. The lines show the connections between the cones and the mechanisms. One type of connection is excitatory and the other inhibitory; which is which is arbitrary. The connections coming in from the right represent lateral interactions from other similar mechanisms. [From Hurvich, L. M., and Jameson, D. Opponent processes as a model of neural organization. *American Psychologist,* 1974, *29,* 88–102. © 1974 by the American Psychological Association. Reprinted by permission.]

tions of red and green than would a normal trichromat. Some anomalous trichromats require more green and some need more red than normal. There are three types of dichromats; protanopes lack sensitivity in the red end of the spectrum, deuteranopes have a decreased ability to perceive green, and tritanopes are deficient in the blue region. Tritanopia is quire rare. Monochromats, persons who have no color vision, are also very rare and usually have other visual deficiencies.

Anomalous trichromatism affects about six percent of the male population and is the most frequently found type of color deficiency. Since these persons have trouble with red and green, these colors are about the worst possible choices for traffic lights and warning lights of various types. However, since most colors seen in real life are not pure hues but mixtures, there are other clues to help these persons. Green grass for instance reflects some yellow and blue wavelengths along with green. A red ball may appear darker than a blue ball. A color-deficient person learns to associate a particular set of clues with each color name. In fact, some men and women who learn to discriminate and name colors on the basis of such clues during their childhood are quite surprised when they are tested as adults and learn that they do not have normal color vision.

It is difficult to determine what the color defective person actually sees when presented with different parts of the color spectrum. Color experience is not easily communicated (could you describe the color green to someone who is blind?); in addition, it is subject to cultural and psychological distortions. Color-matching experiments provide the most information about color defects. In this type of experiment, the subject might determine the amount of green and red light that must be mixed together to match a standard yellow stimulus. Color matching tells us, for example, that for the protanope there are many proportions of green and red that appear to match the standard whereas for the normal subject, only one combination matches. The protanope evidently has only one (receptor type for red and green) and thus these two colors are not coded independently as they would be in normal color vision. Each type of dichromat lacks one of the cone pigments. In the anomalous trichromat, there is an unusual distribution of the pigments, perhaps a deficiency, but not the complete absence of any of the three pigments.

Trichromatic theory accounts very well for the varieties of color defects. The areas of decreased sensitivity in each type of defect generally correspond to the receptor types of the Young-Helmholtz theory.

AUDITORY QUALITIES

The Physics of Sound

The stimulus for audition is any vibration that will set the ossicles of the ear in motion between about 20 and 20,000 Hertz (cycles per second). Ordinarily this means vibrations of the air but vibrations transmitted through the bones also contribute to auditory sensation. (Having a tooth extracted or drilled will almost convince one that the jaw was designed to transmit vibrations to the ear in the most efficient manner possible.) It is convenient to consider the stimulus for sound to be made up of successive compressions and rarefactions of air that follow a sine wave function over time (Figue 3-14). There are at least two reasons for using the sine function. The first is that a pure tone produced by an electronic oscillator or a theoretically perfect tuning fork is a sine wave. The second, and more important, reason is that theoretically a wave of any shape whatever can be analyzed into components that will be sine waves. This is known as Fourier analysis. Thus, we can say that a sound stimulus is made up

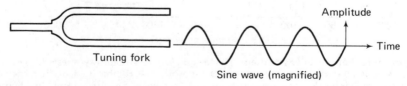

Tuning fork

Amplitude

Time

Sine wave (magnified)

Figure 3-14 Production of a sine wave by a tuning fork. If a tiny stylus were attached to the end of the tuning fork and made to trace a line on a moving piece of paper, the result when magnified would look like the curve in the figure.

of various sine waves having three important parameters (characteristics or values): the frequency, the amplitude, and phase of each sine wave component. The first two are fairly obvious but phase may require some comment. Two sound waves may have the same frequency but be out of phase so that the effect of adding one stimulus to the other will produce a *decrease* in the amplitude of the combined wave because the condensation produced by one sound wave will be counteracted by the rarefaction of the other.

The Sensations of Sound

There are three dimensions of the sensation of sound that correspond in a fairly straightforward manner to physical parameters (and some others that do not). Loudness of the sensation is largely dependent on the amplitude of the wave. However, the ear is not equally sensitive to all frequencies as shown by Figure 3-15. The pitch of the tone depends primarily on the frequency of

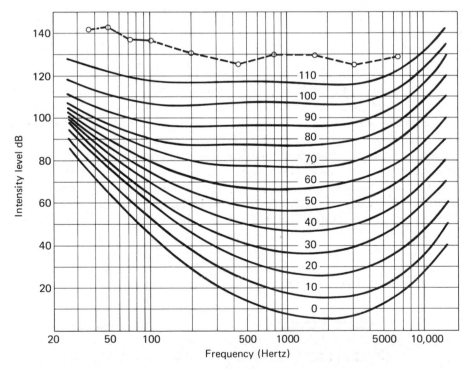

Figure 3-15 Equal loudness contours. The lowest curve is the auditory threshold. The other curves each represent the locus of points for which the combination of frequency and intensity sounds as loud as a particular standard frequency, e.g., 10, 20, etc. dB, above the threshold. The top curve represents the "threshold of feeling," the point at which a sound is felt rather than heard by the ear. [From Stevens, S. S., and Davis, H. *Hearing.* New York: Wiley, 1938.]

We said that the ear performs a Fourier analysis of the auditory stimulus, separating a complex wave into its sine wave components. However, there are certain situations for which this analysis breaks down. One of these is when two stimuli of approximately equal intensity and frequency are presented to the ear at the same time. Instead of hearing both tones, as a linear Fourier analysis should permit, a single tone is heard that varies in loudness in a periodic manner. You have probably heard this when two people sang together or two instruments were played together. The effect can be pleasant or unpleasant depending on the frequency of the beats.

The basis of beats is the following. Take one pure tone of 256 Hz and another of 257 Hz. Each one separately would produce a steady pitch that would be difficult to distinguish from the other. When the two are played together the condensations and rarefactions of the air produced by the two tones will at some point be in phase (synchronised) and the two tones will add together. However, since the frequency of one is slightly greater than the other, they will get out of phase after a while and their effects will cancel each other out. Now, they will come in and out of phase as many times per second as the one tone has more cycles per second. In this example, it would be once per second and so you will hear one beat per second. This provides a very accurate way of measuring the difference between two tones, far better than the ear could discriminate if the two tones were presented separately. This fact is used to good effect by a piano tuner. He tunes one note until it no longer beats with his standard tuning fork. Then he tunes the other notes until their harmonics do not beat with the first note. It is well worth watching a piano being tuned to hear this effect demonstrated. Another easy way of producing beats is singing almost the same note as another person with your mouths close together.

the sound wave, but not completely. Pitch is also dependent on amplitude; the pitch of high-frequency tones will increase with increasing amplitude, but the pitch of low tones decreases with increasing intensity. As described in the section on beats, the loudness of a tone depends on the phase relationships of the component frequencies of the stimulus. Timbre is a quality that depends on the purity of the tone. A tuning fork has a relatively pure tone and therefore little timbre. On the other hand, a piano or other musical instrument has the quality of timbre because of the other frequencies present in the tone.

Some Musical Terms

Each note on the musical scale and on the piano corresponds to a certain frequency. You may have heard an orchestra or choral group tuning to a 440 Hz tone, which is the A above middle C. The letters assigned to notes repeat; the A above middle C (440 Hz) is twice the frequency of the A below middle C (220 Hz)—this doubling of frequency is called an *octave*. Interestingly, these two A's an octave apart sound much more similar than do the much closer A at 440 Hz and B at 500 Hz. No explanation has been found for this phenomenon in what is so far known about auditory coding.

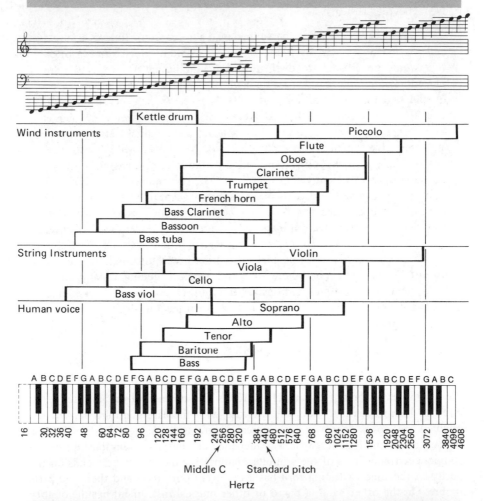

The frequency in Hz of each note on the musical scale in relation to the piano keyboard.

The same note played on the violin, the piano, and the trumpet, does not sound the same. The quality of the sound, or *timbre,* is what enables us to distinguish the three instruments. Timbre is actually due to the complexity or impurity of the sound, but it is very important in music. Among musical instruments the flute makes a sound closest to a pure tone; in the laboratory, a tuning fork is used to produce a nearly pure tone. Since each instrument is constructed in a different way, a different combination of tones results from the playing of one fundamental tone. The frequencies of these tones bear certain mathematical relationships to the fundamental tone. Some are *harmonics* of the fundamental tone—that is, multiples of the base frequency. For example, harmonics of a 200 Hz tone would be 400 Hz, 600 Hz, and so on. In addition to giving each musical instrument a distinctive sound, timbre along with pitch helps us to distinguish one person's voice from another.

That quality of the tone from a stringed instrument which makes the music pleasing to the ear is *vibrato.* An experienced violinist learns to move his hand and wrist in such a way that his moving finger on the string produces a modulation in frequency. The listener hears a rapid variation in pitch.

The modulation in intensity of a tone is called *tremolo.* This effect is employed in organ music where the variation in air supply to the organ pipes actually adds a "trembling" aspect to the music due to the changes in loudness heard by the listener.

Besides these dimensions of sensation that are relatively simple functions of the physical stimulus, there are several others that defy description in simple physical terms. These include volume and density. Low tones of equal loudness seem to occupy more space and thus are said to have more volume than high tones. On the other hand, high tones have greater density than low tones of equal loudness. The volume and density of tones are each a joint function of intensity and frequency of the tones. However, they seem to be as real psychologically as pitch and loudness which have simpler physical bases. By "real," we mean that subjects have no difficulty making reliable judgments of volume or density of tones that differ in frequency and intensity when asked to do so.

Anatomy of the Ear

Unlike the eye where color sensitivity has a chemical basis in the photosensitivity of the cone pigments, the coding of frequency is owing largely to the physical properties of the ear. For this reason a discussion of the structure of the ear is necessary at this point.

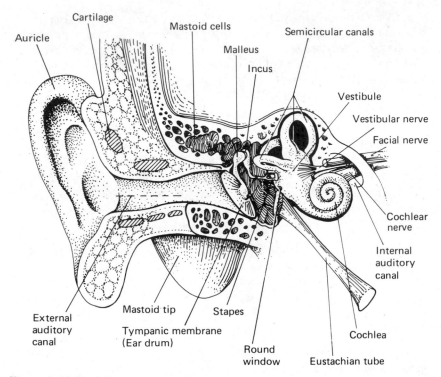

Figure 3-16 Semi-diagrammatic drawing of the ear. [From *Hearing and Deafness,* Third Edition, by Hallowell Davis and S. Richard Silverman, Copyright 1947, © 1960, 1970 by Holt, Rinehart-Winston, Inc. Reprinted by permission.]

The pinna, or outer ear, is largely decorative in man but does serve to gather sound energy in other animals. The tiny bones (ossicles) of the middle ear transmit the vibrations of the air from the tympanic membrane or eardrum to the oval window of the cochlea in an essentially rigid and mechanical manner, but their construction and muscle control allow unwanted vibrations, whether from the head or excessive noise, to be dissipated without being transmitted to the cochlea. The tympanic membrane is much larger than the oval window and the amplitude of movement of each is about the same so that the pressure exerted by the oval window on the fluid of the cochlea is much greater than the pressure with which the air moves the tympanic membrane. Since the fluid is, of course, much more dense than the air, there is a very good impedance match (roughly defined as resistance) between the air and cochlear fluid.

The cochlea, or inner ear, is a coiled canal that lies in the bone of the skull (see Figure 3-16). It is divided into three sections along most of its length by a tube, the scala media, that contains the sensory structures proper. At the tip, the upper portion, the scala vestibuli and the lower, the scala tympani, communicate via the helicotrema.

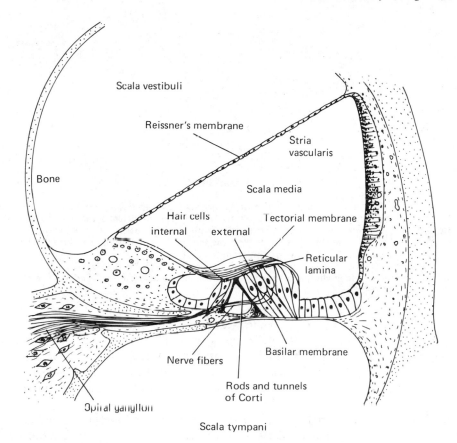

Figure 3-17 Cross section of the cochlea. [From Davis, H., Benson, R. W., Covell, W. P., Fernandez, C., Goldstein, R., Katsuki, Y., Legouix, J. P., McAuliffe, D. R., and Tasaki, I. Acoustic trauma in the guinea pig. *J. Acoust. Soc. America*, 1953, *25*, 1180-89.]

Figure 3-17 shows a cross section of the cochlea. The basilar membrane is set in motion by the fluid of the cochlea. Movement of the basilar membrane relative to the tectorial membrane causes a shearing action on the hair cells that produces an electrical potential, the cochlear microphonic. This in turn is believed to be the stimulus for the auditory nerve fibers that synapse on the hair cells. This potential was first recorded in 1930 by Wever and Bray from the auditory nerve during stimulation of the ear by sound. Later it was discovered that an electrode placed outside the cochlea near the round window could pick up the same potential and reproduce with surprising fidelity the vibrations of the sound to which the ear was exposed. Because of this property, the potential was called the "cochlear microphonic." There is evidence that the source of the cochlear microphonic is the hair cells; however, it has not been established whether the cochlear microphonic represents the receptor potential of the hair cells in the inner ear.

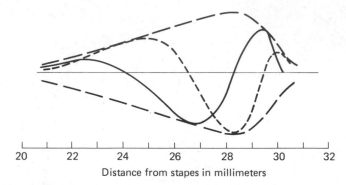

20   22   24   26   28   30   32

Distance from stapes in millimeters

Figure 3-18 The traveling wave. This figure represents the deflection of the basilar membrane as a function of distance from the oval window. The solid line represents the deflection of the membrane at one instant; the line with the short dashes shows the position of the wave shortly afterward. The lines with the longer dashes show the envelope of the wave, the maximum displacement of the membrane at each point along the membrane. The wave moves from the oval window to the helicotrema. [From Békésy, G. von. The variation of phase along the basilar membrane with sinusoidal vibration. *J. Acoust. Soc. America*, 1947, *19*, 452-60.]

The basilar membrane varies in width as it runs the length of the scala media, being narrowest at the oval window and widest at the helicotrema. In addition to this gradation in width, the basilar membrane is stiffer at the base of the cochlea and more flexible at the helicotrema. This property causes the displacement of the fluid at the oval window to produce a wave motion (traveling wave) in the basilar membrane that moves from the base of the cochlea to the helicotrema. The amplitude of the wave increases as it travels from the base until it reaches a maximum and then falls off rapidly, as shown by the envelope of the wave (see Figure 3-18). When the frequency is low the whole basilar membrane is set in motion by the motion of the oval window. As the frequency is raised, the maximum of the traveling wave moves back from the helicotrema, until at very high frequencies only that portion of the basilar membrane nearest the oval window is stimulated. If you were to study successive slices or planes through some of the neural structures to which the auditory nerve projects, you would find that the cells that are maximally responsive to a certain range are located together. Thus, the spatial relationships in the cochlea—high-frequency coding at the base and low-frequency at the apex—are projected onto some higher auditory centers. This is called tonotopic organization.

Recording from a single auditory fiber will give a response profile or tuning curve, as was discussed earlier (see p. 39). The shape of the traveling wave explains why the curve is not symmetrical. The frequency to which the neuron is most sensitive is the frequency that produces a traveling wave whose maximum is located at the point on the basilar membrane that is innervated by that particular neuron. When the frequency is decreased, the maximum of the traveling wave stimulates a point on the basilar membrane farther from the

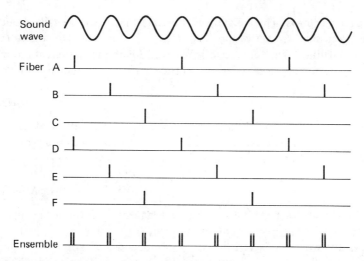

Figure 3-19 The volley principle. The upper trace shows the sound wave to which the ear is responding. At this particular combination of intensity and frequency the individual fibers are unable to respond to each cycle. However, each fiber responds to every third cycle and so the result is a volley of responses at the same frequency as the sound wave even though no single fiber is able to follow the frequency itself.

oval membrane but still stimulates the neuron we are recording from. However, when the frequency is increased, the traveling wave moves back toward the oval window and the amplitude of the traveling wave falls off rapidly beyond its maximum. Thus the threshold of our neuron rises abruptly.

The fibers of the auditory nerve are not able to follow the frequency of a tone above 1,000 Hz. It has been proposed that above this frequency the fibers respond in volleys. Fibers would tend to fire at the same point in the cycle and so even though any single fiber would miss most cycles, an assembly of fibers could follow the frequency of the stimulus tone by the sum of their activity, as shown in Figure 3-19.

TASTE

The term flavor refers to the complete sensory experience of material taken into the mouth and consists of smell, warmth or cold, texture, touch and even pain and visual sensations. It is common knowledge that food seems to have less flavor when a person has a head cold and the sense of smell is reduced. But there are many other, more subtle contributions to flavor. A ripe apple that has recently been bruised repeatedly so that it is mushy will "taste" rotten although the principal difference is in the texture. It is very difficult to identify the flavor of gelatin that has been colored brown with food coloring. The contribution of red pepper to the flavor of foods is largely the result of stimulating pain receptors. These examples illustrate that when we talk about flavor we are discussing an active process involving a number of the traditional sensory modalities. The term taste is reserved for the sensations that are mediated via the taste buds that lie largely on the tongue in the human adult.

Taste Qualities

It is generally agreed that there are only four qualities of taste: salty, sour, sweet, and bitter. All other proposed qualities have been shown to be due to smell, touch, or other sensory modalities.

Taste Stimuli

The stimuli for taste are substances in aqueous solution or readily soluble in saliva, or substances in liquid form, such as glycerine. It is not possible to state exactly what characteristics of a compound will stimulate a particular taste and which will not. The salty quality is typical of salts of alkali metals (such as sodium) and halogens (e.g., chlorine), but not all of these salts are salty and some are bitter or sour. Some non-halogens (sodium nitrate) and some nonalkali metals (ammonium chloride) are salty. The sweet taste is typical of sugars and other carbohydrates, but there are many artificial sweeteners that are not carbohydrates. There is one salt (sugar of lead) that is very sweet (and poisonous!). Sour is the simplest quality to define since it depends largely, although not perfectly, on pH (acidity). The best way to characterize bitter substances is to say that most of them are organic compounds having biological activity, many of them poisonous. However, there are inorganic compounds that are bitter. The bitter taste seems to be a poison detector. In spite of cultural influences that produce preferences for substances like coffee and beer, most bitter substances are rejected by man. If you like some of these bitter things, try to remember your first encounter with them! Thus, unlike vision, audition, and the skin senses where we can easily define the variation in stimulus quality, there does not seem to be a simple physical dimension for taste quality. We will see later that the situation is even worse for smell.

Anatomy of the Taste Receptors

There are four types of papillae on the tongue. One of them, the filiform papillae, is not sensory and serves the same function as the tread on automobile tires. The fungiform papillae (so called because of their resemblance to a mushroom) lie toward the tip of the tongue. They may be seen easily in a mirror, especially if the tongue is coated with a film of milk. The foliate papillae lie along the edges of the tongue about halfway back, and the vallate in a row at the back of the tongue.

The tongue is not uniformly sensitive to taste. The center of the tongue is devoid of taste papillae. Sensitivity to sweet and salty is best on the tip of the tongue. Sour sensitivity is best along the edges, and bitter at the front. It was

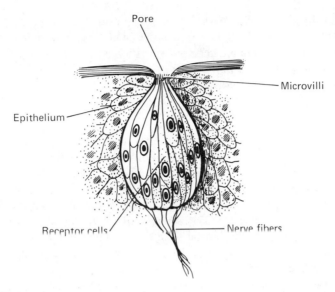

Pore

Microvilli

Epithelium

Receptor cells

Nerve fibers

Figure 3-20 Drawing of a taste bud. There are identifiable differences among cells in the bud but their significance is still unclear. Some may be sustaining cells and not receptor cells. [From Beidler, L. M. Comparison of gustatory receptors, olfactory receptors, and free nerve endings. *Cold Spring Harbor Symposia on Quantitative Biology*. 1965. *30*. 191-200.]

generally believed that the back was most sensitive to bitter but more recent evidence shows that this may be due to inadvertent stimulation of the soft palate, a particularly sensitive area to bitter. These distributions of sensitivity circumscribe areas only relatively; all qualities can be sensed on all parts of the tongue that have papillae (Collings, 1974). A question of some controversy over the years has been whether a single papilla responds to more than one quality. The evidence seems to favor the conclusion that the papillae are not specific for single taste qualities.

Each papilla contains a number of taste buds, about two hundred in the case of the vallate papillae (Figure 3-20). The taste bud itself contains about a dozen cells that are the receptors proper for taste. The taste cells are modified epithelial cells and have a limited life span of about eleven days. Each cell has a small projection (the microvillus) into the pore of the bud where it contacts the taste stimulus. There is a synapse between the taste cell and the taste nerve. The taste neurons branch before entering the taste papilla and branch again inside the taste bud. Thus a single fiber may innervate more than one papilla and a large number of taste cells (Beidler, 1969). The principal taste nerves in mammals are the chorda tympani, which serves the front two-thirds of the tongue, and the glossopharyngeal (IXth) nerve, which serves the back third. These nerves also carry touch and temperature information.

The receptive process in taste apparently involves the adsorption of the taste substance by the taste membrane. As mentioned previously, each papilla seems to respond to more than one taste quality. Electrophysiological recording of individual taste cells shows that each cell also responds to more than one quality. Thus when we recall the considerable branching of each neuron, what is surprising is not that there are very few specific taste neurons, but that we can discriminate tastes at all. A pattern theory such as that illustrated in Figure 3-2 is required to account for the data.

Taste Modifiers

There are several substances that alter the taste of certain other substances in specific ways. These "taste-modifying" substances are of interest for the information they provide about the quality coding mechanism for taste. The taste-altering properties of the leaves of the plant *Gymnema sylvestre* were discovered many years ago in tropical regions of the world but have only recently been studied systematically. The application of the active principle of this plant, gymnemic acid, to the tongue selectively eliminates the sweet taste without affecting sour, bitter, or salty. Thus, after gymnemic acid, granular sugar placed on the tongue is as tasteless as grains of sand.

The berry of an African plant with taste-modifying properties is called "miracle fruit." A substance isolated from these berries, when applied to the tongue, makes sour substances taste sweet. The natives of Nigeria and Ghana chew miracle fruit berries before eating their sour maize bread or drinking sour palm wine or beer. Taste qualities other than sour are not affected.

Flavor enhancers such as monosodium glutamate (MSG) have an effect on the taste of foods but not on simple chemical solutions. MSG is used extensively in Oriental recipes. It makes foods more palatable, presumably by accentuating the flavors that are present. Whether this seeming enhancement is the result of an actual change in the food taste or the addition of a taste such as salty has not been determined.

OLFACTION

For a number of technical reasons, less is known about olfaction than any of the other sensory systems. First, the receptors are hidden deep in the head and are difficult to get at. Then the aerodynamics of the nasal cavity makes it difficult to present a known quantity of stimulus to the receptor. Also, the receptors are very tiny and are thus difficult to record from. Finally, researchers have not been able to analyze the qualities of smell sensations into a small number of types so that the development of a coding theory has been thus far impossible.

Olfactory Stimuli

The stimuli for smell are airborne molecules of volatile substances that are either water or fat soluble. As with taste, it is not possible to state the physical or chemical basis for olfactory quality. Many compounds that have similar smells have dissimilar chemical structures. In general the more volatile a substance, the more odorous it is, but notable exceptions are the musks which are very good olfactory stimuli but have very low volatility.

Olfactory Qualities

A number of attempts have been made to categorize odors into a small number of types. The most recent system is that of Amoore (1962a), who proposed seven categories—camphoraceous, pungent, ethereal, floral, pepperminty, musky, and putrid. However, further work has convinced Amoore that these may not be primary odors, but rather classes of odors, since many kinds of floral odors, for example, may be distinguished. It has not been possible to match odor samples by using mixtures of odors from these seven categories. For this reason there may be a large number of primary odors.

The Olfactory Receptor

The olfactory epithelium lies in the upper part of the nasal cavity. It covers about 5 cm^2 in man on each of the two cavities (Moulton and Beidler, 1967). Turbinate bones project into the nasal cavity and direct most of the air below the level of the receptors during nasal breathing. During sniffing or when air refluxes from the mouth, eddy currents carry more of the odorant to the receptors. The eddying of the air in the nasal cavity makes it practically impossible to state exactly what amount of the stimulus has reached the receptor.

The olfactory epithelium is a relatively simple structure compared to the retina but it is not well understood. The receptors proper are the olfactory cells which project into the mucous layer where they contact the stimulus. The cells send very fine fibers through the cribiform plate of the skull into the olfactory bulb. Thus, there are no specialized receptors and no synapses before the bulb. The olfactory cells have cilia that serve to enlarge the surface area of the cell enormously so that it is about the same as the total skin area for man. A generalized diagram of the mammalian olfactory epithelium is shown in Figure 3-21.

The passage of odor-laden air over the olfactory mucosa gives rise to a slow negative potential that may be recorded from the mucosa, the electro-olfactogram (EOG). There is debate about the nature of the EOG, but it is believed by some to represent at least in part the generator potential that initiates the nerve impulse in the olfactory cells. All-or-none activity has been recorded from the mucosa that is believed to arise from the olfactory cells. The activity of the olfactory nerve has been recorded as well as that of the structures in the olfactory bulb.

Theories of Olfactory Coding

There have been several types of theories proposed to account for the coding of olfactory quality information. Radiation theories propose that the

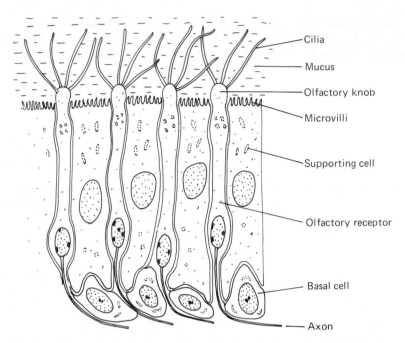

Figure 3-21 The olfactory epithelium. [From Moulton, D. G., and Beidler, L. M. Structure and function in the peripheral olfactory system. *Physiol. Rev.,* 1967, *47,* 1-52.]

frequency and intensity of oscillations within an odor molecule stimulate the olfactory receptor in a certain way and this determines how each odor is coded.

The sterochemical theory of Amoore (1962b) originally stated that each type of odorant had a distinctive shape and size which snugly fit into a receptor site on the olfactory epithelium. This theory was later modified on the basis of experimental evidence so as not to require the fit of the whole molecule into specific receptor sites.

A gas chromatographic model of olfaction (Mozell, 1966) has been suggested based on spatiotemporal differences in response to odorants across the olfactory mucosa and in the olfactory bulb. It appears that different chemicals excite different areas on the mucosa and bulb; each odorant has different characteristics such as latency, rate of movement across the mucosa, and binding strength. The receptors thus signal the molecular movements and each odor is coded as a different spatiotemporal pattern. This model is rather well supported by electrophysiological evidence.

Hedonics of Taste and Olfaction

Hedonics, or the study of the "pleasantness dimension" of a sensory system, is of great importance in taste and olfaction. A major function of these two modalities concerns preferences and approach-avoidance choices. Taste provides clues about poisons (bitter and sour), nutrition (sweet), and essential substances (salty). Rats prefer some concentrations of salt (0.1 M) but reject stronger solutions; they reject quinine, which is bitter, but accept sweet solutions. Olfaction can serve to identify social relationship or territory, signal alarm, and communicate sexual receptivity.

Humans today do not depend as much on taste and olfaction for survival as other animals. However, the pleasantness dimension is still of considerable importance as witnessed by the prospering deodorant and perfume industry. There is a certain amount of individual variation in odor preferences, since a person's judgments are affected by a variety of factors such as past experience and the context within which each odorant is presented. However, subjects are able to make magnitude estimates (see Chapter 2) of the pleasantness of odors. It is interesting to note that although the range of subjective intensity for odors is only about 5:1, the range for pleasantness has been found to be much greater—on the order of 125:1 (Engen and McBurney, 1964).

The senses of taste and smell often operate together to create the sensation of pleasure. In fact, one reason for fortifying foods with vitamins and minerals is that man does choose what he eats largely on the basis of how it tastes. The enjoyment of gourmet foods (or even a good hamburger) comes from both taste and smell which contribute to the appreciation of flavor. Obviously, the food industry is much concerned with hedonics. Food processors must know the preferences of persons in different areas of the country and different age ranges (think of the number of varieties of breakfast cereal) in order to market their products successfully.

CUTANEOUS SENSES

The skin is innervated by large myelinated, A, and small, unmyelinated, C neurons. These neurons terminate in various kinds of encapsulated endings, hair follicles, and as free endings. For many years a concerted effort was made to correlate specific sensations such as cold with the types of encapsulated endings, but this has proven fruitless. The maps of modality distribution on the skin (see section on skin mapping) do not even correlate with the presence of encapsulated endings, let alone a particular type. Although the effort to correlate sensations with type of nerve ending has been generally unsuccessful, certain things may be said about the type of ending involved in particular sensations. The mediation of the touch sensation is generally considered to be accomplished by either the hair follicle endings (in hairy skin) or the free nerve endings. The stimulus for touch appears to be displacement or deformation of the skin above a certain threshold. Note that free nerve endings, such as found in the cornea of the eye, respond not only to touch but to all of the usual modalities of sensory quality.

Other efforts have been made to correlate quality with the diameter of

Your skin is not equally sensitive at all points to all types of stimuli, e.g., pressure, temperature, and pain. In addition, sensation is not continuous on the skin but can be localized at discrete points. This may surprise you, but it can be confirmed by mapping the sensitivity of the skin, searching point by point for spots that are sensitive to different stimuli.

To do this, we stamp a small grid on the skin—on the arm, for example. To determine sensitivity to pressure, a stiff hair would be pressed against the skin in each box of the grid, and the person would indicate when he felt it. We can then repeat the procedure with a brass cylinder heated or cooled to test for warm and cold, and with a needle for pain. Some spots will prove sensitive to more than one type of stimulus, for example, pressure and warmth.

By comparing our sensitivity we can determine the relative sensitivity for many areas of the body to specific stimuli. It turns out that there are more pressure-sensitive spots at the tip of the tongue and on the fingertips than on the back of the body. For any given body area, there are usually more pain than pressure spots, and more pressure than temperature spots.

Since there are more pressure spots on the fingertips than on the back, we ask ourselves in what way the fingertips are more sensitive to pressure. This we can determine by means of a measure called the *two-point threshold*. The instrument we will employ has two points that can be adjusted to span different distances on the skin. If the points are close together they feel like one; if they are far enough apart, they feel like the two points they actually are.

This two-point threshold varies widely depending on the part of the body stimulated. To be felt as two points, the tips of the instrument must be *34 times farther apart* on the middle of the back than on the fingertips! When we study things with our hands, we usually manipulate them with our fingers, a situation that is not really comparable with our two-point threshold experiment. Nevertheless, a low two-point threshold on individual fingers is essential to the use of braille, the appreciation of the texture of fabrics, and so on.

A strange thing happens when we stimulate cold spots on the skin. They are not only sensitive to a brass cylinder cooler than skin temperature, but they are also sensitive to a hot stimulus. A hot stimulus placed on a cold spot will feel cold. This phenomenon, called *paradoxical cold*, usually occurs only with the stimulation of a small area. An exception is the sensation of cold you sometimes feel when you touch something very hot before realizing that the object is actually hot.

The sensation of heat is not the same as the sensation of warmth. The feeling of heat can be aroused by placing your arm across a grill composed of alternating hot and cold bars. Because the sensation can be aroused in this way, it has been proposed that the feeling of heat results from the simultaneous stimulation of hot and cold receptors. However, another theory suggests that there may be receptors which mediate heat only.

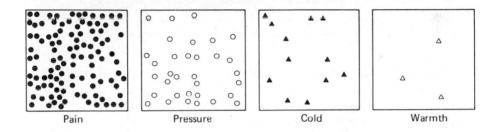

Pain   Pressure   Cold   Warmth

Typical results of mapping a small area of the skin for sensitivity to pain, pressure, cold, and warmth.

the fiber. Although some modalities tend to be represented in different ranges of fiber diameter, no clear distinction can be made on this basis. The small C fibers, which were presumed to subserve pain, have been found to respond to light touch (Hunt and McIntyre, 1960). The nerve fibers that respond to temperature are often referred to as "warm fibers" and "cold fibers." However, most of these fibers respond to more than one quality of stimulus; for example, touch and temperature.

An alternative to specific receptors or fibers would be some form of pattern theory for cutaneous coding. An example is the gate control theory for pain proposed by Melzack and Wall (1965) and illustrated in Figure 3-22. Both large and small fibers enter the spinal cord and synapse on cells in the substantia gelatinosa.

The T or transmission cell signals pain to the brain. Both large and small fibers have excitatory synapses with the T cell, so both large and small fibers might be expected to mediate pain sensations. Note, however, that the large and small fibers both synapse on the S.G., or substantia gelatinosa cell. The large fiber's synapse is excitatory (+) but the small fiber's synapse is inhibitory (−). Notice that the S.G. cell synapses on the termination of both the large and small fibers

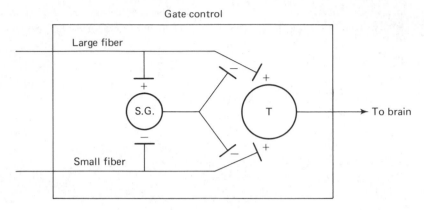

Figure 3-22 Schematic diagram of the gate-control theory of pain. [Modified after Melzack, R., and Wall, P. D. Pain mechanisms: A new theory. *Science,* 1965, *150,* 971–79. © 1965 by the American Association for the Advancement of Science.]

just before they synapse with the T cell. The S.G. cell's synapses are inhibitory. The effect of the S.G. cell is therefore called *presynaptic inhibition.* Now the system looks somewhat complicated, but the key is the S.G. cell. Large fiber activity will excite both the T cell and the S.G. cell. The S.G. cell in turn inhibits the termination of both the large and small fibers on the T cell. Note that small fiber activity excites the T cell, but inhibits the S.G. cell. Therefore the effect of activity in the small fiber on its own termination is inhibition of inhibition or *disinhibition* through the intermediate step of inhibiting the S.G. cell. The point is that it is not correct to say that the small fiber is for pain and the large fiber is for something else, like touch. The sensation of pain, signalled by activity of the T cell, depends on the *ratio* of activity in large and small fibers. If there is more large fiber activity, the S.G. cell is excited, which in turn inhibits the effect of both large and small fibers on the T cell, thus shutting off pain. (The theory thus explains why pressure on a wound will relieve pain.) If there is more activity in the small fibers, the T cell is stimulated. But the S.G. cell is also inhibited, which results in disinhibition of large and small fiber terminations, resulting in continued activity of the T cell. Although the theory was specifically designed to handle pain, it implies that touch and other modalities of skin sensation may be coded by similar mechanisms.

OTHER SENSES

We have now completed our discussion of the coding of sensory qualities associated with the traditional senses. We must, however, not overlook such other senses as that of orientation (to be discussed in Chapter 9). In addition,

An adequate consideration of extrasensory perception is far beyond the scope of this book. However, it seems reasonable to spend a little time in a book on perception discussing why most psychologists do not believe in the existence of extrasensory perception. We will consider only one aspect of the question: that is the fact that ESP is defined by exclusion perception not mediated by the known sensory receptors. But research has shown that it is extremely difficult, if not impossible, to rule out the possibility of information entering via the senses. There are several well understood reasons for this. First, we know from Signal Detection Theory that there is not a threshold below which no information is received by a receptor. Any finite amount of stimulus energy will have some effect on the receptor, although it may take many thousands of trials for it to stand out from the chance level. Second, we know that a person's lack of awareness of the source of his information is no criterion that he did not receive the information by some ordinary means. There are many experiments in which subjects performed at very high levels to stimuli whose presence they were totally "unaware" of (see the section on perceptual learning, Chapter 14). Third, to define a phenomenon simply by the absence of some process is philosophically very weak. It may well be that there is some type of sensory receptor whose existence is unknown, or that one of the ordinary senses has abilities that we have not considered. By defining certain phenomena as *extra* sensory perception, the emphasis is no longer placed on understanding the mechanism of a puzzling effect but simply on proving that it did not occur in certain particular ways. This is a scientifically sterile procedure. The fruitful procedure is to relate new phenomena to known principles of perception or to discover a new principle. A particularly good example is Makous' study of cutaneous color perception (1966), to be treated in a later section of this chapter. He was able to burst a large bubble of interest in the possibility that persons can "see" color by ESP by first calculating and then demonstrating that the skin is sensitive enough to temperature that it can detect color by sensing differences in the heat energy reflected onto the skin from objects of different colors.

There are many other objections one can raise to the possibility of ESP, but the profitable approach is to ask "exactly what can we learn about perception from purported examples of *extrasensory* perception?"

there are a number of other senses such as the sense of time or rhythm, for which we do not even know what receptors might be involved. In some of these cases the sensations are no doubt based on inferences from other sensations that are better understood. For example, Boring and Boring (1917) awakened subjects at different times during the night and had them estimate the time. It was concluded that subjects inferred the time from sensations of fatigue or restedness and sensations from the intestinal and excretory systems. Another class of sensations of which we are not normally aware can be perceived by attention or training. Perceiving the heartbeat requires careful attention in quiet surroundings during periods of rest (except after strenuous exercise or fright). What we actually perceive is not the heartbeat but its consequence, the dilation of the blood vessels. It is easier to perceive the heartbeat even more indirectly by arranging for the pulse to provide a tactile stimulus to the skin. An example of a "sensation" that requires special training is hunger. Children who have missed a meal may get restless and irritable without realizing that they are hungry. This implies that the stimulus consequences of hunger are subtle and need to be conditioned to internal events, like stomach contractions, or external cues like the reading of a clock. If hunger is a sensation, what are its stimuli? It would perhaps be better to refer to it as the perceptual capacity of responding to a state of food deprivation!

A Note on Sensation and Awareness

The term "sensation" seems to connote the idea of awareness for the layman and many psychologists. The problem of awareness has been a perplexing one in psychology. The usual definitions of awareness rely heavily on the subject's verbal report. However, the level of awareness that a subject will reveal by his verbal report depends greatly on how he is questioned. In addition, the ability of subjects to agree on a verbal description of their sensations puts practical limits on verbal report as the criterion of awareness. For these reasons, although verbal report is an extensively used tool, it must not be relied upon as incorrigible or infallible. It should be viewed as an *inference* by the subject of what his sensation *was*. Verbal report frequently disagrees with the electrical potential evoked in the brain by the stimulus or with a motor response to the stimulus on a given trial.

A Note on the Senses as Perceptual Systems

We have treated each sense separately in this chapter as if there were no interaction among them. That this view is not completely accurate can be seen from our discussion of "flavor," that everyday term combining sensations of taste and smell. Moreover, we have treated the senses as essentially passive recorders of energy that impinges on them. Gibson (1966) has made a distinction between the senses as receivers of energy and the perceptual systems as *active*

Every now and then someone claims to be able to read utilizing only the sense of touch. A flurry of interest in this supposed ability arose in the United States in the early sixties following sensational claims made in the Russian press that, among other things, certain persons were able to read newspapers while securely blindfolded. An American investigator, Youtz, tested one woman whom he found able to detect color with her fingers (see Gardner, 1966). How could this be done? One explanation might be to call this an amazing example of some unknown power beyond the normal sensory channels. Gardner argued that most of the feats were accomplished by cheating, because it is well known to magicians that blindfolds are very easy to circumvent. However, Youtz was convinced that his subject was basing her ability on temperature sensitivity.

Makous (1966) seems to have settled the question. He did so by first calculating the amount of heat that would be absorbed or reflected from objects of different colors when the hand was held near the object. Colors toward the red end of the spectrum reflect more heat than those from the blue end. *These differences in reflected heat are several times greater than the difference threshold for temperature!* Thus, if a person held his hand near an array of objects all of which were at room temperature, those from the red end would feel warmer because they would reflect back to the skin more of the heat originally radiated from the hand. Makous then gave further proof of the color sensing phenomenon by taking a metal plate and polishing one half so that it would reflect heat and painting the other so that it would absorb heat. Subjects found it easy to discriminate the two sides by holding their hands above them.

This is an effect that you can easily demonstrate yourself. Metal is best because it will absorb more heat without changing temperature, but you can observe the effects, at least briefly, from colored paper. Makous' work is an especially good example of how one should approach a new and strange phenomenon. He was able to relate it to the known properties of a sensory system without having to invoke any new mysterious powers.

perceivers of energy, defined by the type of stimulus that is being perceived. The haptic system, for instance, groups the senses of touch, temperature, and proprioception into a system for perceiving things by touching or handling them. This view does more justice to the way the sensory systems operate than a passive-independent view. The savoring system involves not only taste, smell, and skin senses, as mentioned earlier, but also the muscles and other structures involved in sniffing and chewing. Other receptors for chemical stimuli that are not usually discussed under taste and smell but contribute to savoring include the trigeminal nerve component of smelling and the common-chemical sense, which contributes a general irritability of the whole skin including the inside of the mouth. It was necessary to treat the senses as independent for a discussion of sensory coding. However, the rest of the book is organized around perceptual systems as much as possible in order to emphasize the integrated nature of perception.

4

Energy Relationships

Everyone has had the experience of trying to judge the temperature of bath water. The water may appear comfortably warm to a small area of the body, such as the hand, wrist, or elbow. But when one steps all the way in it may suddenly feel very hot and, after a few seconds, unbearably so. This example illustrates two phenomena: first spatial, then temporal summation. To a large extent, the magnitude of response to a stimulus depends on the total amount of energy in the stimulus and is independent of how the energy is distributed over time or space. A weak but long lasting stimulus over a large area may have the same effectiveness as a short, intense stimulus on a smaller area. Such an inverse relationship between the variables which describe a stimulus is called a trading relationship. Various types of trading relationships will be discussed in the sections that follow.

INTENSITY AND TIME

A photographer knows that if he is taking a picture on an overcast day, the exposure time will have to be increased in order to have enough light for a good picture; conversely, in bright sunlight, a short exposure time would be in order. The same total amount of light is necessary to expose the film properly in each case. This relationship is known as the Bunson-Roscoe Law in photo-chemistry. A similar relationship known as Bloch's Law holds true in vision up to a certain length of time. It states that intensity and duration can be traded

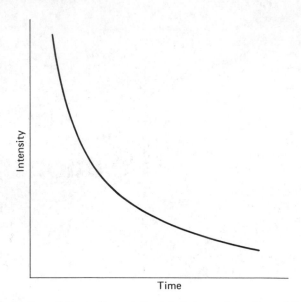

Figure 4-1 Illustration of the trading relationship between intensity and time. Any point on the curve represents a combination of intensity and duration that will produce a certain response. This curve is fit by the equation $I \times T = k$. If we substitute area for time ($I \times A = k$), it also describes the trading relation between intensity and area. [From Graham, C. H., and Margaria, R. Area and the intensity-time relation in the peripheral retina. *Am. J. Physiol.*, 1935, *113*, 299–305.]

off as long as the amount of total energy required to produce a response of predetermined magnitude remains invariable. In other words, intensity times time is a constant.

$$I \times t = k$$

Equation 4-1

This reciprocal relationship between intensity and time is illustrated by Figure 4-1. If we take the logarithm of Eq. 4-1, we obtain Eq. 4-2.

$$\log I + \log t = \log k$$

Equation 4-2

which is plotted in Figure 4-2. There is a linear relation between $\log I$ and $\log t$ up to a time known as the critical duration, t_c. The slope of the line in Figure 4-2 is -1, which means that the relationship between I and t is exactly reciprocal. For vision, t_c is generally about 0.1 second (Graham and Margaria, 1935). Beyond this time, the absorption of more light will be of little or no use because

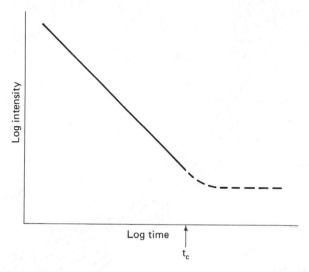

Figure 4-2 Trading relationship between intensity and time. This graph shows the same relationship as Figure 4-1 except that here the logarithm intensity is plotted against the logarithm of time. The big advantage of this plot is that we can make a precise test of the form of the equation. If it is actually of the form $I \times T = k$, then it will be a straight line when plotted in logarithmic coordinates. The point at which the curve deviates from the straight line, t_c (indicated by the change from a solid to a dotted line), can be located with considerable accuracy. The trading relationship no longer holds beyond this critical duration point.

the effects of the earlier absorption will have deteriorated and the nervous response has already been initiated.

Temporal summation manifests itself in a number of situations, including the threshold, sensation magnitude, and reaction time. In general, given a constant response criterion, intensity and time will trade off. The first example was for threshold. The following example is particularly interesting because it shows that as the task is made more difficult, the same trading relation holds but the amount of energy required is increased. This application of the Bunson-Roscoe Law is known as the "span of apprehension," the classic problem of estimating how many objects one perceives in a given brief period of time. An everyday analogy to this would be a quick glance in the rear-view mirror while driving on a superhighway and then an attempt at estimating the number of vehicles seen. In an experimental situation, the subject's task is to estimate the number of dots presented briefly to his visual field. Up to a criterion of eight dots and with durations below one second, the intensity of the field and the exposure time required for detection are reciprocally related (Hunter and Sigler, 1940). Thus, with higher intensity, a shorter time would be required in order to perceive the number of dots, with lower intensity, a longer time. Figure 4-3 shows a logarithmic plot of intensity as a function of duration of exposure for

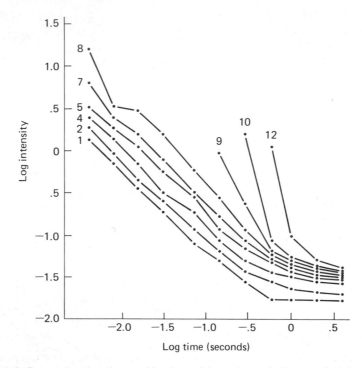

Figure 4-3 Curves showing the combinations of intensity and time required in order to see various numbers of dots. Note that, although all the curves have the same shape, they are displaced from each other by a certain amount. This simply indicates that it takes a greater amount of intensity-times-time to see two dots than one, and so forth. [From Hunter, W. S., and Sigler, M. The span of visual discrimination as a function of time and intensity of stimulation. *J. Exp. Psych.*, 1940, *26*, 160–79. © 1940 by the American Psychological Association. Reprinted by permission.]

criteria of different numbers of dots. In order to maintain a constant "span of apprehension" as shown by any one of the curves for one to eight dots, time of exposure must increase as intensity decreases, or vice versa. Up to a certain duration, a constant amount of stimulus energy ($I \times t = k$) is required for any given apprehension span. With eight dots or more, the subject must count in order to correctly detect the number of dots and $I \times t$ is not a constant; time is then more important than intensity up to one second beyond which time has no effect on threshold.

That temporal summation occurs in the auditory system is indicated by the influence of the duration of a stimulus on its threshold. As tones of middle frequencies become progressively briefer than 200 milliseconds, the power (for audition, power or I^2 is the proper measure of energy) of the tone must be increased to achieve threshold (Garner, 1947). This trading relationship is shown in Figure 4-4. In other words, with increasing time less power is required to reach threshold. The auditory system is able to add up the effects of the stimu-

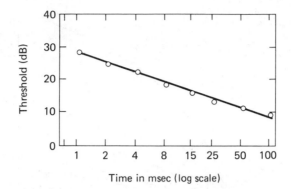

Figure 4-4 Trading relationship between time and intensity at threshold for audition. The intensity of a 4000 Hz was plotted on a logarithmic axis, but time, rather than log *t*, is plotted on the abscissa. [From Garner, W. R. The effect of frequency spectrum on temporal integration of energy in the ear. *J. Acoust. Soc. America*, 1947, *19*, 808-15.]

lus over a period of 200 msec. The system performs the summation best if the sound is continuous, but it can also be accomplished with short periods of time between bursts of stimulation.

The rest of the examples in this section use magnitude of sensation to illustrate temporal summation. Perceived cold increases continuously and markedly with duration (Marks and Stevens, 1972). This conclusion was obtained by having subjects who were exposed to cold for various amounts of time assess their perception of cold numerically. Perceived cold as a function of duration of stimulation is shown in Figure 4-5 for several levels of cooling (ΔH). By drawing a horizontal line across all the functions at a magnitude estimate of, say, 4, we see that in order to produce this level of perceived cold, duration of cooling must vary inversely with amount (intensity) of cooling.

When we compare the previous figure with Figure 4-6, which shows magnitude estimates of warmth as a function of duration of stimulation, we see that the time course for warming is much different. Perceived warmth at the two highest stimulus levels increases only slightly with duration; at lower levels of warming there is no increase with duration (Marks and Stevens, 1968). On the other hand, even at low intensities, perceived cold increases steadily with exposure time.

The understanding of temporal summation of warmth is complicated by the fact that the stimulus to the skin and the stimulus to the warmth receptor do not have the same temporal characteristics. The heat must be conducted from the surface of the skin to the depth of the receptors, the identity of which is unknown, let alone their depth. Thus the summation found will depend on the assumed depth of the receptors. It appears that temporal summation in the warmth sense is due to the heat-transfer properties of the skin and does not have a neural basis (Marks and Stevens, 1973).

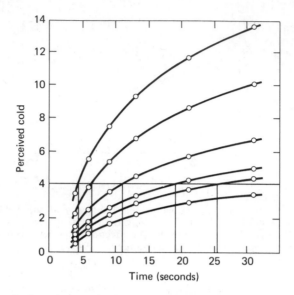

Figure 4-5 Magnitude estimates of cold as a function of duration of cooling. Each curve is for a different intensity of the cooling stimulus. [From Marks, L. E., and Stevens, J. C. Perceived cold and skin temperature as functions of stimulation level and duration. *Am. J. Psych.*, 1972, *85,* 407–19.]

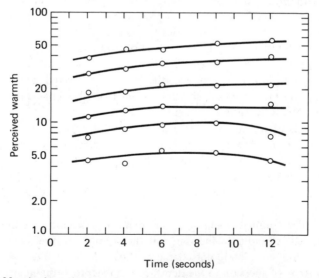

Figure 4-6 Magnitude estimates of warmth as a function of duration of the warming stimulus. Each of the curves is for a different intensity of the warming stimulus. [From Marks, L. E., and Stevens, J. C. Perceived warmth and skin temperature as functions of the duration and level of thermal irradiation. *Perception and Psychophysics,* 1968b, *4,* 220–28.]

Temporal summation can be demonstrated in other areas. Stevens and Cain (1970) instructed subjects to squeeze a hand dynamometer at different levels of force for various lengths of time. The perceived effort, as judged by the subjects, was found to be a power function of both force of contraction and duration. An everyday example of this phenomenon is the effort necessary to carry a heavy object like a suitcase for a certain time in an airport. The suitcase gradually seems to become unbearably heavy. In Figure 4–7, perceived force as scaled by magnitude estimates is plotted as a function of the length of time the force is held. Each function represents a different level of force. Looking at any function, it may be seen that the perceived force is approximately doubled by tripling the duration. The exponent of the power function relating perceived force to duration is 0.7.

There is a trading relationship here between level of force and duration. If, for example, we draw a horizontal line across all the functions in Figure 4–7 at the magnitude estimate level of 10, we can see that these combinations of force and duration yield equivalent amounts of perceived force: 98 newtons of force for 3.5 seconds, 67 newtons for 9 seconds, and 36 newtons for 60 seconds. Interestingly, this means that if a subject is told to maintain a constant *subjec-*

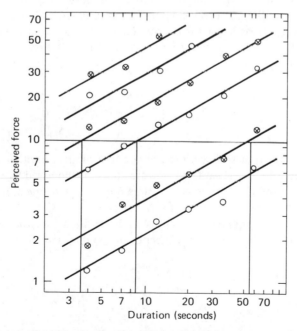

Figure 4–7 Magnitude estimates of perceived force as a function of duration of the effort. The intersections of the horizontal line with the three vertical lines show the combinations of force and time that would be perceived as equally effortful. [From Stevens, J. C., and Cain, W. S. Effort in isometric muscular contractions related to force level and duration. *Perception and Psychophysics*, 1970, *8*, 240–44.]

tive force (effort level) over time, he will actually exert less and less physical force as time goes on. A situation with which you are probably familiar is that of pedaling a bicycle up a hill with constant slope. You find yourself gradually slowing down even though your pedalling effort seems constant.

INTENSITY AND AREA

In vision there is a reciprocal relationship between the intensity and area of a stimulus at threshold. Ricco's Law, stated in Eq. 4-3,

$$I \times A = k$$

Equation 4-3

says that the greater the area of the stimulus on the retina the smaller the intensity required for threshold. Thus a constant total amount of energy is necessary for threshold in spite of differences in area. The area over which complete summation occurs varies from $30'$ to $2°$ depending on which part of the retina is being stimulated. Complete summation means that there is no loss in efficiency in spreading light over a large area as opposed to concentrating it on a smaller area. At areas larger than about $2°$ of visual angle in the periphery of the retina, there is only partial summation and Piper's Law holds. This law, $I \times A^{.5} = k,$ or

$$I \sqrt{A} = k$$

Equation 4-4

says that intensity trades off with the square root of area. In other words, if the intensity is reduced by a given factor the area must be increased by the square of the factor; or if the intensity is halved, area must be quadrupled. Beyond about $24°$ of visual angle there is no further summation.

The relationships between intensity and area hold for other senses as well as vision. For taste, the product of concentration and area at threshold is

$$C \times A^{m} = k$$

Equation 4-5

The effects of area and concentration on taste intensity have been studied simultaneously by having subjects make magnitude estimates of the intensity of a solution presented to different sized areas on the tongue (Smith, 1971). Each taste quality has its own value for the exponent m, and this consists of the ratio of two other exponents (p/n), p the exponent for area and n the exponent for concentration.

$$C^n \times A^p = k$$

Equation 4-6

Smith's experiment allowed for the independent measurement of n and p. He found that compounds of all qualities have the same slope or exponent for taste intensity (p) as a function of tongue area. However, the exponent n, relating taste intensity to stimulus concentration, differs for each taste quality; that is, bitter, sour, salty, and sweet compounds each have a characteristic slope value. Thus the trade off between stimulus concentration and size of the area stimulated depends on the taste quality tested; in other words each quality shows its own characteristic degree of spatial summation.

Probably no sense modality shows spatial summation quite as impressively as the sense of warmth. Complete summation of warmth at threshold occurs for areas of exposure of the body up to 12 square centimeters (Kenshalo, Decker, and Hamilton, 1967). Eq. 4-7 summarizes the data.

$$I \times A = k$$

Equation 4-7

Figure 4-8 plots warmth thresholds as a function of the size of the stimulated area. The curves for different parts of the body all have the same slopes, indicating the same degree of summation, but each has a different intercept, perhaps because of varying densities of innervation among the areas stimulated. As the area of stimulation is increased, the intensity of the stimulus can be decreased and a constant level (threshold) of perceived warmth will still be maintained. So also, then, will changes in the areal extent of stimulation, given a constant stimulus intensity, be perceived as changes in warmth. From other data it is known that, at levels of stimulation above threshold, area makes a weaker and weaker relative contribution to warmth. At these levels it takes an increasingly larger change in area to balance a given decrease in intensity.

It is interesting to note that reaction time depends on intensity and area in about the same way as do threshold and sensation magnitude for the various senses. For example, the reaction time to radiant heat decreases with increases in the areal extent as well as the intensity of the stimulation (Banks, 1973). Area and intensity can be traded off to maintain the same response latency.

Putting areal and temporal summation together, we now know that in vision the important thing in determining thresholds is the total amount of energy (intensity $\times$ time $\times$ area) as long as we keep the exposure time short and

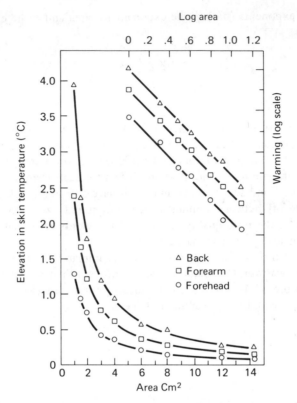

Figure 4–8 Warmth thresholds as a function of area for three different parts of the body. The same data are displayed twice, once on linear coordinates and once on logarithmic coordinates. The scales to the left and bottom are for the curves on the lower left, and the scales on the top and right-hand side are for the curves on the upper right. [From Kenshalo, D. R., Decker, T., and Hamilton, A. Spatial summation on the forehead, forearm, and back produced by radiant and conducted heat. *J. Comp. and Physiol. Psych.,* 1967, *63,* 510–15. © 1967 by the American Psychological Association. Reprinted by permission.]

the area small. For the dark-adapted eye a very small quantity of energy is actually needed for threshold. In a classic study Hecht, Shlaer, and Pirenne (1942) determined that five to fourteen quanta of light provide a threshold stimulus. The area of the retina over which spatial summation is complete contains approximately 500 rods and the five to fourteen quanta could be spread over these rods. One quantum of light is enough to excite one rod, but according to these experimenters' calculations, the responses of five to fourteen rods must summate to reach the response threshold. The anatomical basis of

There was a rather puzzling controversy in the world of taste investigation for some years. Early investigators in taste reported that single taste papillae showed broad sensitivity to chemical solutions. A half century later, Georg von Békésy repeated these experiments (Békésy, 1966) using a new method of stimulation. He devised a special stimulator to place a very small amount of chemical solution on a single papilla on the human tongue. He found each papilla to be specifically sensitive to only one of the four basic taste qualities.

Other investigators (Harper et al., 1966, McCutcheon and Saunders, 1972) found, in replicating Békésy's experiments, that most human taste papillae had a wide range of sensitivity in agreement with the older literature. However, it was also noted that the concentrations of the solutions used by Békésy were near the thresholds for the whole tongue whereas these other investigators were using much stronger solutions. It has been known for some time (Bujas and Ostojcic, 1941) that there is spatial summation in the taste system. Because of this spatial summation, the whole-tongue threshold for any substance should be much lower (perhaps one to two log steps) than the single papilla threshold for the same substance. So, then, Békésy was using very weak solutions and finding specific papillae whereas others, using stronger solutions, found nonspecific papillae. How could this happen? If we think of the responsiveness of each papilla as being represented by a tuning curve such as that shown in the figure below, then we can see that, if all solutions presented were at very weak concentrations (C_1), each papilla might respond to one taste quality only. This is the result obtained by Békésy. On the other hand, if we present solutions at a higher concentration (C_2), we will find the papillae responding over a broader spectrum.

Actually, in relation to unsolved problems regarding sensory coding in the taste system, the specificity of individual papillae may very well be a trivial matter. In-depth studies of the individual taste cell or the first-order neuron are more likely to be informative. However, a resolution of this controversy would prove interesting in light of trading relationships and, in particular, Smith's (1971) work on the relation of concentration and area.

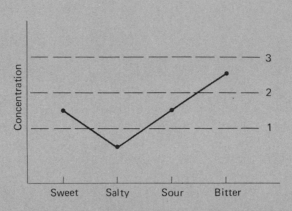

Hypothetical tuning curve for a taste papilla. If the stimuli are all weak (concentration 1) as illustrated by the dotted line labelled 1, then only salty would be perceived. If the concentrations were all increased (concentration 2), then sweet, salty, and sour would be perceived. At the strongest level of all stimuli all qualities would be tasted. This graph should not be interpreted to mean that there is a continuum along which the taste stimuli fall or that there is a way to equate the concentrations of different taste stimuli except for effectiveness in stimulation of some particular area of the tongue.

spatial summation in the rods has been discussed in Chapter 3. The requirement that the responses of several rods summate to produce a threshold response is an important control mechanism. Single receptive elements in the eye (and in many sensory systems) often fire spontaneously, and if the response of one rod were sufficient to cause a response in the visual system, a person in dim viewing conditions would constantly see a chaotic flashing of lights.

INTENSITY AND ACUITY

It should be noted that to the extent that a sensory system trades off space or time against intensity, the system must give up the ability to discriminate spatial or temporal characteristics of the stimulus. Thus a sensory system such as warmth, which has a high degree of spatial summation, will be extremely poor at telling whether two stimuli or one are being presented or where they are being presented. The sense of warmth also shows great temporal summation and is thus largely incapable of distinguishing between a steady or a flickering stimulus. On the other hand, the eye has more modest ability to summate over space or time and is, of course, very good at spatial discrimination and fairly good at temporal discrimination (see Chapter 7). And the same sense may show either high or low degrees of spatial summation depending on the intensity of the stimulus. As Cain (1973) points out, at low intensities of thermal stimulation there is almost perfect spatial summation and very poor localization. At higher intensities there is better localization and less summation. This has great functional significance for the organism. At lower intensities the system is very sensitive to heat load at the expense of location of the load. At potentially damaging intensities it is more important to localize the stimulus in order to facilitate escape from it.

We have discussed the spatial summation that occurs in the rod system of the eye. This summation is the basis of the great sensitivity of scotopic vision, the ability to see at low levels of illumination such as at night. Acuity, the ability to resolve two stimuli separated in space, is more important for daytime vision. Visual acuity is related not only to the density of the receptors in the eye per se, but to the synaptic organization of cones and ganglion cells. The cones have nearly a "one-to-one" relationship with optic nerve fibers, and it is in this way that the high resolving power of the eye is achieved.

Visual acuity improves as a function of illumination. Figure 4-9 shows two curves; the lower represents the rod results and the upper, under higher

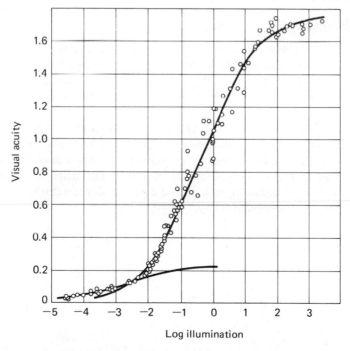

Figure 4-9 Visual acuity as a function of illumination. The shallow line in the lower left is the theoretical curve for the rods. The other curve is for the cones. [From Hecht, S. Vision: II. The nature of the photoreceptor process. In C. A. Murchison (ed.), *A handbook of general experimental psychology*. Worcester, Mass.: Clark University Press, 1934; reprinted New York: Russell & Russell, 1969.]

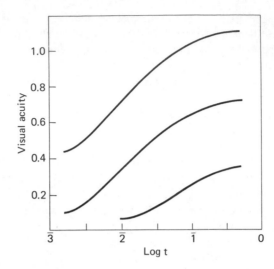

Figure 4-10 Visual acuity as a function of log duration of the stimulus. Each curve is for a different level of intensity; the greater the intensity the higher the curve. [From Graham, C. H., and Cook, C. Visual acuity as a function of intensity and exposure-time. *Am. J. Psych.*, 1937, *49*, 654–61.]

illumination, the cones. Acuity at night under rod vision is very poor; you have probably experienced difficulty in reading a map or the face of your watch at night. As illumination increases, the cone system comes into play and acuity increases. Reading and sewing are everyday situations that require good acuity. The layman tends to think that if there is enough light to see the book, any amount in excess is unnecessary. In fact speed and accuracy of reading continue to improve with increasing illumination. The more light, the better, almost without limit. An old friend that we run into here is the Bunson-Roscoe Law. As illustrated in Figure 4-10, intensity and time can trade off to maintain any specific level of acuity up to a critical duration. Beyond this time, intensity is the only factor determining acuity.

5

Adaptation

Adaptation is one of the most profound and pervasive sensory phenomena. You may have had the experience of entering a theater from the bright outdoors and stumbling in the darkness to your seat over the feet of persons already seated. A few minutes later you were annoyed by late comers stepping on your feet in what, by then, seemed to you to be adequate light. In the time that you had been in the theater your eyes had adapted to the darkness; that is, they had become more sensitive to light. An opposite effect occurs when one enters a room that is permeated by the odor of bacon, eggs, and coffee. After a few minutes the odor is less noticeable. These two examples demonstrate that after exposure to a stimulus, the sensitivity to that stimulus is decreased and after removal of the stimulus the sensitivity returns. Although these are the most familiar results of adaptation, and adaptation is usually defined in terms of them, there is a good deal more that occurs when adaptation takes place. Adaptation may be defined as the various outcomes of the operation of repeated or steady presentation of a stimulus to an organism.

OUTCOMES OF PRESENTATION
OF A STIMULUS

(1) *Response decrement.* This outcome is a universal finding among the sensory systems. The decrement is negatively accelerated, meaning that it occurs rapidly at first and then more slowly. Not all sensations decrement to zero but may asymptote (level off) well above zero. This is the reason one occasionally

finds statements that certain sensations "do not adapt," i.e., they do not adapt completely. The adaptation response to more intense stimuli takes longer, but the slope of the decline (in linear coordinates) is faster. Thus the question of how adaptation varies with intensity depends on whether one refers to the time to reach zero sensation or the slope of declination over time. However, the *rate* of decline may be independent of level as shown by the constants of an exponential decay function (see Figure 5-1).

Smell and taste are generally considered to show rapid and complete decrement. However, this may be more folklore than fact. Ekman et al. (1967) and Cain (1974) found that adaptation to odors reached an asymptote at about one-third of the initial perceived magnitude. Although weak tasting solutions seem to adapt completely, stronger ones do not decrement to zero (Meiselman, 1974).

In vision and audition the response decrement is slower and not complete. Indeed, there is some question as to whether there is a loudness decrement over time. If a subject attends for a period of time to a constant-amplitude sound, he will say that the loudness remains constant. However, if a subject is required to make periodic interaural loudness matches between a constant-intensity tone and a tone of variable sound pressure, adaptation appears to occur. Hood (1950), for example, found a decrease of approximately 35 db in about 5 minutes. The question of loudness adaptation is a puzzle that has not been resolved. It appears that those results that indicate the existence of loudness

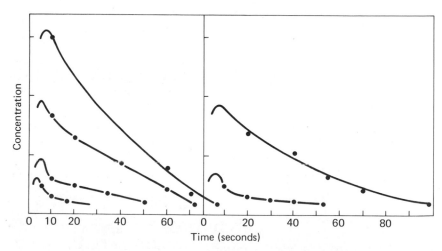

Figure 5-1 Adaptation of the taste of sodium chloride (table salt). The ordinate shows how strong a solution presented to one side of the tongue had to be in order to taste as strong as the solution remaining on the other side of the tongue for the length of time indicated on the abscissa. Each curve is for a different concentration of the solution to be matched. [From Bujas, Z. L'adaptation gustative et son mecanisme. *Acta Instituti Psychologici*, Zagreb, 1953, *17*, 1-11.]

adaptation are the result of differences in binaural interaction following the steady presentation of an auditory stimulus (Marks, 1974).

The extent of brightness adaptation depends on the intensity of the stimulus. There is little adaptation for low intensities but the most intense stimuli may decline in brightness by 90% (Stevens and Stevens, 1963). Under conditions of uniform unpatterned stimulation, such as the *Ganzfeld,* in which temporal variations in intensity are prevented, brightness declines markedly. The *Ganzfeld* is produced by placing the head inside a uniformly lit dome. Similar effects can be produced by placing half of a ping pong ball over each eye.

In the cutaneous temperature sense, complete adaptation occurs within about 30 minutes to stimuli between 29° and 37° C (Kenshalo and Scott, 1966). Outside this temperature range, the adaptation is not complete no matter how long the temperature stimulus is presented; in other words, cold or warm sensations can persist indefinitely.

An unusual situation exists with the adaptation of sense of touch. As you know, adaptation to touch does occur. Shortly after putting on your clothes you are no longer aware that they are touching your body. (Heavier touch stimuli of course require a longer adaptation period.) Interestingly enough, experiments have shown that adaptation in the touch sense is a function of stimulus failure not the receptor (Nafe and Wagoner, 1941). The touch receptors respond to a moving stimulus and thus when a stimulus ceases to deform the skin the receptors no longer respond.

Does pain adapt? This question has not been adequately answered and will probably not be answered until the stimulus(i) and receptor(s) for pain are better understood. In light of the fact that it is very difficult to present a constant pain stimulus, this sensation apparently does adapt to a steady stimulus.

(2) *Threshold increase.* This outcome is similar to response decrement except that instead of measuring the decreasing response to a steady stimulus, the stimulus is varied so as to maintain a constant (threshold) response.

In an experiment to maintain constant response a subject is generally given control over the intensity of the stimulus and is instructed to maintain a constant sensation such as "just perceptibly warm," "just perceptibly salty," and so on. Figure 5-2 demonstrates that the same relationship between adapting intensity and rate of decrement holds for thresholds as for the response decrement. The threshold increase and response magnitude decrease are not strictly reciprocal because the magnitude function exhibits a warmup phase. During the initial period of stimulation the response magnitude is increasing at the same time that the threshold is rising. This may be seen by comparing the two figures.

(3) *Recovery.* The response recovers and the threshold returns to its preadapted level when the adapting stimulus is removed. The recovery is negatively accelerated and takes longer with more intense adapting stimuli. In taste the rate of recovery is about the same as the rate of threshold increase as may

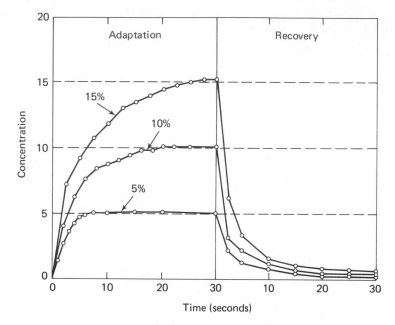

Figure 5-2 Adaptation and recovery from adaptation to sodium chloride. The threshold was measured after adaptation to some concentration for the amount of time shown on the abscissa. Each curve is for adaptation to a different concentration of sodium chloride. The right-hand side shows the time course of recovery from adaptation to the same concentrations. [From Hahn, H. Die adaptation des geschmacksinnes. *Zeitschrift für Sinnesphysiologie*, 1934, *65*, 105–45.]

be seen by comparing the left- and right-side of Figure 5-2. In vision, however, dark adaptation (recovery from light adaptation) takes up to 30 minutes or more depending on the level of prior light adaptation whereas the light adaptation takes only about one minute.

(4) *Steepening*. After adapting to a stimulus of moderate intensity, the slope of the function relating response magnitude to intensity becomes steeper. This means that adaptation has a greater effect on stimuli near the intensity of the adapting stimulus than on stronger stimuli. The response to intense stimuli may be normal. This result has been found in every sense for which the appropriate experiment has been performed. Figure 5-3 shows the results of visual adaptation on magnitude estimates of brightness (Stevens and Stevens, 1963). For magnitude estimation data, the effect of adaptation on the function may be accounted for by a constant S_o, subtracted from the values of the stimulus in the power function $R = k (S - S_o)^n$. In most cases the value of the constant approximates the threshold that would obtain in the particular situation under the given conditions of adaptation. (See section on scaling, Chapter 2.)

The steepening that is produced by adaptation is similar to that produced by certain types of damage to the nervous system as in sensory-neural deafness.

This type of deafness, which is characteristic of aging, exhibits the phenomenon of recruitment in which threshold is increased but loudness is normal at higher intensities. Since loudness grows more rapidly than normal with increasing intensity it is a common experience when talking to older persons to have them complain that one is not speaking loudly enough to be heard. When the speaker cooperates by raising his voice the complaint is made that the speaker is shouting.

(5) *Sharpening.* The size of the difference threshold (DL) for a particular stimulus intensity is not a fixed quantity, but varies with adaptation. The DL for a given standard stimulus is smallest when the receptor is adapted to that standard stimulus. This means that the organism is more sensitive to changes in a given stimulus intensity after adaptation to that stimulus than before. Perhaps more than any other outcome of adaptation, sharpening illustrates that adaptation is not principally a loss in sensitivity to a stimulus. The sharpening effect has been likened to a tuning mechanism that adjusts the point of maximum sensitivity to the level of the stimulus to which the organism is adapted. The increase in sensitivity in the case of taste is as much as two to one (McBurney, Kasschau and Bogart, 1967). In other words, the DL for 0.1 M NaCl

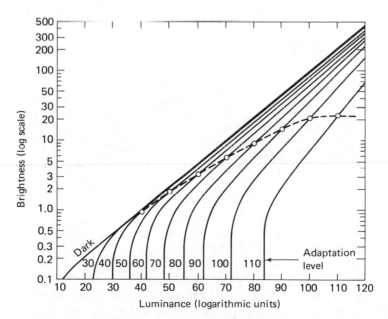

Figure 5-3 Effects of adaptation on brightness. Magnitude estimates of brightness are shown as a function of the intensity of the light. Each curve is for a different level of previous adaptation. The dashed line is the brightness of a steadily viewed light; these functions were obtained with brief flashes of light. [From Stevens, J. C., and Stevens, S. S. Brightness function: Effects of adaptation. *J. Optical Soc. America,* 1963, *53,* 375–85.]

Most people who take pictures for the first time with a camera having a fixed lens opening and shutter speed are surprised that the film is much less forgiving about variations in light intensity than is the eye. The quality of the picture will suffer if the exposure is off by as little as 2:1. On the other hand, the eye has much more "latitude" as illustrated by the need for a light meter in order to obtain the correct exposure. Looking at the limits of dark and light to which our eyes can adapt, we find an incredible range of 13 log units—or one trillion to one! This adaptation is not instantaneous; you have had the experience of being dazzled upon emerging into the sunlight from a dark theater, and we have already referred to what happens when you enter a theater from the outdoors. In both cases you are temporarily blind until the adaptation takes place. This section deals with the mechanisms and time courses of dark and light adaptation.

First the *mechanisms.* You are probably aware that the pupil of the eye becomes larger as the amount of light decreases and vice versa. Most people assume that this is an important mechanism of dark and light adaptation, but the actual variation in area is only about 16 to one—nowhere near the amount needed to explain dark adaptation. Researchers now believe the principal function of the pupil is to allow a sharpening of the image and an increase in depth of field (the range of distances perceived sharply at any one setting of a lens' focus) in bright light and to allow some increase in sensitivity at lower illuminations (Rushton, 1965). The size of the pupil also seems to function as a social stimulus (pp. 158–59). More about the mechanism of dark adaptation later.

Time course. Light adaptation is very rapid, being complete in a minute or so. Dark adaptation, however, takes much longer. The results of a typical dark adaptation experiment are shown in the accompanying figure. The subject is first adapted to a strong intensity of light. Then he is placed in darkness and his threshold is measured over time. It is found that the threshold drops very rapidly at first, until it is within about a log step of the first plateau shown in the curve. Then it approaches the first asymptote more slowly and by about 10 minutes it appears not to be dropping any further. Then a curious thing happens. The threshold drops again fairly rapidly for a while and then, after about twenty minutes, it reaches a new asymptote about three log units below the first (temporary) asymptote.

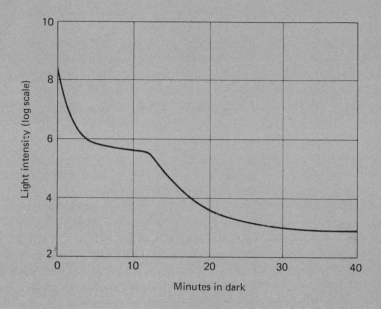

Minutes in dark

This in itself is interesting, but there are some other phenomena associated with the break in the curve. If a colored light is used, the color will be seen until the break, after which the light appears colorless. If a small target light is used to stimulate the fovea only, the break will not appear but the curve will continue along the first asymptote. However, if the small light is then viewed extra-foveally the curve will continue to drop. These phenomena may suggest to you that the break is related to duplicity theory. Remember that the fovea contains only the color sensitive cones. The rods, located in the periphery, are color-blind but are more sensitive to low intensities of light. We now need only one other fact to explain the rod-cone break. And this is that the rate of dark adaptation is faster for the cones, but the cones, of course, cannot reach the same absolute sensitivity. What actually happens is that in the first phase of dark adaptation the cones are more sensitive than the rods and we see the light (in color) with the cones. After the rod-cone break we see only with the rods, because the threshold of the rods is below the limit of the cones.

More about the mechanism of dark adaptation. It has been known since the work of Hecht in the thirties that there is a close connection between the bleaching of the rod pigment, rhodopsin, and the experience of vision. There is also a close relationship between the bleaching and regeneration of rhodopsin and certain aspects of the dark adaptation curve. For some time it was assumed that dark adaptation could be accounted for entirely by the amount of bleached rhodopsin. But we now know that there are important contributions of the neural portions of the retina as well. One line of evidence for this is the fact that light adaptation and the very early part of dark adaptation occur much too rapidly for the chemical steps in bleaching and regeneration of rhodopsin to take place.

Rushton has proposed a retinal "summation pool" hypothesis to account for the neural part of dark adaptation (1965). This summation pool receives input from the rods and affects the sensitivity of the system by continuing to act as if it were receiving activity from the rods even when there is no light falling on them. In addition to the bleaching of rhodopsin and the decay of activity in the summation pool, it is believed that the receptive fields of ganglion cells may undergo reorganization during the course of dark adaptation. So we see that the mechanisms of dark adaptation form a complex topic—too complex to do justice to here—and they are still only being glimpsed by present theory.

Why War Movies Use Red Light in the Briefing Rooms for Night Missions

This practice is solidly based on visual science. As we recall from our discussion of the Purkinje shift (Chapter 3) the rods are relatively less sensitive to light in the red end of the spectrum than the blue. Therefore red is the best color to use if one wishes to dark adapt the eye without totally depriving it of light. The rods begin dark adapting because they are relatively insensitive to the longer wavelength, dim red light. (Rods and cones are equally sensitive to red light.) Thus the pilots can begin adapting to the darkness in red light as they are simultaneously being briefed for the mission. Then they can go directly out into the dark without having to wait to adapt to the darkness before taking off. The same principle explains why red light is used in certain animal laboratories and zoo displays of nocturnal animals.

when the tongue is adapted to water is twice the DL value when the tongue is adapted to 0.1 M NaCl.

(6) *Generalization of adaptation (or cross adaptation).* The response to stimuli differing qualitatively from the adapting stimulus may be reduced after adaptation to a given stimulus. After adapting to a red stimulus, an orange stimulus will have less saturation and brightness than it had prior to adaptation. After adaptation to sodium chloride (table salt) the salty taste of other salts is reduced. Since in general taste substances of the same quality cross adapt, the occurrence of this outcome of adaptation is taken as evidence that the same receptor mechanism is responsible for coding both stimuli. Figure 5-4 (Smith and McBurney, 1969) shows the extent to which the taste intensity of certain salts is reduced by prior adaptation to sodium chloride.

(7) *Successive Potentiation.* After adaptation to one stimulus the response to another stimulus may be enhanced. The most familiar example of this effect is the case of visual negative afterimages. After looking at a red stimulus for about a minute, a normally white stimulus will appear green and the saturation and brightness of a green stimulus will be enhanced.

Successive potentiation also occurs with taste, temperature, and motion but not with audition or smell. This effect may be demonstrated by a simple

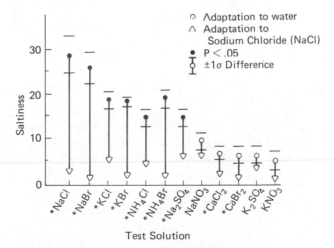

Test Solution

Figure 5-4 Generalization of adaptation between salts. The ordinate shows magnitude estimates of saltiness of the twelve salts listed on the abscissa. The circles show the saltiness of the salts after adaptation to distilled water. The triangles show the saltiness after adaptation to sodium chloride. The distances between the circles and triangles thus indicate the reduction in saltiness as a result of adaptation to sodium chloride. All of the compounds were of the same overall subjective intensity before adaptation to the salt. The differences in the intensity of saltiness before adaptation to salt reflect the fact that most of the salts have other qualities besides salty. [From Smith, D. V., and McBurney, D. H. Gustatory cross-adaptation: Does a single mechanism code the salty taste? *J. Exp. Psych.,* 1969, *80,* 101–5. © 1969 by the American Psychological Association. Reprinted by permission.]

Visual afterimages are a common experience. Anyone who has had his picture taken with a flash camera with recall the persistent afterimage of the flash unit in his visual field. Usually a bright afterimage is followed by a dark one. The bright or positive afterimage takes on various colors in sequence, a phenomenon known as the "flight of colors." The appearance of the afterimage depends on the background against which it is viewed so that the hue, saturation, and brightness of the image can all be changed by looking around the room or even by blinking the eyes. Actually, the topic of afterimages is quite complicated and it would be impossible to summarize the phenomena here. We will consider only the negative afterimages in the paragraphs that follow.

If you fixate a stimulus of a certain hue for 30 to 45 seconds, and then shift your gaze to a white surface, you will see the complementary hue in the white area. Thus if you stare at a yellow patch, a white area will then appear blue. You can also affect the hue of a colored patch by viewing it after adapting the eye to some hue. A yellow patch would look orange after adaptation to blue-green because the red afterimage resulting from adaptation to blue-green would combine with the yellow. The saturation of a yellow patch would be increased after adaptation to a blue stimulus because the yellow afterimage would summate with the yellow patch. You can demonstrate negative afterimages by using a colored piece of paper. Or you can check in almost any introductory psychology textbook for more complicated demonstration figures.

Why do afterimages occur? To explain them we must refer to our discussion of visual mechanisms. When a bright light is presented to the eye, the photopigments in the retinal receptors are bleached, resulting in a neural message in the optic nerve. Positive afterimages presumably result from continued activity in the visual receptors and firing of the optic nerve following stimulation. Negative afterimages, on the other hand, result from the selective bleaching of the photopigments. After being exposed to intense light, those retinal elements bleached by the stimulus will be less responsive to light than unbleached parts of the retina. Thus we see a dark area where the light stimulus was formerly focused on the retina.

Negative afterimages involving color can be best explained within the framework of an opponent process theory. The result of exposing the eye to a certain wavelength of light is that one of a pair of opposing responses becomes weaker and the other relatively stronger. So, for example, the diminished response to a yellow stimulus is accompanied by an increased response to its complement, blue. Because the two responses are incompatible, we cannot see the stimulus and its complement in the same patch of light, but when a neutral patch is viewed, we see the complement.

experiment with temperature. Simultaneously place your right hand in cold water and your left hand in hot water for a few seconds and then place both hands in lukewarm water. The same water will feel warm to your right hand and cool to your left hand. The analogous result in the case of motion after-effects will be discussed in Chapter 9.

These seven outcomes of adaptation constitute the detailed operational definition of adaptation or the "laws of adaptation." Not all of them occur in each sensory system but the regularity with which they occur makes it arbitrary to define adaptation by only one of the outcomes or to ignore the relationships among them.

Mechanisms of Adaptation

We have defined adaptation as the behavioral outcomes of the operation of steady stimulation. It might appear desirable to define the process physiologically as a particular type of change in a receptor. However, this is not possible for the reason that sensory organs accomplish the process of adaptation in many different ways. The response decrement in touch is largely a function of stimulus failure. In vision it is the function of a number of effects including a change in pupil diameter, bleaching of the photopigments and reorganization of the neural receptive fields. In taste the decrement seems to take place not in the receptor but at the synapse between the taste receptor cell and the taste nerve. Adaptation, like the similar physiological processes of learning, respiration, and reproduction, must be defined functionally. The study of the mechanisms of adaptation is important from a comparative point of view but is not necessary for a behavioral understanding of the phenomena themselves.

Similarities to other behavioral phenomena

Adaptation is frequently distinguished from habituation on the basis of presumed differences in mechanism, locus, or time course. Just as adaptation cannot be defined in terms of a particular mechanism, neither is it possible to define adaptation as an exclusively peripheral or receptor phenomenon or by its time course. In vision, audition, and the vestibular senses adaptation

It is often assumed that pure water is tasteless. However, if you have ever tasted distilled water you may have noticed a "flat" taste that is different from ordinary tap water. There was a controversy for many years concerning the taste of water, some believing that it had some intrinsic taste and others believing it to be tasteless. This controversy was ended when it was found that water will take on a bitter-sour taste as a result of adapting the tongue to salt (Bartoshuk, McBurney, and Pfaffmann, 1964). A concentration of salt as weak as is found in saliva is effective in producing this taste.

It was already well known that adapting to sour will cause water to taste sweet and vice versa. Later it was found (McBurney, 1969) that adapting to urea and certain related substances would cause a salty taste in water. Thus, all four taste qualities can be produced in pure distilled water simply by prior adaptation of the tongue to the appropriate substances. We conclude therefore that water is neither tasteless in the ordinary sense nor does it have its own taste. The taste of water depends on the adapting state of the tongue. If the tongue is adapted to water, then the water will be tasteless (McBurney and Bartoshuk, 1972). The taste produced by adapting to a particular substance will contribute to the taste of other compounds tasted after such adaptation. If you have adapted to something sweet, water will taste sour and the taste of something sour will be potentiated. Thus, as is well known, if you are going to have orange juice and Sugar-O's cereal for breakfast, it is better to drink the orange juice first.

The water taste phenomenon also seems responsible for the aftertaste of artichokes. Gourmets have known that artichokes will cause wine, for example, to taste unpleasantly sweet. Bartoshuk et al. (1972) have isolated a compound from artichokes that causes a strong, sweet water taste. Interestingly, the effect is found more in females than males.

takes place centrally to some extent. There are a number of examples of adaptation that have time courses well beyond the typical examples. In the McCollough effect visual negative aftereffects are seen for as long as an hour. The effects of wearing distorting lenses develop over days and may last for days. (See the section on rearrangement studies in Chapter 10.) For these and other reasons it is not possible to distinguish adaptation sharply from other similar concepts such as habituation or satiation. These categories may be regarded as artificially distinguished members of a larger category of behavioral plasticity that con-

We pointed out that adaptation is simple neither in its effects on perception nor in the physiological mechanisms by which it occurs. A particularly good example of this is the McCollough effect (McCollough, 1965), which is produced in the following way. Vertical red and black stripes are presented to the eye for a few seconds. Then horizontal green and black stripes are presented for a few seconds. The two patterns are alternated for several minutes after which vertical or horizontal *white* and black stripes are presented. Now the vertical white stripes will appear green and the horizontal stripes will appear red, apparently ordinary negative afterimages. However, there are several reasons why the mechanism of the McCollough effect must be different from ordinary afterimages. First, two complementary afterimages are built up in the same portion of the visual field at the same time. Second, the effect appears only when a pattern is viewed. Third, the same degree of stimulus stability and intensity is not required as in afterimages (Harris and Gibson, 1968). Finally, the McCollough effect lasts longer than ordinary afterimages (Hajos, 1967, cited by Murch, 1973)—up to two days. This interesting phenomenon is fairly easy to demonstrate because the stimulus conditions are easy to arrange and the parameters of the stimulus are not critical. Unusual effects can also be produced by rotating a single pattern of stripes or by looking at different patterns such as a radiating set of stripes. In the case of a rotating pattern of stripes, the same black and white stripes will appear colorless, green, or red as they come to be oriented in the appropriate directions.

The McCollough effect may result from the adaptation of cortical neurons responding to contours of certain colors. These are believed to be the same as, or similar to, the cells studied by Hubel and Wiesel (see Chapter 7). Another explanation, however (Harris and Gibson, 1968), postulates the existence of fatiguable cells, known as "dipoles," that respond selectively to differences in color at two points in the retina. Although this is a simpler explanation, such dipoles have not been shown to exist in the brain. The long duration of the McCollough effect suggests that it may be related to prism adaptation, specifically the adaptation to color fringes seen at edges between bright and dark areas (see Chapter 10).

tributes to the fitness of the individual organism for survival. Such a category might be called behavioral adaptation with sensory adaptation, habituation, learning, etc. as conveniently labelled subcategories.

6

Interactions
Between Stimuli

Many of the sensory experiments performed in the laboratory use simple stimuli, such as pure tones or solutions of chemicals having only one taste quality. However, most stimuli we encounter in everyday life are more complex. In this chapter we will discuss the ways that stimuli interact when they are presented simultaneously or successively to receptors.

AUDITORY MASKING AND MIXTURES

Two basic kinds of interaction are possible when stimuli are presented simultaneously. First, the stimuli may interact in such a way that a sensation different from that normally produced by either of the components occurs and the separate effects of each stimulus are lost. Color mixing (see Chapter 3) is an example of this type of interaction. For this reason vision is classified as a *synthetic* sense in contrast with audition which is *analytic*. We are able to analyze a complex acoustic stimulus into its components; that is, we can hear "two tones at once" and describe the loudness, pitch, and other aspects of one of the tones while effectively ignoring the other. You can listen to a flute and oboe duet, for example, and quite easily pick out the melody line played by one instrument and follow it separately. However, analysis is not perfect, and sometimes the presence of one tone obscures or masks the other. Then we have the second basic kind of interaction, *masking*. Masking as a result of simultaneous presentation of two stimuli occurs in analytic senses. A synthetic sense generally fuses two stimuli to produce a new sensation quality. This kind of masking must not be confused with backward and forward masking, in which a stimulus presented before or after another stimulus masks the perception of the target stimulus. (See the section on temporal interaction, below). Backward and forward masking occur widely among the senses without regard to the analytic-synthetic distinction. Still another sort of masking involves a patterned stimulus as the masker. Masking by patterns can occur either simultaneously or successively.

Auditory Masking

You have probably had the experience of trying to carry on a conversation at a party over loud band music. You may have to shout to be heard and understood by other people because the music masks your voice. Running water is another excellent masker of sounds such as voices and the ring of the telephone. Most of our everyday listening is done in the presence of noise of various types; therefore understanding of the facts of masking has practical importance.

Weak stimuli are masked more than more intense stimuli. The amount of masking is often determined by measuring thresholds. The intensity at which a signal is just audible without the masking stimulus is its absolute threshold. The masked threshold is the intensity at which it is just audible in the presence

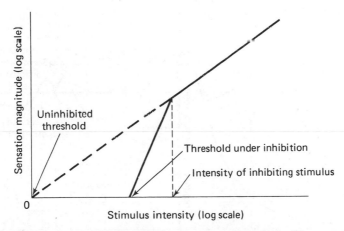

Figure 6-1 Effect of an inhibitory stimulus on sensory magnitude. The same figure can be used to illustrate either the effect of a masking stimulus on loudness or the effect of a bright surround on brightness. The ordinate is the sensation magnitude as measured by magnitude estimation. The abscissa indicates the intensity of the test stimulus. Both axes are plotted logarithmically. The straight line that continues as a dotted line is the function that would be found in the absence of an inhibitory stimulus, the solid line that obtained in the presence of such a stimulus. The inhibitory stimulus steepens the slope of the function up to the point at which the test stimulus overtakes it in intensity. [Modified after Stevens, S. S., and Guirao, M. Loudness functions under inhibition. *Perception and Psychophysics,* 1967, *2,* 459–65.]

of the masking stimulus. The threshold shift is the amount of change in decibels between the absolute threshold and the masked threshold. Not only is the threshold of the signal raised in the presence of the masking stimulus, but the absolute loudness grows more rapidly with each increase in signal intensity above the masked threshold. Thus, as shown in Figure 6-1, the loudness function of a masked tone has a steeper slope than the loudness function under normal listening conditions (Steinberg and Gardner, 1937). The masking effect actually decreases as the intensity of the signal is increased until the point where the signal and the masker are the same intensity. Thereafter they have the same slope or rate of growth of loudness. This phenomenon, called *recruitment,* occurs not only with masking but also with certain types of deafness.

The masking effects of pure tones on pure tones, noise on pure tones, and other combinations have been studied experimentally. Figure 6-2 summarizes the various ways that two pure tones may interact. One tone is constant at 1200 Hz and 80 db above threshold, and the other is variable in frequency and intensity as indicated by the coordinates. The main facts about masking are evident from this figure. The solid line in the figure indicates the threshold of

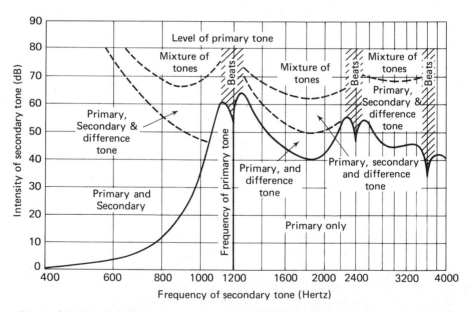

Figure 6-2 Interactions between two pure tones. The ordinate shows the intensity of the secondary, or test, tone in decibels above threshold; the abscissa its frequency. The contours demarcate areas in which the labelled phenomena are heard. [From Wegel, R. L., and Lane, C. E. The auditory masking of one pure tone by another and its probable relation to the dynamics of the inner ear. *Physical Review,* 1923, *24,* 266–85.]

the masked, or secondary, tone. Masking is greater for tones in the same general frequency range than for tones widely separated in frequency. For example, the threshold for the secondary tone is highest when its frequency is close to 1200 Hz. Also, a low-frequency tone is more effective in masking a high-frequency tone than vice versa. This is indicated by the large proportion of the area to the right of 1200 Hz which is under the solid line in contrast to the area under the line to the left of 1200 Hz. Under the solid line, only the primary tone is heard; that is, the secondary tone is masked. One prominent feature of the graph is the presence of areas in which beats are heard. Beats, the waxing and waning in loudness of a tone, result when two similar frequencies are presented to the ear. In the above example, beats occur when the secondary tone is approximately 1200 Hz, or when the secondary tone is an approximate multiple (harmonic) of the primary tone; i.e., around 2400 Hz or 3600 Hz.

The situation above the masked threshold is further complicated by combination tones. Combination tones, such as difference or summation tones, occur when two intense frequencies are presented to the ear. The frequencies of difference tones are proportions between the higher (H) and the lower (L) frequencies, e.g., $2L - H$, $3L - H$, etc. Summation tones are of the sort $L + H$, $2L + H$, $3L + H$, etc. The auditory system is nonlinear at high intensities of stimulation; that is, the displacement in the system is no longer linearly proportional to the force of stimulation applied to it. The nonlinearity can be shown mathematically to lead to the production of different types of combination tones, depending on the input to the system. We will not discuss these interactions in detail, but simply mention that they are examples of distortions produced by the auditory system similar to the distortion problems you are probably familiar with in sound systems.

Taste Mixtures

The sense of taste is analytic. Thus, when acetic acid and sucrose are mixed, the resulting solution is sweet and sour, not, say, salty or bitter. In fact a mixture of these compounds is what is responsible for the taste of sweet-and-sour sauce (vinegar and sugar). If taste were synthetic, and sweet and sour were opponent tastes, as is sometimes assumed, the mixture should be tasteless. In general, each component of a taste mixture is tasted, but there is mutual suppression. If one is stronger than the other, the weaker may not be tasted. The laws of mixture suppression are not well worked out, even in broad outline. The amount of suppression varies among taste qualities. Different compounds having the same taste (e.g., sugars) may add their tastes as if the concentrations were being added together, not the sensations (i.e., $R = S_1^{.5} + S_2^{.5} > R = (S_1 + S_2)^{.5}$). This may account for some of the apparent mixture suppression (Bartoshuk, 1975).

Much of the information about taste mixtures has come originally from cooking tradition and folklore. Cooks know that certain tastes can be enhanced or suppressed depending on the particular ingredient added and the amount used. A pinch of salt is frequently added to enhance or "bring out" the sweet taste, as in candies. It is also recommended in cooking tradition that if soup is made too salty, adding the right amount of sugar will suppress the saltiness without making the soup noticeably sweet. A small amount of sugar is sometimes added to mask the bitter taste of some vegetables. Certain substances, called taste enhancers, are said to enhance whatever taste is present. Perhaps the best known taste enhancer is monosodium glutamate (MSG). MSG does seem to improve flavor of food, but there is some question as to how it operates—perhaps it just adds a salty taste to the flavors already present. Surprisingly, while most of this information has had practical application in the kitchen and in reference to food and flavor, much of it has not been confirmed in controlled laboratory conditions using simple taste solutions.

The effects of temperature upon taste sensations have been experimentally tested. McBurney, Collings, and Glanz (1973) determined thresholds for representatives of the four basic taste qualities at six temperatures in the range between the pain thresholds for cold and hot. For all four taste qualities, our sensitivity is greatest at some temperature between 22° and 32° C (approximately 71° to 89° F). This confirms the advice given in the cookbooks that food should be seasoned at the temperature at which you intend to eat it. If you salt the soup when it is at room temperature and serve it much hotter, it will not taste salty enough. Likewise, tea sweetened before the ice is added will need more sugar when it is cold. On the other hand, lemonade that is too sour may taste fine once it is chilled.

Odor Mixtures

As in taste, a more nearly additive mixture results when similar odors are mixed than when the odor qualities are quite different. If the component odors are different, there is usually suppression; that is, the total intensity will be less than the sum of the individual components (Berglund et al., 1973). When two odors are present together, the stronger odor may mask, or cover up, the other odor. Masking is one of several ways to get rid of unpleasant odors and it is the principle underlying the use of some air fresheners and perfumes.

SPATIAL INTERACTION

In general, the response to a stimulus depends on the way the energy is distributed over the receptor. Thus the receptor is not just a collector of energy, but responds to differences in the energy from one place to another. In this section we deal with the spatial interactions between relatively simple stimuli. More complex interactions, some functioning by means of the same mechanism, are dealt with in the next chapter under the topic of pattern perception.

The interactions that we deal with here are of two general types. First are those that involve bilateral stimulation. The various sense organs are bilaterally symmetrical and there are interactions that occur when stimuli are presented to corresponding loci on the two sides of the body. Interaural auditory masking and auditory localization will be considered under this category. The second type of interaction takes place within a single receptor, such as one eye or on the skin of one arm.

Auditory Interaural Masking

We have shown that one auditory stimulus may be masked by another stimulus presented to the same receptor. Does "cross masking" also occur?— that is, can a stimulus presented to one ear be masked by a sound at the other ear? As an everyday example, does it help to put your hand over your other ear when you are talking on the telephone in a noisy room? The answer is that there is very little "cross masking." A very intense high-frequency tone in one ear can mask somewhat a low-frequency tone to the other ear (Ward, 1967). However, the masking can be mostly attributed to direct stimulation of one ear by sound conducted to it across the head. So, putting your hand over your ear may cut down distraction a little, but it would be more useful to put your hand over the mouthpiece to prevent conduction of sound from it to the earpiece.

Although there is little cross-masking, stimuli presented simultaneously to the two ears do interact; their effects summate under certain conditions. When the same threshold-level tone is presented to both ears simultaneously, the effectiveness of binaural summation is in the range of 3 to 6 decibels. This is true for the person whose two ears are equally sensitive. For the average listener, however, the two ears differ in threshold sensitivity by as much as 6 db; therefore the binaural threshold will probably be about the same as that for the most sensitive ear. Above threshold, the binaural loudness function is steeper than monaural. The slope of the binaural function is 0.6 whereas the slope for monaural listening is 0.54 (Reynolds and Stevens, 1960). For maximum summation, two tones of the same intensity heard by both ears must be of the same frequency (Hellman and Zwislocki, 1963). Such a tone heard binaurally sounds twice as loud as the same tone heard monaurally.

Vision

On a dark night, you can see better if you use two eyes rather than one. If there were complete binocular summation, you would expect the binocular threshold to be as low as one-half the monocular threshold. Such is not the case; however, the monocular threshold is slightly lower than what would be expected on a purely probabilistic basis of two eyes against one. Thus, summation of the two receptor areas is a less significant effect in vision than in audition. It turns out that there are advantages to having the two eyes behave differently from the two ears. For one thing, with binocular summation, the world would darken every time you closed one eye. The greatest problem would come from the fact that the visual fields of the two eyes do not overlap completely. On the periphery, there are areas that stimulate only one retina. If we were to look directly at a white screen, for example, and there were binocular summation, we would see a bright center area bounded on each side by darker bands. This would undoubtedly create problems in the coding of visual information.

Brightness Contrast

We have discussed the interactions that occur in the visual system when stimuli are presented simultaneously to different eyes. It is also important for us to consider interactions that result from the stimulation of adjacent areas of the same retina. Such interactions affect both the brightness and the hue of what we see. The effect of light falling on part of the retina is not confined to the retinal elements stimulated. Stimulation of adjacent areas affects brightness. In Figure 6-3, compare the appearance of the scene against a black background and its appearance against a white background. The scene appears light gray against the black background but very dark against the white background. This is the phenomenon of simultaneous brightness contrast. The use of different intensities of surround illumination produces two different brightness impressions from the two identical grey areas. There are many examples of contrast. You have probably noticed when looking out the window at dusk that the outside (the target) appears darker when the light is on in the room where you are (the surround) than when it is off. You may also have noticed that the brighter the light, the darker a black object appears; thus, paradoxically, an 8-ball looks much blacker in the sun than in a dark room. Contrast therefore serves to accentuate differences in apparent brightness between adjacent areas of different luminances.

Figure 6-3 Simultaneous brightness contrast. The two scenes have identical average intensity. The effect is much greater in life than we can depict in the figure because the range of intensities is greater than can be produced on paper.

One method for studying brightness contrast psychophysically consists of presenting to one dark-adapted eye a test field surrounded by an inducing field. The other dark-adapted eye sees the matching field. The subject is required to make a binocular match of brightness between the two fields. Increasing the inducing luminance generally leads to decreased perceived brightness of the test field. This is true, however, only when the inducing field has higher luminance than the test field. When the brightness of a disc surrounded by an annulus is scaled, the results are as shown in Figure 6-1. As the brightness of the annulus is increased above the level of the disc, the slope of the brightness function increases. This recruitment-like phenomenon is similar to that observed in auditory masking.

Closely related to brightness contrast is a visual phenomenon called glare, which is of great practical importance. Bookkeepers used to wear green eyeshades to keep the glare of an exposed light from interfering with seeing their writing and figures. Now the upper part of the car windshield is often tinted to protect the driver from the glare caused by the sun. You have probably found that at night objects visible on or along the highway (and the road itself) disappear when headlights flash into your eyes as an oncoming car approaches.

The mechanism of glare is essentially masking by scattered light plus ordinary masking. It is generally assumed that light from the glare source is scattered in the eye by structures such as the cornea, the lens, and the media of the eye (humors). Any part of the retina which is illuminated tends to result in the scatter of some light into surrounding regions.

Color Contrast

Simultaneous color contrast is analogous to brightness contrast. Here there may be a change in hue or saturation due to the influence of a nearby inducing color. A colored inducing field surrounding or adjoining a neutral grey test field can cause the complement of the surround hue to appear in the neutral area. The contrast color will be most vivid at the border region. Thus, a grey patch on a yellow background will appear blue and on a red background, green. If the test field is already colored, it will look like a mixture of its hue and the complement of the inducing area. Color contrast, like brightness contrast, serves to accentuate differences, since any color placed beside another tends to look more like the complement of the adjacent color. (Recall that complementary colors are opposite each other on the color circle.) This leads to a subjective exaggeration of the physical differences between the two colors. In Chapter 5 we discussed the visual phenomenon of successive contrast (afterimages) which is based on the adapted state of the retina. Simultaneous color and brightness contrast, on the other hand, are thought to be the result of lateral inhibitory interactions in the retina, to be discussed in Chapter 7.

Several variables are important in the observation of color contrast. A large inducing field and small test field give the best results, and it is best if the two fields are contiguous, or at least very close. The most effective situation is one in which the two fields have approximately equal brightness, and the inducing hue is at a high level of saturation. It is important to eliminate any contour between the two fields as well as any textural cues in either field. For example, in a simple demonstration of color contrast, a small grey square is placed in the center of a piece of colored paper; a piece of tissue paper placed over the papers enhances the color contrast by obscuring both contours and texture.

Contrast in Taste

Early experimenters in taste sought to find simultaneous contrast in that modality analogous to the phenomena that we have discussed in the visual system. When two areas on the tongue were stimulated with taste solutions of different qualities, enhancement of the taste sensation on one area resulted from the stimulation of an adjoining area on the tongue. Earlier experimenters (Kiesow, 1894; Bujas, 1937) reported contrast between salty and sweet, and salty and sour. When the two stimuli were the same quality, on the other hand, increasing the concentration of the inducing stimulus raised the threshold for, or masked, the taste stimulus on the test area (Bujas, 1937). However, as in all sensory systems, it was impossible to measure a subject's sensitivity independent of the subjective criterion he adopted to judge the stimuli presented. If control is not exercised, the subject may change his criterion over time. More recent experiments employing new psychophysical methods suggest that the reports of taste contrast may have been the result of a criterion shift when the two stimuli were presented simultaneously to the tongue.

TEMPORAL INTERACTION

We have discussed the results of stimuli presented simultaneously to the same or to different receptor areas. These are spatial interactions. In the next sections we will consider those interactions that occur from the successive presentation of stimuli to the same or different receptors.

Backward and Forward Masking

In vision, if a brief test flash containing readily perceivable information is preceded by a brighter masking flash, the brief second flash may not be perceived. This is called forward masking. Backward masking occurs when the test stimulus occurs first and is masked by the following brighter masking flash. In both types of masking, masking may be complete up to a certain time delay between the two stimuli; beyond that interval it is only partial.

Although most studies of auditory masking involve the simultaneous presentation of the masking stimulus and the signal, forward and backward masking also occurs in audition. The maximum delay between the two stimuli for complete backward and forward masking is about 20 msec. (Elliott, 1962).

Forward and backward masking have also been demonstrated in the cutaneous senses. The threshold for tactile stimulation to one finger, for example, can be raised by presenting similar masking stimuli to another finger. Different delays hold for backward and for forward masking, and the delay also varies with the body locus studied; for example, much longer delays are effective on the forearm than on the fingers.

For most people, the concept of forward masking seems consistent with normal temporal relationships between stimuli as they impinge on sensory receptors. It is quite logical that a prior event could influence an event occurring later. A retroactive suppression as is found in backward masking is more difficult to grasp, however. It is surprising that a prior stimulus can be made less effective by subsequent stimulation. There have been several theories proposed to account for this phenomenon. Most assume that the neural activity caused by the later intense masking stimulus "overtakes" the neural activity caused by the earlier test stimulus.

When stimuli are presented successively to adjacent localities in the retina, metacontrast and paracontrast can result. These phenomena are combinations of spatial and temporal masking. In paracontrast, the brightness of a stimulus is reduced when it is preceded by a masking stimulus to an adjacent area. Paracontrast is a type of forward masking; metacontrast is backward masking. Since the experiments and theories in this area become quite complicated, we will refrain from discussing them in greater detail here. (See Breitmeyer and Ganz, 1976.)

Auditory Localization

Auditory localization is aided by the relative positioning of the ears on either side of a solid mass and the resulting fact that each ear receives somewhat different stimulation. Let us consider localization in the most important plane, the horizontal. There are three major cues for localization in the horizontal plane. First, the sound will reach one ear before the other unless a sound source is centered straight ahead. If the sound must travel farther to one ear than the other, there will be a difference in time of arrival at the two ears of about 0.029 msec for each cm of difference. (Here we are assuming that the listener is in an area relatively free of reflected sound.) If the sound is directly opposite one ear, it will be 0.6 msec later arriving at the other ear. Amazingly, we are able to discriminate a difference in time of arrival of as little as 1.0 μsec (microsecond). Second, due to the "shadowing" effect of the head, there are intensity differences at the two ears when the sound comes from one side of the head. The head serves to attenuate the sound to the farther ear, and the intensity difference is thus the greatest when the sound source is directly opposite one ear. The difference in intensity tends to be greater for high-frequency than for low-frequency tones, so this shadowing effect becomes an important cue for high-frequency sounds. Expressed in another way, low tones bend around corners better. If you are down a side street when a parade passes an intersection, for example, you will hear the bass drum and the tubas when the band is out of sight. Only as the band enters the intersection will the trumpets and piccolos be heard. The same effect will be produced by a band some distance directly down the street but for a different reason: low tones carry farther in a straight line than high tones. The third cue is the phase angle of the tone at the two ears. If the sound must travel farther to one ear than the other there will be a phase difference in the signal received by the two ears. This is a useful cue for frequencies less than about 1500 Hz. For higher frequencies phase difference is not a useable cue.

All three of these cues are used to locate the source of a sound, depending on its frequency spectrum. We can study these cues in a somewhat artificial situation by considering a person wearing headphones so that the sounds to each ear can be manipulated easily. A sound will be localized to the right if it arrives earlier at the right ear than at the left. If, however, succeeding stimuli are made louder at the left ear, the source will be perceived as moving back toward the midline, thus demonstrating the trading relationship in localization between time and intensity.

Auditory localization has been studied not only by psychophysical procedures but also in terms of central neurophysiology. It is obviously essential for localization to occur that there be binaural input to some higher centers

We pointed out before that there are three cues to localization of a sound source in the horizontal plane: differences in arrival time, intensity, and phase angle at the two ears. Phase angle is more effective for low tones, and intensity differences are greater for high frequencies. Time of arrival is about equally effective for all frequencies, if the onset is sudden enough. (To be a little more precise, the sudden onset of a tone has high frequency transients and these are necessary for onset time to be an effective cue.) Birds make excellent use of these facts of localization in producing their calls. The territorial call of a bird in signalling his location to a rival contains low and high frequencies presented with many abrupt bursts or chirps. On the other hand a bird's alarm call will contain medium frequencies which are at the same time too high for phase angle and too low for intensity differences to be useable by a predator. Also the intensity of the call will rise and fall very gradually so that time of arrival is not a useable cue (Marler, 1959). What about foghorns? There are probably two reasons for the low pitch of foghorns. First low tones allow the use of phase angle in localization. But, equally important, low tones carry farther than high tones.

in the auditory system. The lowest level at which impulses from the two ears converge is the superior olivary complex of the brainstem. There is evidence that cells in the accessory olive of this complex respond to differences in time of arrival of sound at the two ears (Galambos, Schwartzkopff and Rupert, 1959). In other words, the probability of a cell's firing is greater if the contralateral ear is stimulated before the ipsilateral, or vice versa for other cells. Some cells at this level and at some higher levels (e.g., inferior colliculus, medial geniculate) respond to interaction between the input from the two ears (Hall, 1965; Rose, et al., 1966). For example, some cells fire only when they receive stimulation from both ears; some are excited by input from one ear and inhibited by input from the other ear; others are excited only by ipsilateral or contralateral input. There are other neurons in the superior olivary complex that respond to frequency differences in the makeup of the sound reaching the two ears (Masterton and Diamond, 1974).

7

Sensitivity
to Spatial and Temporal
Patterns of Energy

In our introductory chapter we stressed that organisms respond more to patterns of energy than to amount of energy. For example, the amount of light falling on an object in direct sunlight is about 1,000,000 times greater than that cast by the full moon. Nevertheless, it is not difficult to recognize a face or to read a page of this book under either condition. The absolute amount of energy is practically ignored by the visual system for purposes of pattern recognition. This is an extremely useful property for a system that must operate under widely varying conditions of stimulation. The ear is not very sensitive to the absolute pressure on the eardrum, except when pressure changes such as those resulting from large changes in altitude cause minor discomfort. However, the ear is exquisitely sensitive to vibrations in the frequency range of 1,000 to 4,000 Hz, which, not incidentally, is the most important range for the discrimination of speech.

These examples involve perception of patterns of energy at the receptor; spatial patterns in reading and temporal patterns in speech. The purpose of this chapter is to discuss some perceptual problems that involve patterns of energy and to introduce some concepts that have been applied to these problems with considerable success in recent years. The methods come from a branch of electrical engineering known as linear systems analysis. A detailed understanding of this highly technical area requires more math background than can be assumed for readers of this book. However, since the insights provided by linear systems can be applied to understanding perceptual problems, we will try to give an intuitive grasp of some of them.

METHODS OF LINEAR
SYSTEMS ANALYSIS

Fourier Analysis

This is a technique that allows one to take a complicated function of time or space and separate it into simpler functions. Fourier's theorem says that it is possible to take any periodic function and analyze it into a set of sine wave functions. (If you haven't had college trigonometry, some sinusoids are shown in Figure 7-1). For example, consider the sound produced by a person saying the sound "ah" that is picked up by a microphone and displayed on an oscilloscope. It will look like Figure 7-2 where the amplitude of the sound energy is displayed as a function of time. This periodic wave may not look much like a sine wave to you, but it is possible to analyze this sound into a number of component sine waves of various frequencies.

Modulation Transfer Functions

These are mathematical representations of the way that a system responds to various stimulus inputs. Most basically, a modulation transfer function describes the extent to which every frequency that is input to the system is either lost by the system or faithfully reproduced. The transfer function can be thought of as a measure of the limitations of the system in following the input. One kind of transfer function you may be familiar with is the frequency response curve of an audio system. A typical one such as that in Figure 7-3 shows, on the ordinate, the amount by which a stimulus is attenuated as a function of the frequency of the input. Attenuation refers to the percent by which the input is reduced in passing through the system. A high fidelity system should be nearly flat over a wide range of frequencies, indicating faithful representation of the stimulus in the output. A cheaper system would show more attenuation at the high and low frequencies. For our purpose, obtaining a transfer function involves measuring something very similar to the frequency-response curve of the audio system (actually the phase shift should also be measured for each frequency but this has not been feasible in most sensory work). Sinusoidal stimuli of various frequencies are input to the system and the amount of attenuation is measured at each frequency. Unlike Fourier analysis, which is a mathematical procedure, determination of the transfer function is an experimental problem. The transfer function, once known, allows one to predict the response of the system to any arbitrary stimulus whatever. In other words, it is a complete description of the temporal (or spatial) frequency response of the system. This is possible because we can also take a number of sinusoids and combine them to produce a more complex waveform. This is exactly the opposite of Fourier analysis and is known as *Fourier synthesis.*

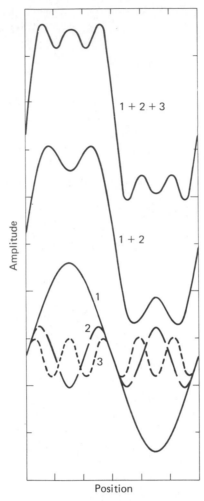

Figure 7-1 Illustration of a periodic wave that can be broken down into separate sine waves. The curve at the top is the result of adding together the three sine waves shown at the bottom. When curve numbers 1 and 2 are added together the result is the function shown in the middle. The addition of curve 3 yields the result at the top. You can see that the curve becomes progressively more squared. If you keep on adding sine waves that are successive odd multiples of the fundamental frequency (1F, 3F, 5F . . .) and they have the corresponding amplitudes A, 1/3A, 1/5A . . . . eventually the curve will approach a square wave (see Figure 7-4).

Why would one want to do this? Having analyzed the signal into sinusoids and having discovered via the transfer function to what extent each of these sinusoids is attenuated by the system, we now want to recombine those attenuated sinusoids and predict the output of the system. We have summarized the steps of this process as follows: (a) Fourier analysis of the stimulus (find what frequencies the stimulus is made up of); (b) measurement of the transfer function

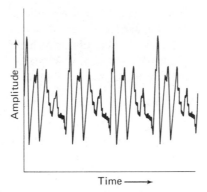

Figure 7-2 Typical waveform of the speech sound "ah." This wave can also be broken down into component sine waves. [From Denes, P. B., and Pinson, E. N. *The speech chain.* ©by Bell Laboratories, 1963. Reprinted by permission of Doubleday & Company.]

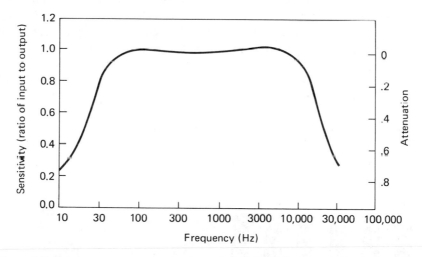

Figure 7-3 Frequency-response curve of a typical high fidelity system, showing sensitivity and system response to stimuli composed of various temporal frequencies.

of the system (find what frequencies the system tends to lose); (c) comparison of the results from Fourier analysis of the stimulus with the transfer function of the system to see what frequencies are left (you can think of this as a multiplication of the results of step one by the results of step two); and (d) Fourier synthesis of what is left (put the pieces of the stimulus back together) to see what it should actually sound like. The following will serve as an analogy. Suppose you have a favorite rock record that you have listened to often on a very good high fidelity system. This is analogous to step one. you know what frequencies the record contains. Your friend has a cheap record player. You have heard many records played on this machine so you are familiar with its limitations. This is analogous to measuring the transfer function of the record player. But you have never heard your particular record on his player. You can still predict what your record will sound like on his machine before you ever play it even if he only plays Bluegrass music and Wagnerian operas. We will now describe some areas of application of transfer functions to sensory problems.

MODULATION TRANSFER FUNCTIONS
FOR SPATIAL FREQUENCIES

The example of the audio system discussed above concerned temporal modulation (intensity as a function of time). This was used because most readers are probably more familiar with the concept of temporal frequencies. However, these techniques are equally applicable to spatial frequencies or patterns, such as we touched upon when we mentioned reading under different conditions of illumination. The intensity of the stimulus now varies as a function of space rather than time. An example of a spatial frequency pattern with which you are no doubt familiar (if not by that name) is the square wave, which alternates in an all-or-none fashion between two values. Figure 7–4 shows a plot of reflectance as a square wave function of distance. What such a function would look like in the case of a visual pattern is shown in the left part of the same figure. As one goes from left to right the reflectance of the paper varies in an all-or-none fashion between maximum and minimum (white and black). The pattern looks like an ordinary set of stripes, which it is.

The square wave pattern is an interesting one for several reasons. First,

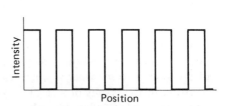

Figure 7–4 A square wave pattern and a graph of the pattern. The graph on the right represents the intensity of the light from the pattern as a function of position. The graph is made by drawing a horizontal line across the pattern of stripes and plotting the intensity of light reflected from the pattern at any point. If you have trouble going from the pattern to the graph, remember that the striped pattern has three dimensions—horizontal, vertical, and reflectance. The graph represents only two, horizontal and reflectance.

it can be shown by Fourier analysis to consist of a series of sine components, all of which are harmonics of the fundamental frequency. Second, it is an easy pattern to produce as a stimulus and so has been extensively studied in sensory as well as other work. Third, if one is studying the response of a system at the upper limits of frequency, the square wave becomes equivalent to the sine wave when the system can no longer perceive the higher frequencies.

Figure 7-5 shows an interesting pattern that differs in three important ways from the last figure. First, it is a sine function instead of a square wave function. Second, the frequency of the pattern is not constant across the figure, but increases from left to right. Third, the amplitude of modulation, that is, the contrast, is not constant but decreases from the top down. A horizontal line drawn on it will pass through sine waves having the same amplitude of modulation (but different frequency). A vertical line will pass through points where the frequency is the same (but with different amplitude of modulation). This pattern illustrates very clearly that the sensitivity of the eye to spatial frequency modulation is a function of frequency. This is demonstrated by the fact that a number of vertical stripes are seen extending from the top of the figure, but they do not all seem to extend the same distance down the figure. The bands will seem to extend farthest down the page at about six cycles per degree of visual angle (the calibration of the figure is based on the book's being held approximately at arm's length). The point at which the lines seem to end can be considered to be the threshold for detection of spatial frequency modulation. The percent modulation can be read directly from the ordinate. If you were to trace a line along the loci of the threshold as a function of frequency, you would have a crude spatial-frequency modulation-transfer function.

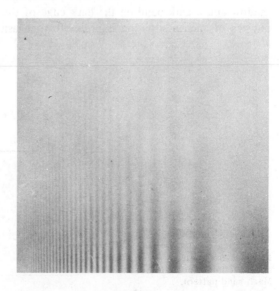

Figure 7-5 Demonstration of the human spatial frequency modulation transfer function. [From Cornsweet, T. N. *Visual percep tion.* New York: Academic Press, 1970.]

SOME RESULTS OF THE SPATIAL-MODULATION TRANSFER FUNCTION—THE MACH BAND PATTERN

Ernst Mach, who was mentioned in the first chapter, was the first to study a very interesting phenomenon, which has been given his name. Consider the pattern of light that is graphed in Figure 7-6. This pattern has constant reflectance from the left up to a point at which there begins a gradient, or steady decrease in reflectance, that continues to another point after which reflectance is again constant at a lower level. We showed the graph of the reflectance before showing the pattern itself because it does not look much like what the graph would lead you to expect. Figure 7-7 is such a pattern. Looking at it, you will see that it seems brighter on the left and darker on the right, and in the middle the brightness decreases from left to right. So far, so good. However, there are two lines in the figure that should not be there; a bright line at the edge of the bright side just before the gradient begins (actually the brightest area in the figure), and a dark line at the edge of the dark side that is darker than any other part of the figure. These lines are usually very compelling. In fact, students often refuse to believe that they are not physically present. If you were to take a light meter and read the amount of light reflected from the surface of the figure and graph it you would obtain something of the form of the previous figure, with nothing to suggest bright or dark lines. These patterns are very common in nature and there are almost certainly some in the place where you are now reading this book. Look around for a shadow cast by a fairly small light source such as a single light bulb, or the sun. If it is the principal source of light in the room, you will probably see a light band on the bright side of the shadow and a dark band on the dark edge of the shadow. Consideration of the physics of such a situation is probably the easiest way to convince you that

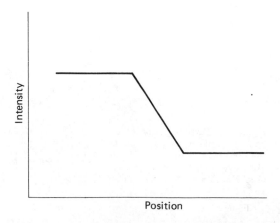

Figure 7-6 Graph of reflectance as a function of position from the Mach-band pattern.

Figure 7-7 Demonstration of Mach bands.

there is not any more light falling on the bright line, or less on the dark line, than the nearby bright or dark side respectively. Refer to Figure 7-8, which shows a shadow cast by a light source large enough to cast a fairly large penumbra, or half shadow. The unshaded portion, of course, will receive light from

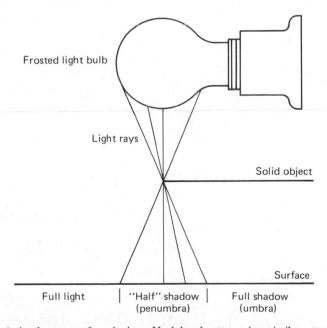

Frosted light bulb

Light rays

Solid object

Full light   "Half" shadow   Full shadow
              (penumbra)   (umbra)

Surface

Figure 7-8 A simple means of producing a Mach-band pattern. Any similar setup will do.

the whole source, and the full shadow will receive no light directly from the source. In the region of the penumbra or "half shadow," the amount of light falling on the surface decreases from the unshaded to the fully shaded portion in direct proportion to the amount of the source that is "seen" by the surface at that point. There is no way that more light can fall on the bright edge of the shadow than on the unshaded portion to cause the bright line or, conversely, no way less light can fall on the dark edge than on the rest of the full shadow to cause a dark line.

If the Mach bands are not present physically in the stimulus, how can they be explained? There are two ways in which we can approach their explanation. The first is based on the idea of the transfer function, and the second on the physiology of lateral inhibition. These two explanations are actually two sides of the same coin. The first is a mathematical model that could represent a number of physiological mechanisms. The second is the mechanism of the Mach band in those organisms that have been studied physiologically. It is not certain, but the evidence is very strong, that the physiological mechanisms are similar, if not identical, in man.

The spatial frequency modulation transfer function for the human visual system is shown in Figure 7-9. You can see that this is quite similar to the line that could be obtained by tracing the loci of the thresholds for stripes of varying frequencies and modulation depths in Figure 7-5. From this we can see that the eye is not particularly sensitive to very high spatial frequencies. This refers to the upper limit of resolution of the visual system which is a limit imposed by the optics of the eye. Neither is the eye sensitive to very low spatial frequencies, from which we infer that the visual system will respond to a gradual

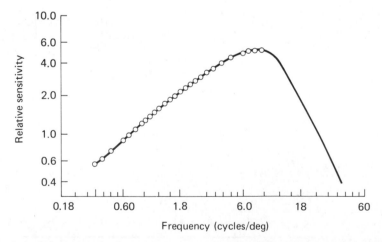

Figure 7-9 The transfer function of the human eye for spatial frequency modulation. In this figure sensitivity is plotted as a function of spatial frequency, an inversion of the relationship in Figure 7-5. [From Cornsweet, T. N. *Visual perception.* New York: Academic Press, 1970.]

change in intensity as if it were constant. Going back to the Mach band, a Fourier analysis of the pattern would show that a number of different frequencies taken together would constitute the Mach band pattern. Generally speaking, it is possible to say that the low frequencies determine the intensity in the area where intensity is constant or changing gradually. The medium and higher frequencies determine the shape of the function in the region of the change from steady intensity to the gradient; in other words, at the locations at which the Mach bands occur. The reason the Mach bands are seen, therefore, is that the visual system is more sensitive to the frequencies that determine the shape of the pattern in these transition areas than to the lower frequencies. The very high frequencies are not seen, but that mostly eliminates some information on the sharpness of the contours. The lower frequency information is also thrown away. That is what minimizes the differences in brightness between the more and less intense areas and also in the gradient, leaving the differences in brightness along the edges exaggerated.

We have gone into the transfer function in some detail considering that its application to sensory work is rather recent and its usefulness is still debated. Nevertheless, we feel its potential for sensory work has warranted the discussion. We will consider transfer functions again in the context of brightness and color contrast and constancy and also in the study of temporal resolution in vision.

LATERAL INHIBITION

The spatial transfer function of the visual system is determined by two basic processes. The high frequency cutoff is, as we said, due to the limits of the eye as an optical system. The attenuation, or lack of sensitivity, at the low-frequency end is due to the neurophysiological process of lateral inhibition. This is an extremely important concept for sensory processes because it is of great generality among the sensory systems and it accounts for many important perceptual phenomena. Recall the anatomy of the retina, as discussed in Chapter 3. There are the bipolar cells that connect cones and rods to the ganglion cells. In addition, there are horizontal cells that connect the receptors together and amacrine cells that communicate among the ganglion cells. Such lateral connections allow for considerable interactions between neighboring areas in the retina. Exactly how these connections function is now being unravelled. In a classic study, Kuffler (1953) recorded the electrical activity of the ganglion cells of the cat while a small spot of light explored the retina. He found that the light caused an increase in the activity of the ganglion cell when it fell within a fairly small area of the retina. However, there was a larger area surrounding this first area in which the light caused a decrease in the activity of the ganglion cell. In between these two areas there was a region in which there were responses to both the onset and the offset of the stimulus, indicating a mixing of the two other areas. These three areas together constitute the receptive field of the ganglion cell, which is defined as that area of the retina which, when stimulated, will influence the activity of the cell. There were also some receptive fields which instead of having an excitatory center and an inhibitory surround had an "off" center and an "on" surround. These results indicate clearly that there is inhibitory interaction in the cat's retina, presumably the result of activity in horizontal and/or amacrine cells.

The mammalian retina is rather complicated for quantitative study of these effects which, incidentally, have been obtained in many different species besides cats. Hartline, Ratliff and others have done extensive analysis of lateral interactions in a much simpler preparation, the compound eye of the Horseshoe crab, Limulus. This creature is familiar to anyone who has spent much time near the ocean. It is very interesting from a taxonomic point of view because it is considered a living fossil, related to the spiders. It has two pairs of eyes. The one we are interested in is the lateral eye, a typical, but very large, compound eye. Each ommatidium, or individual receptor, receives and focuses light independent of the others and contributes its own private neuron to the optic nerve. However, there is a plexus of fibers that connects the nerve fibers

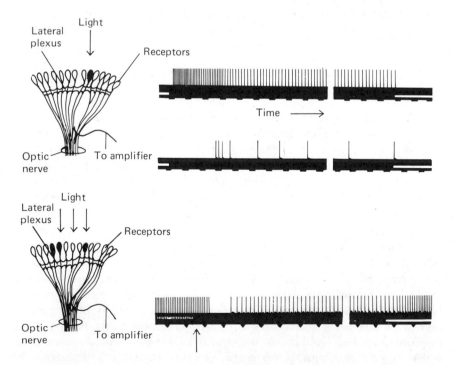

Figure 7-10 Action potentials from the eye of Limulus showing the influence of lateral inhibition. On the left is a schematic diagram of the eye of the Limulus. On the right are three records (to be read from left to right) taken from an oscillograph of the response of a single ommatidium (element) of the Limulus eye. [From Ratliff, F. *Mach bands: Quantitative studies on neural networks in the retina.* San Francisco: Holden-Day, 1965.]

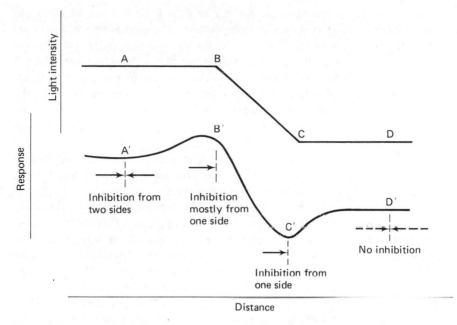

Figure 7-11 Prediction of the appearance of the Mach-band pattern from the facts of lateral inhibition.

together just below the ommatidia. Activity in this plexus inhibits the activity in the neurons leaving neighboring ommatidia.

Elegant quantitative studies have shown that the amount of inhibition produced by an ommatidium is a function both of the amount of light falling on it and the distance at which the inhibitory effect is measured. The more light falling on the ommatidium, the more the inhibition. However, the inhibitory effect decreases with increasing distance between the ommatidium producing the inhibition and the one at which the effect is measured. From these studies it can be shown that the Limulus must see the Mach band pattern in essentially the same way we do.

Figure 7-10 illustrates the inhibition produced in one nerve fiber by light falling on its neighbors. The upper record shows the activity in a single fiber as the result of a bright light falling on its ommatidium; the second, the response to a weaker stimulus. The lower trace shows what happens when the same amount of light is shone on this particular ommatidium, but with stimulation at the same time of neighboring ommatidia. The presentation of light to a larger part of the eye *reduces* the activity in the fiber being recorded from. This occurs because each ommatidium, besides sending excitation along its nerve fiber, sends inhibition to all the neighboring fibers by way of the plexus referred to above.

Figure 7-11 illustrates how such an effect would produce the Mach band.

Suppose that we are recording the activity of a single nerve fiber originating in the ommatidium that is shown in bold outline. The distribution of light over the whole eye is represented by curve 1. We will continue to record from the same fiber as we move the pattern to different places across the eye. Curve 2 shows the activity in our fiber as each particular part of curve 1 falls on the same ommatidium. You will notice that the input, or the curve indicating the original distribution of light on the eye, is not faithfully represented in the output, the response of the ommatidium. The reason for this is the action of inhibition, as follows.

If the part of the pattern labelled A is located over the ommatidium being recorded from, there will be a certain amount of activity in the fiber as indicated by point A' on curve 2. Then we move the pattern of light to the left until point B is over the same ommatidium. There we find the amount of activity indicated by point B', which is more than at A'. The reason that the B' response is greater is that, even though there is the same amount of light at the two points on the pattern, when A was over the ommatidium, inhibition was being received by the ommatidium from both the right and left of the point. The amount of inhibition an ommatidium exerts on its neighbors is proportional to the amount of light falling upon it. Thus when B is over the ommatidium, the same amount of inhibition is received from the left as when point A was located there. But less inhibition is received from the right of B because less light is falling on the ommatidia to the right of B than to the right of A. The converse of this argument explains why C' responds less than D'. Both receive the same amount of light (but less than A and B). But when point C falls on the ommatidium, the ommatidium receives more inhibition from the more highly responding left side. However, when point D falls on the ommatidium, there is little inhibition coming from either side. Thus, the response at D' is greater than at C'. We have gone into this explanation in some detail because it provides a relatively simple physiological model of a very important principle of sensory processes. Of course, the human visual system is more complicated but the same sorts of phenomena operate and similar physiological processes are believed to account for them.

PATTERN PERCEPTION BEYOND
THE RETINA

We have seen that the retina is a highly organized structure that has important functions in beginning the process of pattern analysis. In some lower vertebrates such as the frog we know that even more analysis takes place in the retina. Lettvin and associates (e.g., 1959) have shown that optic nerve fibers code information about form that corresponds in a close way to the ecological niche of the frog. Thus, there are fibers that respond to small concentric contours, popularly known as "bug detectors." Other fibers respond to larger contours (predator detectors) and dimming or brightening of the entire field. But in higher vertebrates, the information leaving the retina consists of the types of receptive fields described by Kuffler. This in itself is, of course, a major step in the analysis of visual patterns.

The major projection from the retina in higher animals is to the lateral geniculate body of the thalamus. We will pass over this interesting structure because, for the purpose of form perception, the properties of the cell bodies that comprise it are essentially the same as the optic nerve fibers that innervate it. However, when we reach the visual cortex we find a striking difference between the responses of cortical cells and previous levels. We have already pointed out that the visual system does not pay much attention to absolute levels of intensity and that this filtering begins in the retina. However, both ganglion cells and lateral geniculate cells respond very sensitively to abrupt increases or decreases in intensity.

When we get to the cortex, we find that there are very few cells that respond at all to illumination of the whole retina. In a classic series of studies, Hubel and Wiesel (e.g., 1959) have made recordings of single cortical cells of the cat and monkey in response to illumination of the retina with patterns of light. They find cortical cells that respond very selectively to particular patterns. These cells are called simple, complex, or hypercomplex on the basis of their receptive field properties. Simple cells respond to light or dark bars, or to

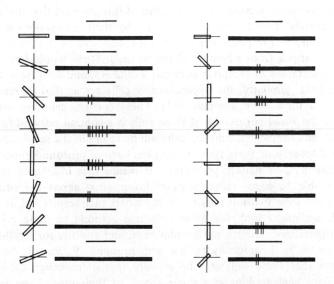

Figure 7-12 The response of a simple cortical cell to a bar of light presented to the visual field of the cat's eye. On the left of each column is the orientation of the bar of light in relation to the center of that cell's receptive field. The cell responded maximally when the bar was oriented vertically and centered. [From Hubel, D. H., and Wiesel, T. N. Receptive fields of single neurons in the cat's striate cortex. *J. Physiol.*, 1959, *148*, 574-91.]

edges between light and dark areas. These bars or edges must be oriented at particular angles and in particular areas of the visual field, depending on the cell. Edge-detecting simple cells also respond to movement in the appropriate direction. Simple cells can be identified by exploring the visual field with a spot of light and mapping those areas in which the spot produces excitation or inhibition of the cell. An example of the response of one simple cortical cell is shown in Figure 7-12. It is believed that the properties of a simple cell responding to a bright bar can be accounted for by assuming that a single simple cell receives the output (by way of the lateral geniculate body) of a number of ganglion cells that are arranged along the retina with their "on" centers in a straight line. Thus, illumination of a part of the retina that includes an "on" center that projects to a particular cortical cell will produce excitation of the cortical cell, and darkening will inhibit it. Likewise darkening of any of the areas that include "off" centers will excite the cortical cell and illuminating them will inhibit it.

Complex cells are similar to simple cells, with the following difference. Complex cells are not specific to location in the visual field but will respond to a bar or edge, depending on the type of cell, anywhere in the visual field. The last category, hypercomplex cells, are like complex cells except that the stimulus to which they respond must be limited in length. Some hypercomplex cells (lower order hypercomplex) respond to lines and some (higher order hypercomplex) respond to lines in two orientations in such a way as to suggest that they are really angle or corner detectors. Just as it is assumed that the properties of simple cortical cells can be accounted for by their connections with lateral geniculate cells, so the properties of complex cells can be attributed to their receiving the input from a number of simple cells. These would have the same type and orientation of receptive field but would respond to different parts of the visual field. Similarly, the hypercomplex cells act as if they receive their input from a number of complex cells. These cortical cells are arranged in columns in the visual cortex. All of those cells in a column respond to the same orientation, and simple and complex cells will be found in the same column.

The discovery of these types of cells has been of profound importance for the understanding of pattern perception. It means that individual cells in the cortex are able to signal rather abstract information about the visual input. At the present time it is not possible to say where such results will lead. On the one hand, we might look for other cells that respond to more complicated visual configurations, one for my grandmother, and another for a yellow Volkswagen. The list is theoretically endless and, presumably, absurd. Another approach says that these cells may be actually spatial frequency detectors and we have only been looking at a single aspect of their more basic properties. This requires that there be ways of translating information about spatial frequency in two dimensions into recognition of patterns. Some progress has been made along these lines. This area is one that is developing rapidly and is still controversial. There are some workers who believe that either one or both of the possibilities outlined above are ridiculous and others who are working hard to substantiate them.

For obvious reasons the neurophysiological evidence on feature detectors has been obtained from nonhuman subjects. There exists a fairly large body of behavioral evidence that suggests that similar mechanisms must exist in the human. The evidence comes from experiments in which the appearance of various features of targets is studied before and after adaptation to, or masking by, a particular type of target.

Weisstein and Bisaha (1972) have shown that a bar stimulus presented to the eye will mask a square-wave grating that follows it. The reverse also holds. A square-wave grating, you will recall, looks like a set of black and white stripes. They argue that such masking is evidence that there are units in the visual system that respond to the spatial frequencies represented in both the bar and the grating. Exposure to a stimulus with particular spatial frequencies will mask another stimulus having the same spatial frequencies even though the two stimuli do not have the same shape or location because the same neural units are used to code the information about spatial frequency in the two stimuli. This suggests that the units stimulated are spatial frequency analyzers rather than feature analyzers. Feature analyzers would respond to stimuli of various sizes, shapes, and orientations. A spatial frequency analyzer would operate, as the name implies, by responding to stimuli containing certain spatial frequency information.

Another line of evidence for some kind of spatial frequency analysis in the visual system is provided by Harmon and Julesz (1973). Consider Figure 7-13. This is a photograph that has been computer processed by dividing the

Figure 7-13 Can you see a face in this figure? See the text for discussion. [From Harmon, L. D., and Julesz, B. Masking in visual recognition: Effects of two-dimensional filtered noise. *Science*, 1973, *180*, 1194-97. © 1973 by the American Association for the Advancement of Science.]

original picture into blocks. Each block is then given the same density (darkness) as the average of that part of the original picture. What this does is to remove the high spatial frequency information that was present in the original. In addition, some high-frequency noise is introduced because of the sharp edges between the blocks. Can you make out the face in the picture? If you cannot, squint, take off your glasses, or move away from the picture. You might expect that these procedures would make it more difficult to recognize the face, but they actually make it easier. What these various suggestions have in common is that they result in reducing the high-frequency information that enters the visual system. Figure 7-14 is the same photograph that has had the high-frequency information removed by further computer processing. Harmon and Julesz conclude that the reason high-frequency information makes it more difficult to recognize the face is that higher frequencies mask the lower ones in a manner analogous to auditory masking. This suggests a new way of interpreting the old expression about not seeing the forest for the trees. The way to see the forest is to step back and "get some perspective." What you are really doing when you step back and look at a scene from some distance is changing the spatial frequencies that represent the various features of the scene. The farther away, the higher the spatial frequencies representing any particular object. In this way we lose sensitivity to the trees and gain sensitivity to lower frequency components, the forest. You may have noticed in an art museum that each painting has an optimal viewing distance. Closer than the optimum you lose

Figure 7-14 The same photograph after removal of high-frequency information. [From Harmon, L. D., and Julesz, B. Masking in visual recognition: Effects of two-dimensional filtered noise. *Science,* 1973, *180,* 1194-97. © 1973 by the American Association for the Advancement of Science.]

the overall effect of the painting and farther away you lose detail. How do you suppose the artist was able to include those spatial frequencies necessary for viewing at the correct distance when he, of necessity, painted it close up? Along the same line, art teachers sometimes instruct students who are learning to sketch to squint at their subject, or take off their glasses. This has the effect of removing high-frequency information so that the student will see and draw only the more important intermediate frequency information.

Another line of evidence for feature detectors comes from adaptation to movement, rather than to patterns per se. If there are neurons in the human visual cortex that respond to movement then it should be possible selectively to adapt them. In a series of experiments, Sekuler (e.g., Sekuler and Pantle, 1967) studied the effects of adaptation to movement. In one experiment it was shown that after a person watched a moving target, the luminance threshold for seeing the same target move in the same direction was higher than before. In addition, the threshold for targets moving in the opposite direction was lower. This adaptation was selective for various target velocities. These results argue that neurons that responded to movement in the adapting direction were rendered less sensitive than normal and those that responded to movement in the opposite direction were relatively more sensitive. They also suggest that different neurons are sensitive to different velocities.

The earliest experiments relevant to the question of spatial frequency detectors are those involving stabilized retinal images. There are two basic techniques for producing stabilized images on the retina. The first, that of Riggs et al. (1953) and Ditchburn and Ginsborg (1952) manages to compensate for movements of the eye by means of a tiny mirror mounted on a contact lens and a system of mirrors through which the light is projected to the eye. Those are arranged in such a way that an image remains stationary on the retina when the eye moves. The other, used by Pritchard (1961) mounts a tiny projector on a contact lens that maintains a stabilized image by riding along with all of the movements of the eye. The first device has the advantage of providing better stabilization of the image; however, the second also controls for torsional movements of the eye.

A very interesting phenomenon was discovered by two independent researchers. Riggs and Ditchburn both found that stabilized images could be seen for only a few seconds before they began to fade. How is it that we can steadily fixate objects under natural viewing conditions without experiencing fading? The answer is that a tremor of the eye with a frequency of about 150 Hz and an amplitude of about 2 minutes of arc (1/2 the diameter of a cone) protects against this adaptation. One might think that such a tremor would degrade the sharpness of the image seen by the eye, as is the case with a camera held by an unsteady hand at slow shutter speeds. But the tremor is necessary to protect against the rapid process of adaptation. Actually, the effect of a stabilized retinal image can be seen without any special apparatus. Refer to

Figure 7-15 Stare at the spot in the picture on the left for a number of seconds. The Cheshire cat will disappear except for his smile. Then try to do it with the one on the right. Why doesn't this cat fade and why doesn't the smile on the other one fade?

Figure 7-16 Selective fading of the HB monogram on the left yields patterns such as those on the right [After Pritchard, R. M. Stabilized images on the retina. *Scientific American,* 1961, *204* (b), 72-78.]

Figure 7-15. The reason this figure fades with steady viewing is that there are fuzzy edges in the picture (no high spatial frequency information). When the eye moves with respect to a target, spatial frequencies are translated into temporal frequencies. If the movements of the eye are limited to those of the frequency of the involuntary tremor (high temporal frequency) then this movement does not produce the temporal frequencies to which the eye is sensitive. In other words, the image is stabilized as far as concerns those temporal frequencies to which the eye responds. It is possible to produce similar effects with letters produced by spray painting in such a way that the edges are very fuzzy.

Back to the reason for bringing up the stabilized image. Pritchard found that the images did not fade uniformly or randomly. Patterns such as those in Figure 7-16 faded in such a way that meaningful units such as lines, edges, and the like were left. If a letter were used as a target, parts of the letter would sometimes fade in such a way to leave other letters in the remaining portions. Pritchard concluded that this was evidence for the existence of neural elements in the brain for the perception of meaningful elements of figures. These results have been somewhat controversial because some have felt that the selective fading could have been produced by slippage of the contact lens that held the projector. However, Pritchard points out that if slippage were causing the selective reappearance, or protection from fading, it would be expected that not just one feature of a figure, but those features in parallel would also reappear.

TEMPORAL PATTERNS—FLICKER

As indicated earlier, the linear systems approach can be applied equally well to temporal as to spatial patterns. In fact, the stabilized image work just described concerns the reduction of temporal frequency information to the retina and belongs under the temporal frequency heading. It was discussed above because of its relevance to the question of spatial frequency analyzers. One traditional problem in vision has been that of sensitivity to flicker. Most people are aware that when a light is turned on and off at a high enough frequency the individual pulses of light are perceived as a steady stream of light. This is what makes it possible to use fluorescent lights without discomfort because, even though these lights flicker at a frequency of 120 Hz, this rate is above the threshold of fusion at ordinary intensities. Similarly, movies and television depend on the fusion of successive discrete images, presented at 72 Hz in the case of most movie projectors. It has been known for a long time that the highest rate of flicker that can be detected as flickering, the so-called critical flicker frequency (cff) is dependent on the intensity of the flickering source. The more intense the source, the higher the cff. This fact is illustrated in Figure 7–17 which also shows that wavelength has an effect at illuminances below the level of the transition from rods to cones. In the cone region of intensities, the cff increases approximately in proportion to the logarithm of the intensity of the light, a relation known as the *Ferry-Porter law.* There are a number of factors that influence the cff, including retinal locus. For reasons that are not completely understood, the periphery of the eye is more sensitive to flicker than is the fovea. You may have noticed that a fluorescent light that is going bad will seem to flicker if you are looking at it with your peripheral vision, but that this disappears when you fixate it foveally. Similarly, it can be very annoying to try to read with a TV set operating in your peripheral field of vision where flicker is manifest.

Above the cff, the appearance of a flickering light is indistinguishable from a steady light of a certain lower intensity. The brightness of the flickering light above cff can be matched by a steady light that has the same intensity as the time-averaged intensity of the flickering light, a relationship known as the *Talbot-Plateau law.* For example, if the flickering light is on half of the time it can be matched by a steady light of one-half the intensity of the flickering one. This is not surprising in terms of what we know about Bloch's law (see Chapter 4).

It may seem a little more surprising that at certain frequencies below cff the brightness of the flickering light is greater than that of a steady light of the same intensity. This is known as brightness enhancement or the Brücke effect. The frequency at which this occurs is about 10 Hz.

These results have been obtained from classical methods using square-wave stimuli varying between some particular intensity and zero intensity. Linear systems techniques have revolutionized the entire topic of flicker. This is another example of the point mentioned earlier: that when the transfer function has been determined using sinusoidal stimuli it is possible to predict the results using any other kind of stimuli. Thus, the results of the newer methods can predict the earlier results but not vice versa. Kelly (1971) measured the temporal modulation transfer function using sinusoidally varying fields of light. His results are shown in Figure 7-18. Here we have the threshold for the detection of fluctuations in intensity plotted as a function of frequency. Each curve is for a different average intensity. You will notice that, except for the lowest

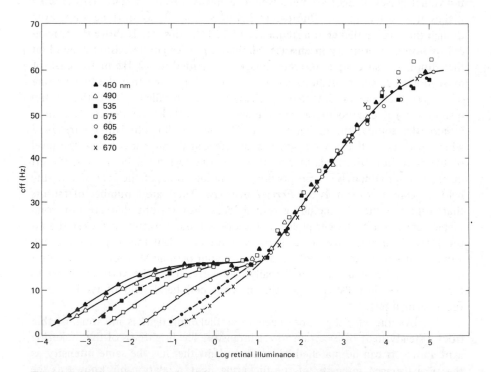

Figure 7-17 Dependence of the cff on the intensity of the light. Below a certain intensity, corresponding to the rod-cone break, the function depends on wavelength. [From Hecht, S., and Shlaer S. Intermittent stimulation by light. V. The relation between intensity and critical frequency for different parts of the spectrum. *J. Gen. Physiol.,* 1963, *19*, 965–79.]

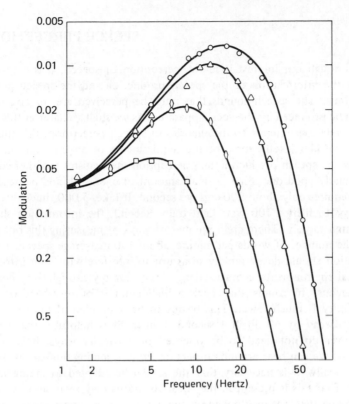

Figure 7-18 Sensitivity of the eye to temporal modulation of light intensity. The abscissa shows the frequency at which the light intensity was varied in a sinusoidal manner. The ordinate shows the proportion by which the light had to be modulated in order for the modulation to be detectable. Each curve is for a different average intensity about which the light was varied; the lower curves are for weaker average intensities. The lines drawn are the curves predicted by the theory. [From Kelly, D. H. Theory of flicker and transient responses, I. Uniform Fields. *J. Optical Soc. America*, 1971, *61*, 537–46.]

intensities, the modulation sensitivity peaks in an intermediate region between about 5 and 30 Hz, depending on intensity. This predicts the brightness enhancement, or Brücke effect. Also, you will notice that the cff point, at which sensitivity is lowest (essentially zero), is reached at higher frequencies with higher average intensity. This predicts the *Ferry-Porter law*. And finally, at any given frequency, increasing the average intensity will yield a smaller relative modulation threshold. The theories or models of the visual system which these methods lead to are beyond our scope, but suffice it to say that they have produced a fundamental advance in our understanding of the phenomenon of flicker.

SPEECH PERCEPTION

Although our interest is in the perception of speech, it is helpful to remember the interrelation of the speech production and the speech perception mechanisms. The speech sounds that must be perceived are, of course, those that can be produced by the vocal apparatus. As we shall see later in this section, this interrelation extends to the theories of speech perception. For this reason we will consider briefly some of the requirements of an information channel and how the speech production and perception mechanisms together constitute a particularly good one. First, a small amount of energy should be needed, and speech requires only about 200 ergs per second. It takes 5,000 times this amount of energy to light a 100 watt light bulb. Second, the information should be transmitted rapidly. There are a number of ways of measuring this but a simple one is the number of words per minute, about 150 in average speech. Third, the information should decay rapidly so as not to interfere with later information. In typical environments, acoustic energy decays rapidly enough to be considered instantaneous. In rooms that have a high amount of reverberation, speech intelligibility is much lower. This begins to be a problem if the sound energy does not decay by 60 db in 1 second. Fourth, it is helpful if the sender and the receiver do not need to be oriented in particular ways. It is extremely useful that we can hear around corners or without aiming our ears at the sound source. Finally, it is necessary that the sender be adapted to the needs of the receiver. That this is present in the vocal apparatus may seem an obvious point but it is one that was overlooked by the workers who tried to teach speech to a chimpanzee. Their vocal apparatus is not adapted for making the sort of sounds that are required for speech. These considerations point out that the ear is very well designed for the perception of speech. In fact, one could argue that it seems to have been designed for this purpose!

It is a little arbitrary to compare the rate of reception of speech information by the ear and printed words by the eye, but this is in fact our criterion when we say that the eye is a better receiving device for verbal material than the ear. It is possible to read the same material about two or three times as fast as we can listen to it. Various experiments show that this is a limitation in the speech perception apparatus rather than in the ability to talk fast enough.

The problem of speech perception is a complex one. It basically involves the question of how acoustic information gets processed into linguistic information; that is, how patterns of sound are transformed into words and sentences. This is actually a rather involved question and an adequate consideration of it would be beyond our scope. As an example of the complexity of the question, consider what is the basic unit of speech that is being processed. It is generally considered to be the phoneme, which may be thought of as the simplest acoustic

There have been a number of attempts to build some sort of device for the blind as a substitute for reading. Since we can read two or three times as fast as we can speak, it would seem natural to try to speed up the listening process by tape recording speech and playing it back at a faster speed. This, however, produces a "chipmunk" effect: a high-pitched voice that is difficult to understand. (This mechanism was employed by one of the popular children's radio programs of the late 'forties, "Big John and Sparky." The first author remembers his disillusionment when he learned that "Sparky" was only Big John's voice speeded up.)

In order to avoid the chipmunk effect, devices have been built to faithfully reproduce the message in the following way: very many short sections of the tape are removed electronically and what is left is "respliced" so that the words are present at the same pitch as before, only shorter. These "speech compressors" are now commercially available. It is possible to compress speech by about 30 percent before intelligibility is significantly impaired. It is impossible to specify a precise compression limit because the tolerable level of compression will vary with the type of material and the method of measurement. There is a range of compression in which the amount of material comprehended is increased even though the percent heard is less than normal. In other words, you hear more because more is coming in per unit time, but you catch a smaller percentage of the input, sort of an auditory scanning. When speech is presented faster than 275 words per minute, comprehension deteriorates markedly. This is due to a limitation of the rate of processing auditory information rather than the loss of critical speech sounds by the compressor (Foulke and Sticht, 1969).

unit in a spoken word. This may be generally correct, but it is known that the same phoneme will have different physical properties depending on the context in which it appears. This problem will come up again when we consider the theory of speech perception, but for the moment we will consider the phoneme to be the unit of speech perception.

Speech sounds have been analyzed by means of the *sound spectrograph*. This is a device that takes the speech sound and passes it through a number of filters that are selectively tuned to various frequencies. The sound is then represented visually on a graph that shows the amount of energy in each frequency

139

range by the darkness of the trace over time. This device has yielded a great deal of information about the physical basis of speech sounds. Figure 7-19 shows the sound spectrogram of the sentence, "I can see you." The first thing one notices in such a record is that the energy is located in several bands known as *formants* (Figure 7-20). Each vowel phoneme has its own distinctive pattern of formants. Consonants are a little harder to characterize but also have unique patterns.

One way to analyze this speech is to make a simplified pattern from the spectrogram by presenting it to another machine that can be thought of as doing the reverse of the sound spectrograph. The *pattern playback machine* takes such a pattern and produces a sound that has energy in the various frequencies in proportion to the darkness of the pattern in the various areas. Listening to the output of this device makes it possible to determine which aspects of the sound spectrogram actually contribute to the perception of speech. The simpler the pattern that is put in, the more artificial the sound becomes but, up to a certain point, recognizable speech is produced. Pure vowel sounds have about four formants but they are easily recognizable with only the first three formants present. The spectrogram representing the sound of the letter *I* illustrates the change that takes place in *diphthongs*, vowel sounds that begin like one pure vowel and glide into another. With diphthongs one or more of the formants will show the glide from one frequency to another.

As mentioned earlier, the physical basis of the consonants is more difficult to specify. One reason is that their sounds last a very short time. A second and more important reason is that the exact physical description of the consonant

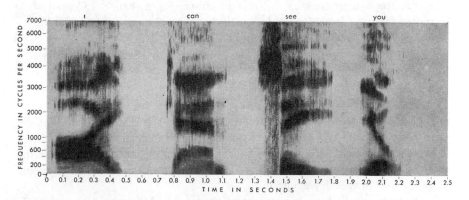

Figure 7-19 Sound spectrogram of the sentence, "I can see you." The dark patches are the frequencies at which the sound intensity is located at various times. [From *The speech chain* by Peter Denes and Elliot N. Pinson. © 1963 by Bell Telephone Laboratories, Inc. Reproduced by permission of Doubleday & Company, Inc.]

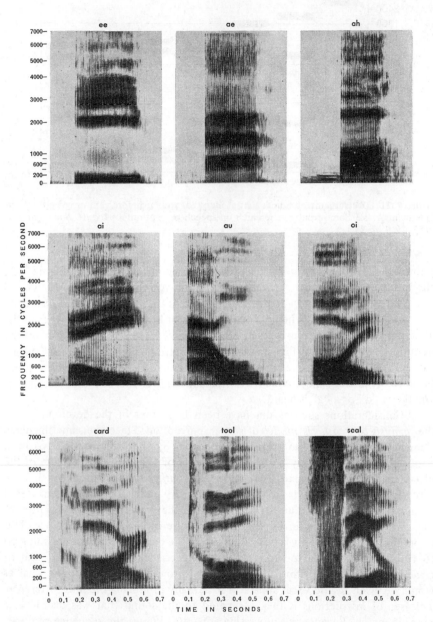

Figure 7-20 Sound spectrograms of typical speech sounds and words. [From *The speech chain* by Peter Denes and Elliot N. Pinson. © 1963 by Bell Telephone Laboratories, Inc. Reproduced by permission of Doubleday & Company, Inc.]

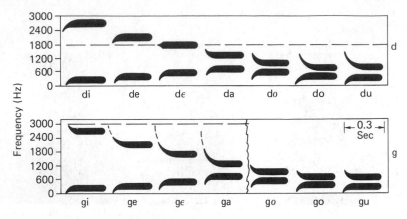

Figure 7-21 Spectrograms of sounds that produce /d/ and /g/ before various vowels. [From Liberman, A. M. Some results of research on speech perception. *J. Acoust. Soc. America,* 1957, *29,* 117–23.]

phoneme will differ depending on what vowel phoneme follows it. Figure 7-21 shows the spectrograms of a number of different vowel phonemes having what is called a *formant transition* at the beginning. It is the second formant transition that is of interest here. Whether a "d" or a "g" is heard does not depend on the direction of the transition or even the frequency of the transition but on the frequency at which, if the transition were extrapolated back, the formant would have begun. A frequency can be imagined that the formant seems to point back to. This frequency, which was not sounded, is the one that determines whether a "d" or a "g" is heard.

Considerations such as this have been important in the development of the *analysis-by-synthesis model* of speech perception. Since the same linguistic element (say a "d") is not always represented by the same acoustic pattern, a model that is based only on invariant aspects of the acoustical pattern of the utterance is of limited value. The *analysis-by-synthesis* model proposes that the way we perceive speech is to make a preliminary analysis which is then tested against possible linguistic units for a match. If they match, fine. If they do not, the *control unit* makes an hypothesis about the nature of the utterance. This hypothesis is processed by a stage that knows the pattern of instructions that go to the vocal apparatus to produce various speech sounds. This stage, that of *generative rules,* transforms the hypothesis into a set of instructions such as would be given to the vocal apparatus in actually producing the same utterance. This set of instructions is then compared to the sound that was heard for a possible match. Because the processing apparatus knows the sequence of movements of the vocal apparatus in producing various utterances, it can interpret sounds that vary with context. The model also relates speech production to speech perception via the stage of generative rules that is common to both.

COMPARISON OF SENSITIVITY
TO SPATIAL AND TEMPORAL FREQUENCIES
AMONG THE SENSES

We have pointed out previously that the various senses are exquisitely adapted for the tasks they have to perform. Each sense operates close to the theoretical limits of sensitivity and some are frequently better than any man-made device. This is especially impressive considering that the receptors are very small living devices subject to all of the insults that we give our bodies and limited by their very makeup and structure. If the ear were any more sensitive to low frequencies we would hear the blood flowing in our ears and if the eye were any more sensitive to long wavelengths we would be able to see the heat produced by our bodies as infrared radiation (Békésy, 1957). What we wish to stress now are the differences among the senses in reaction to temporal and spatial patterns of energy. These follow directly from the tasks to be accomplished by the various senses. As Geldard (1970) has pointed out, vision is preeminently a spatial sense and we routinely arrange for fine spatial discriminations to be performed by the eye. Likewise, the ear is basically a processor of temporal information, especially that involved in speech perception. But the eye is not very good at discriminating temporal aspects of stimuli except where time is translated into space as with the Pulfrich effect. The ear is not very good at spatial properties except where space is translated into time as with auditory localization. The cutaneous senses should not be treated as a group because it is difficult to generalize between the temperature senses, where there is very limited temporal as well as spatial ability, and the vibration sense, where temporal and spatial resolution are both quite good. However, the skin senses generally fall somewhere between vision and audition in ability to process temporal and spatial information. The chemical senses are generally considered at the bottom of the heap on both temporal and spatial discrimination.

Can we be a little more specific? The most systematic way to do this would be to present temporal and spatial frequency modulation transfer functions for each sense, where applicable, and let them speak for themselves. Unfortunately, these have not been determined for every sense. Let us do what we can with the data that are available.

First, temporal properties. The transfer function for audition is the familiar plot of threshold as a function of frequency shown in Figure 3-15. We know that the ear is sensitive to temporal modulation between about 20 and 20,000 Hz with the maximum sensitivity between 1,000 and 4,000. The latter frequencies are, not surprisingly, those that contain most of the information required for speech discrimination. The skin is next best. The upper limit is not easy to specify because of technological problems, and the lower limit is dependent on the subject's criterion, but it is generally agreed that vibration between about 10 and 10,000 Hz can be perceived. The frequency at which the skin is most sensitive to vibration is agreed to be about 250 Hz. The relevant data for vision have already been presented in Figure 7-18. Once again, the lower limit is arbitrary but the upper limit is about 60 Hz, with the maximum sensitivity at about 30 Hz depending on intensity. The chemical senses fall far short in temporal sensitivity. For taste the maximum rate of discrimination between two streams of solution flowed alternately on the tongue is 5 Hz for sour, sweet, and bitter. Salt is somewhat faster. The greatest sensitivity is reached at about 0.1 Hz. No analogous data exist for smell, but we assume the situation is similar.

We can see that the various senses differ markedly on temporal sensitivity depending upon their function. No important information about a food seems to be conveyed by high temporal frequency information. But temporal resolution is used by the skin in discrimination of texture of surfaces, and is paramountly important for the ear in speech perception. The eye makes relatively little use of temporal information.

It is harder to make the same sort of comparisons for spatial frequency modulation. The relevant data do exist for vision (refer to Figure 7-9) where the maximum sensitivity is 6 Hz per degree of visual angle. This translates into 0.5 Hz per mm at a distance of 50 cm for the eye. The closest to the proper sort of data for the skin are measurements of the ability to discriminate one point from two. This differs as a function of location on the body, being very poor on the back, arm, and thigh (about 7.0 cm) and very good on the fingertips (about 0.3 cm). Comparing these data with those for vision, we find the threshold for discrimination of two lines to be about 0.1 at a distance of 50 cm. Many other types of data could be summoned here, but we merely wish to point out the great differences among the senses on these measures based upon their principal functions.

8

Attention

It is helpful to approach the topic of attention from an historical perspective. If one surveys earlier psychology textbooks, for example, William James' classic (1890), one finds that attention played an important role in psychological theory around the turn of the century. With the advent of behaviorism, however, this topic suffered neglect along with other "mental" concepts eschewed by the behaviorists. Nonetheless, like imagery, consciousness, and other concepts the pre-behaviorists talked about, attention just will not go away. It is an obvious fact of everyday experience.

Recent discussions of attention, as we will see later in this chapter, seem to skirt what attention "really is" and instead to discuss related but more peripheral topics. Why is this? The behaviorists were correct in saying that attention is not a behavior, but is only inferred from behavior. If an animal responded to a stimulus, then he must have attended to it. If it was not responded to, then he *may* not have attended to it. Superficially it seems that simple. However, other important psychological concepts such as learning and motivation are inferred from behavior and still play important roles in theorizing.

We will define attention as *the capacity to respond to one stimulus at a time.* Although this may not seem to capture the essence of attention it points up the twin thrusts of research in the area: upon focusing and division of attention. Because attention is a familiar fact of everyday experience it is necessary to give only a few examples of what we are talking about.

Students often like to study while doing something else such as listening to music, watching TV, or carrying on a conversation. This is possible to some extent, but it is well known that if one gets more involved in one of the tasks, performance on the other deteriorates. Familiar music or a simple conversation about the weather can be handled along with most reading material but if the reading becomes highly technical or the conversation becomes more involved, then we have trouble. What is happening? It is as if we have the capacity to handle a limited amount of information at one time, and as long as only a little information is coming over the various channels we can handle it all. Once the load of information increases in one channel, information through other channels gets lost. As you read this book there are no doubt a great many physical energies impinging on your receptors. Most of them are ignored and only a very few become stimuli for you. Hopefully only the visual information—and in fact only that small fraction having to do with the meaning of the words and not the color of the ink or paper, or even the shape of the type—will elicit your response. It is a common observation in a perception course that whenever sensations of itching are under discussion a great deal more scratching takes place. Presumably the underwear was just as tight before, but the information was not attended to.

The example of studying while carrying on other activities assumed that it is possible, although difficult, to attend to more than one thing at a time. But this terminology is misleading because we are capable of doing a multitude of things simultaneously; walking, chewing, listening, and humming are all behaviors that can be done at once. An important concept here is the idea of compatibility of behaviors. Do you remember the child's game of trying simultaneously to rub your stomach in a circular pattern and pat your head? These tasks are relatively incompatible, but they can be learned. You might say that you have to attend to one at a time until it is "automatic" but this mostly begs the issue. Recall learning to drive. At first, steering the car was so difficult that when you used the brake or shifted gears the car seemed to want to run off the road. It was as if each task required all of your attention. But when you became a proficient driver you could do all of these plus dial the radio and carry on a conversation at the same time. We could say that as skills become better learned they no longer require as much attention. Perhaps it would be better to say they become less incompatible with other behaviors.

You utilize selectivity of attention very effectively in class when at times you listen very carefully and clearly perceive what is said; at other times, you barely hear the sounds of the lecture and discussion as you think about other things. Another example of auditory selective attention is the "cocktail party effect." In a crowded, noisy room you are able to follow one conversation even though it is no louder than several other conversations going on around you. Eye movements are an important instrument of visual attention. In normal vision where the eye is free to move, the direction of gaze is a powerful determinant of visual selection. We see clearly only what is focused on the fovea, and we obviously do not perceive at all what does not fall in the visual field. For further

You have no doubt had the experience of approaching a room full of people, at least half of whom are talking at once. From outside, the din may be terrific and totally unintelligible but, upon entering the room, you engage in conversation with someone without any difficulty beyond the necessity to raise your voice. Moreover you find it possible to talk with someone who is separated from you by some distance even though there are other speakers closer to you who present a more intense stimulus to your ear. This phenomenon, known as the cocktail party effect, is a striking example of the ability to focus attention on a particular stimulus out of many possible stimuli. The effect depends in an important way on binaural hearing. The reason you could not make out the conversations very well, if at all, from outside the room is that the binaural cues to localization of a sound are destroyed for any sound source that is not in your line of sight. A similar degradation of the ability to listen selectively to one voice out of several occurs when listening to monaurally reproduced material such as TV or a tape recorder. The problem is that there are no binaural cues of arrival time, phase, and intensity differences to help localize a single sound source. When the sound source can be localized, selective listening is much easier.

discussion of visual attention, see the section on Gestalt principles of figure-ground organization in Chapter 10.

THEORIES OF SELECTIVE ATTENTION

What determines what we attend to? This is a question of great practical importance in many areas, notably advertising. We notice those things that are large, loud, colorful, moving, or repeated. These are all stimulus variables. Learning and motivational variables such as novelty, interests, curiosity, and emotional involvement determine attention in different ways, depending on the individual person. Surely you can think of advertisements, especially for automobiles, that seek to appeal to individual factors such as these. One of the most striking examples of the role of individual differences in attention is the effect of hearing one's own name spoken in a noisy crowd of strangers.

Selective attention has been conceptualized in several ways, and models have been proposed to represent the underlying processes. Broadbent's filter theory (1958) proposes that selection occurs by filtering out or blocking information at some level in the information processing system so that only a certain amount of input is allowed at any one time. The sensory content that can pass the filter at one time is determined by whether the total information exceeds the limited capacity of a single "central channel." The input channels correspond to such features as frequency, intensity, spatial location, and sensory modality. Inputs that are blocked by the filter at the time of their arrival may be stored for a few seconds in short-term memory which comes between the sensory input and the filter. These inputs may then enter the central channel, if they are passed by the filter. The filter is biased in favor of input channels in which novel or intense events occur.

As an alternative to the filter theory, which suggests that an all-or-none switch controls the passage of information, Treisman (1969) proposed an attenuator model. The information in a rejected channel would not be blocked completely, but it would be attenuated, or reduced, so that only the most significant units would get through to the person's awareness. Whether a message is attentuated depends upon a partial analysis of its content. For example, a subject wearing headphones may be instructed to "shadow," or repeat, the message received at one ear while paying no attention to an irrelevant message presented to the other ear. He will be able to block the irrelevant message very successfully until it contains words that have significance for him, such as his name, or until the context of the relevant message is switched to the rejected ear. Treisman and others have taken this as evidence that the filter is not an all-or-none block, but that it is an attenuator which reduces input without completely excluding non-attended stimuli of special relevance.

The active processing model is essentially an information-processing approach to attention (see page 150). The primary difference between the attention models is in emphasis. The "active synthesizer" of the processing model constructs an internal image of the environment, and all information acquired about a sensory event must be fitted together into this comprehensive pattern. This determines which of the possible inputs will be selected and which will not. Besides the active synthesizer there are passive automatic devices which perform a continuous analysis of all incoming signals and, in a sense, attenuate the signals until further information corroborates the features expected by the active synthesizing process. The system can then switch channels if there is relevant or significant information on an unattended channel.

Related to the active processing model is the expectancy model (Moray, 1969), according to which the subject develops a model of the temporal characteristics of the information source(s) to which he is attending. Depending on the costs and payoffs associated with the various targets (cf. Signal Detection Theory), he develops strategies of sampling the various information sources of interest. This theory presents a picture of attention as a dynamic process that will change as a result of learning and the operation of reinforcement contingencies. It is also able to account for a wide range of phenomena including our earlier examples of learning to drive and of listening to more than one information source.

VIGILANCE

The area of sustained attention, or vigilance, has been the object of a great deal of research. Vigilance is studied in tasks where the perceiver must remain alert to the possible occurrence of a signal or target, although nothing happens during much of the period of observation. For example, a radar operator must direct his attention to the screen and remain alert in order to notice a blip on the screen if and when it occurs. In an experimental situation, the vigil usually lasts at least half an hour, with signals occurring infrequently and without warning. In the traditional experiment, called the Mackworth clock test, the subject watches a hand moving in jumps around a blank clock face; the hand moves in regular steps once each second and occasionally moves a double step. The subject is instructed to respond by pressing a key whenever a double step occurs. The signal is strong enough or obvious enough that detection failures must be due to failures in attention rather than sensory ineffectiveness. The major effect found in such tests is a drop in the number of correct responses after 15 to 30 minutes to a plateau level, depending on the task. This rapid decrement in performance is rather striking since the subject's work load is very light. Interestingly, some other kinds of tests do not show a performance decrement. These include tests with multiple stimulus sources such as the "twenty dials test" in which the subject must react to an unusual reading on any of twenty dials, with the signal remaining visible until a response occurs. On this test, response time has been observed as constant from the beginning to the end of the watch. Unfortunately, such tasks have not received as much study as those that show a decrement. Recently, however, some investigators have questioned whether a true performance decrement occurs in any of the common vigilance tests. This question was prompted by the use of the Signal Detection Theory methods (see Chapter 2) in order to separate the subject's sensitivity from the decision criterion he adopts in an experiment. It has been suggested that constant sensitivity is maintained, but a more conservative criterion is adopted over the course of an experiment. Current study of the problem includes signal detection analysis of the numerous types of vigilance tasks employed by various investigators.

DIVIDED ATTENTION

So far in this chapter we have been interested in how well a subject could select one stimulus from many, focus his attention on it, and reject other stimuli. The opposite question, that of divided attention, asks how vulnerable

A relatively new development is the application of information processing to the study of perception. It is difficult to summarize the concept of information processing because it is not based on a simple idea but includes a number of related ideas. Basically we can say that the information-processing approach comes largely from the development of the computer and the application of computer concepts to perception. The growth of computer technology after the Second World War suggested to many people that this model might be applicable to the study of perception. A computer receives input (in our analogy, sensory input) and processes it in various ways to yield some output (response). Actually, although the idea of using a computer as a model for the perceptual process was necessarily a novel one because the computer itself was new, the idea of comparing the perceptual process to some man-made device has been a standard scientific technique. For example, before the computer came along, we had the telephone switchboard model of perception. In another area of psychology, Freud's idea of motivation was essentially a hydraulic model.

Most typical of the information-processing approach to perception is the idea of a flow of information from one stage of processing to another. This is represented by flow charts showing boxes indicating stages of processing and arrows leading to other stages and finally to some output. We have already made use of information-processing ideas when we referred to the recent models of speech perception and of attention. We can expect to see a great deal of perception research using the information-processing approach in the future. Perhaps it is worth noting that the approach does not assume that the brain *is* a computer, just that it is profitable to see if it can be modelled by, or compared to, a computer. Similarly, nobody thought seriously that the brain was really a telephone switchboard when that model was in vogue, or supposed that Freud really thought that the mind was a flush toilet. A good introduction to the information-processing approach can be obtained from Lindsay and Norman (1972).

is the brain to overloading—when will our attention be restricted to one stimulus despite instructions to divide it? Three types of divided attention are represented by inquiring how we can (1) handle two or more sensory inputs to different receptors; (2) analyze two or more stimulus dimensions with the same receptor; and (3) test for two or more targets with critical features.

(1) The ability to divide attention between two auditory inputs (messages to both right and left ears) is very limited. When subjects are told to shadow the message to one ear, they are not able to respond to or recall much of the other message. However, a two-input task where two modalities are involved is quite easy. Subjects are able to read a story aloud, i.e., ignoring its meaning, and attend to a conversation at the same time.

(2) When subjects are told to divide their attention between two messages to the same ear in order to detect certain aspects of them, they do considerably worse on either input than if they focused their attention on a single input. An example would be monitoring one auditory message for a certain word and another auditory message for a change in loudness.

(3) Accuracy of monitoring in a selective listening task decreases as the range of potential targets increases (Treisman and Geffen, 1967). For example, subjects detect fewer targets in both shadowed and non-shadowed passages when they are instructed to note "any digit" or "any color" than when they are told to locate specific single words like "nine" or "red." The interpretation of results from this area of research is rather complicated, and many more factors have been considered than we can enumerate here.

It appears, however, that division of attention as it has been studied experimentally is difficult, if not impossible, when there is insufficient time for attention to alternate between inputs or features of the input, or for serial analysis of the input.

FLUCTUATIONS IN ATTENTION

Some evidence for the presence of serial analysis in the performance of perceptual tasks comes from the area of fluctuations in attention. With ambiguous stimuli such as auditory homophones (e.g., bear, bare) and visual figures like the Necker cube (see Figure 10-18), it is not usually possible to perceive both versions at once. Perception seems to alternate and the version that is dominant will change over time as you concentrate on it.

Binocular rivalry results when the two eyes receive different inputs and perception fluctuates between the two. If, for example, a different color or figure is presented to each eye, the images do not fuse but fluctuate so that the viewer sees first one, and then the other, image. With a blue stimulus presented to one eye and yellow to the other, the viewer sees alternating blue and yellow images, never a mixture of the two (unless two similar hues are used). Which form of the input the subject sees is not under his own control although certain factors do have an influence. For example, if one field is plain and one figured, the figured one will predominate. Also, the more familiar or meaningful picture will predominate. Presented with a pair of faces of different nationalities, subjects see predominately the face of their own nationality. A right-side-up face will predominate over an upside down one.

THE PHYSIOLOGY OF ATTENTION

The first evidence that a specific neural structure might mediate attention came from the work of Moruzzi and Magoun (1949). They found that electrical stimulation of the part of the midbrain known as the reticular formation would cause a general activation pattern in the cortical EEG (electroencephalogram). If the reticular formation of a sleeping cat were stimulated, the cat would awaken and its EEG would show an arousal pattern. Other investigators showed the importance of the reticular formation in arousal by demonstrating that animals with midbrain reticular-formation lesions remained comatose and unresponsive to sensory stimulation, even though the main sensory pathways to the cortex (which send collateral branches into the reticular formation) were not affected by the lesion.

More recent studies have shown that other brain structures such as the limbic system, especially the hippocampus, may also be involved in arousal. Thus, there is the possibility that different structures mediate different aspects of attention, and, perhaps, that interactions exist between the reticular formation and the limbic system.

The reticular formation itself is quite a complicated structure, and we are no doubt oversimplifying matters when we speak of it as a single entity. Different parts of the reticular formation are quite specialized functionally and anatomically; in fact, there may be over one hundred histologically distinguishable reticular nuclei. In terms of influence on other neural structures, the reticular formation can be divided into ascending and descending systems. Descending fibers may inhibit or facilitate activity of those motor neurons in the spinal cord that control the skeletal musculature. The ascending system influences the thalamus, cortex, and perhaps other structures. The cortex also acts back on the reticular formation.

Further experimentation (Lindsley, et al., 1950) indicated that behavioral arousal and cortical EEG arousal were closely correlated. The EEG (which can be recorded from the human scalp) shows regular, slow, high-amplitude electrical potentials from the brain when the subject is resting or inattentive; this activity is called alpha. However, if the subject is aroused, alert, or presented with novel stimulation, the EEG changes to fast, low-amplitude, asynchronous activity

Selective attention implies focusing on certain aspects of stimulation while ignoring others. Stroop (1935) developed a test to determine how subjects would perform a visual task when the interference is *between* dimensions of a stimulus. In the Stroop test, subjects are instructed to name the colors of printed words which themselves are the names for different colors. For example, the word "red" might be written in blue ink; according to the instructions the subject should quickly respond "blue." In actuality, however, subjects find it extremely difficult to respond to the colors instead of the printed name.

Various explanations of this interference effect have been offered. What is astonishing is the amount of interference. In a seemingly analogous auditory task, when subjects are asked to shadow one of two messages presented separately to the two ears, the other message causes negligible interference. Broadbent's filter theory (1958), therefore, does not provide an adequate explanation since it postulates that the total information content is the limiting factor in perception.

The auditory shadowing task should contain as much, if not more, information than the Stroop. Treisman (1969) suggests that with the Stroop phenomenon, subjects must select the analyzers for color and reject the analyzers for color words. In other words, they must focus on one dimension of the same stimulus and ignore the other. This is much more difficult than focusing on a selected receptor. Treisman suggests that interference may occur at the response level, when there are two conflicting responses from different analyzers. This interference does not stem primarily from the dual processing of words and colors but, as Klein (1964) has shown, varies with the *type of word* used. Non-color words produce the least interference, while color synonyms and color names produce the most. According to Treisman, interference may also be compounded later in the process; if irrelevant analyzers are involved, they then increase the number of perceptual inputs to be rejected by more central analyzers in the system. In effect, then, according to Treisman's model of attention, the Stroop task is difficult because it involves analyzer selection rather than input selection; that is, we must discriminate between dimensions of a single stimulus rather than between separate sensory messages.

known as beta, or alpha blocking. These observations hold for the normal, awake person.

Other evidence for the role of the reticular formation in attention comes from the study of evoked potentials. The action potential produced in a peripheral nerve by a stimulus is propagated toward the cortex via particular pathways in the spinal cord and from there to specific primary projection areas in the cortex. If recording electrodes are placed near these primary projection areas or the sensory pathways conducting the sensory message to the cortex, an electrical response can be recorded to peripheral stimulation. This electrical response is the evoked potential. The evoked potential is superimposed on the background of spontaneous activity (EEG) of the brain.

The evoked potentials to one stimulus are reduced or disappear when the animal reorients or shifts his attention to a novel stimulus. This finding has been interpreted as suggesting that the reticular formation may exert inhibitory effects on the response of all levels of the sensory system. In the classic study of Hernandez-Peón, et al. (1956), evoked potentials to clicks were recorded from the cochlear nucleus in the auditory pathway of the cat. When a mouse was suddenly presented to the cat, the auditory evoked potentials disappeared or diminished as long as the cat watched the mouse. When the mouse was removed, the auditory potentials reappeared. Evoked responses in the cat to click stimuli also disappear during presentation of olfactory (fish odor) or tactile stimuli (shocks). In each case, the disappearance is assumed to be related to the fact that the animal is paying attention to the novel stimulus and ignoring the click. It appears that input to other sensory modalities is filtered out or attenuated so that the animal can be maximally sensitive to input from the attention-evoking stimulus.

The hair cells of the cochlea receive efferent fibers by way of the olivocochlear bundle, which originates in the superior olivary complex of the medulla. Galambos (1956) showed that electrical stimulation of the olivocochlear bundle would suppress the response of the auditory nerve to click stimuli. Subsequent studies have confirmed and expanded these results to show that stimulation of the olivocochlear bundle produces a proportional reduction in activity at all lower levels of the auditory system. With humans, evoked potentials to brief flashes of light recorded from the visual cortex decrease when subjects are doing math problems; inhibition of the evoked potentials is greater with more difficult problems. On the other hand, if subjects are asked to pay attention to the light source or to count the number of light flashes, the evoked responses in the visual cortex increase. More recent studies have revealed certain methodological problems with Hernandez-Peón's studies (Worden, 1966). In addition, Picton, Hillyard, Galambos, and Schiff (1971) did an experiment in which they took advantage of a new technique that allows one to record the response of the auditory nerve in humans without surgery. They did not find any change in the response of the auditory nerve during changes in attention to clicks even though the response evoked in the cortex did change. These and other findings cast doubt on the idea that alterations in peripheral nerve response play an important part in the physiology of attention. Many investigators feel that attention is a function of central mechanisms that are as yet unknown.

STATES OF AWARENESS IN RELATION
TO PERCEPTION

Arousal

An "alerting," "orienting," or "arousal" response results from the presentation of certain stimuli to an animal (including humans). Included in the response are low-amplitude activity of the EEG, autonomic changes (heart rate and blood pressure), and behavioral responses such as orienting the head toward the stimulus source. The meaning of the stimulus, rather than its intensity, is usually a more important determinant of the magnitude of the activation response. A weak unexpected light may be more effective than a bright, but expected light; a previously reinforced or valued stimulus is better than a novel, but uninteresting one. There are individual differences in the intensity of the orienting response. Also, different animals show maximal responses to stimulation of different sensory modalities. The cat shows the greatest response to auditory stimulation, whereas in man, activation is more prominent from visual stimulation. This suggests that for man the visual system is dominant whereas for the cat the auditory system is of greater importance.

In terms of states of awareness or consciousness, arousal relates to a heightened degree of alertness, a concentration of attention, and increased level of anticipation. Arousal is caused by changes in the stimulus field, but its manifestation depends on both the external environment and the internal state of the animal. The orienting response results in the animal's attention being focused on certain aspects of the environment and prepares the animal for appropriate action.

Sleep

We think of sleep as a decreased state of awareness, among other things. Certainly there is a decreased responsiveness to stimulation. An interesting problem, however, is the selectiveness of the response to stimulation during sleep. How is it that a mother will sleep through loud noise of various kinds but awaken to the slightest cry from her baby? It has been shown that electrical stimulation of the cortex will send messages to the reticular formation and awaken a sleeping animal. Environmental stimuli (noise, smell of smoke, etc.) may arouse the cortex, but the question is what determines the cortical impulse

What happens when an individual is placed in an environment in which he does not receive the normal amount of sensory stimulation? Interest in this area was spurred by reports of brainwashing prisoners of war and other strange phenomena experienced by prisoners in circumstances of enforced solitude or restricted activity. Scientific interest in this topic has been motivated mainly by the hope of learning more about perception by altering the input to the system. A concomitant benefit has been the insight gained in preparing personnel for space travel.

Sensory deprivation experiments have involved different types and amounts of sensory restriction. The greatest total overall reduction in stimulation has been achieved by suspending a nude subject equipped only with a mask and air tube in a tank of water. The subject is instructed to move as little as possible. The water and the subject's air are maintained at a constant temperature. There are essentially no sounds or odors. The mask is blackened to eliminate visual stimulation. The tactile stimulation is constant. Another type of situation is a monotonous environment in which the subject cannot move and sees only the same surface continually, as in a tank-type respirator. A masking noise is used to give monotonous auditory input and the inside tactile stimulation is minimal and constant. A third approach to the sensory deprivation problem has been to have the subject lying quietly on a bed in a sound-attentuated room with his arms and hands encased in cardboard tubes. Translucent goggles admit diffuse light only. The emphasis in these latter two situations is upon the elimination of patterned input. Internal sensations such as the heartbeat prevent the eradication of all sensory stimulation.

Most subjects in sensory deprivation experiments are asked to participate for at least two to three days, but they are allowed to terminate the experiment at any time. Many enter such a situation thinking that it will be a good time to catch up on sleep, think through problems, and so on. This is generally true early on in the experience, but after a while subjects report difficulty concentrating and become restless. Many report disordered thinking and hallucinations. The most frequently studied alterations of perception have involved the visual system. After wearing translucent goggles, various types of movement distortion and apparent movement are experienced (Heron, Doane, and Scott, 1956). Stationary objects seem to be moving randomly, and movement of the environment occurs independently of the subject's own movement. Another study reported a decrease in size constancy (Doane, Mahatoo, Heron, and Scott, 1959). Zubek, Pushkar, Sansom, and Gowing (1961) reported that subjects who had experienced sensory deprivation for a week showed an impaired performance on a visual vigilance task such as the Mackworth Clock Test.

Experiments in sensory deprivation have employed a number of different methods for reducing stimulation, and each method appears to affect different systems and reduce input to a different degree. For this reason, results in many cases are specific to the particular method used. However, it is possible to draw the following general conclusions from these experiments: (1) there is a general disruption of visual perception; and (2) it appears that a certain level and type of stimulation is essential for normal sensory function. We are also led to hypothesize that perception is an active process (see Chapter 9), for hallucinations and increased visual imagery are experienced when the sensory input is reduced and monotonous.

to the brain stem. It has been proposed (Sokolov, 1963) that stimuli received during sleep are matched with a model at the cortical level based on past experience. If they do not match, there is general cortical arousal and impulses are sent to the reticular formation. If the stimulus matches a model, then it is possible that those stimuli that represent unimportant events are ignored, and only those representing important events cause the cortical impulse to the brain stem. Thus, the mother might ignore the rumbling of trucks but awaken to the baby's cry.

The EEG shows characteristic changes during sleep, indicating that sleep is not a homogeneous state physiologically. Four stages of non-dreaming sleep have been defined by the frequency and amplitude of the cortical EEG activity ranging from the low-amplitude fast waves of Stage 1 to the high-amplitude slow activity in Stage 4. Distinct from these stages is a type of sleep known as REM sleep because of the presence of prominent rapid eye movements (REM). During REM sleep the EEG resembles the waking state, but there is a reduction of muscle tone as well as a burst of rapid eye movements. The person is hardest to awaken during REM sleep, but if awakened, he usually reports that he was dreaming.

Dreaming has been called an "approved distortion in awareness" as opposed to the distortions produced by less socially acceptable means such as drugs. Approximately twenty percent of the average person's sleeping time is spent in dreaming; those persons who say that they don't dream generally spend less time in REM sleep, but they do dream. Dream content may be in-

Most psychologists have had the experience of meeting someone socially and having the person say, "I suppose you are reading my mind right now." There are perhaps several appropriate responses to such a statement, depending on the motivation of the psychologist at the moment. But usually he disclaims any such powers. However, the recent vogue in "body language" does have a certain amount of basis in fact. Among other cues to feeling is the size of the pupil of the eye. Most people know that the size of the pupil varies with illumination and assume that its sole function is to control the amount of light entering the eye. Actually, it performs this task poorly because the variation in illumination far exceeds the variation in pupil size (refer to our discussion in Chapter 5).

Hess (1965), for example, noted that pupil size depended on the nature of the object attended to. He found that the pupil dilated to certain pictures and constricted to others even though the illumination was the same on all of them. Pleasant pictures caused dilation and unpleasant pictures caused constriction. He also found that the pupil dilated when the subject performed mental arithmetic or attended to stimuli presented to other senses. Another of his findings indicated that pupil size was not only a response but could actually serve as a stimulus to others. Subjects were shown two pictures of a girl, identical except that in one picture the girl appeared to have very small pupils and in the other, large pupils. Subjects found the version with large pupils much more attractive than the other even though they were unable to verbalize the difference. This may explain why bars and cozy restaurants have the lights turned down low. The pupils of the patrons' eyes dilate because of the darkness and people feel friendlier toward each other. (By the way, the drug belladonna means "beautiful woman" in the original, and one of its effects is dilation of the pupils.)

For obvious reasons these findings stirred up a good deal of interest among psychologists. Here was a response to a stimulus that was entirely involuntary and unavailable to awareness *and* could be measured unobtrusively! One of the many ways it could be used practically was to judge the effectiveness of advertising.

However the research on attitude and pupil size has so far been inconclusive. It has been confirmed that the difficulty of mental tasks can be measured by the degree of pupillary dilation. But it is not at all clear that the pupillary response is a measure of pleasantness-unpleasantness per se. Libby et al. (1973) established that dilation occurs both when viewing pictures of nudes and some unpleasant pictures such as accident scenes or physical deformities. Also, Fredericks and Groves (1971) found more dilation to a sexually arousing picture than to others judged to be more pleasant. Thus it seems likely that the dilation response is more a measure of arousal than pleasantness. This would make sense of the occurrence of dilation to mental arithmetic, a task that most people probably do not consider especially pleasant.

Whether or not constriction occurs to unpleasant pictures is a matter of some dispute. The problem is a technical one deriving from the fact that the pupillary response is under the control of the autonomic nervous system. Like many other autonomic responses, such as the heart rate and the galvanic skin response, the nature of the response depends on the prevailing level of autonomic activity—the so-called law of initial value. When the response baseline is low, a given stimulus may cause an increase in the response, whereas there might be a decrease to the same stimulus if the baseline is higher. Fredericks and Groves believe that the constriction response will be found at the intermediate level of illumination where both increases and decreases from the baseline are possible. However, the point is still moot.

fluenced by recent experience, but it has been difficult to demonstrate experimentally any effect of concurrent sensory stimulation on dreams. For example, sprinkling water on dreaming subjects induced dreams of rain in only a few subjects.

Is learning compatible with, or even facilitated by, sleep? This is a question of some interest for the student who would like to be able to go to sleep while listening to a tape recording and wake up with sufficient recall of the material to pass a test. Unfortunately, those adequately controlled studies that have considered this question have concluded that those who listened to material during sleep are no better at recalling or recognizing material in the morning than those who did not. In studies where some learning has been demonstrated, researchers concluded that the subjects actually did their learning during periods of drowsiness or wakefulness. Simple conditioned responses can occur during lighter stages of sleep (there are anecdotes about soldiers sleeping during a march), but for more complicated cognitive processes, full wakefulness seems to be necessary.

Not only is learning incompatible with sleep, but it appears that forgetting is also. Since there is presumably no new learning during sleep, there would be no new material to replace, or interfere with, old learning. There is a drop in retention during the first two hours of sleep, but none after that, in contrast to the greater and much sharper drop that occurs in the wakeful state. For maximum retention it is best to learn or review the material immediately before going to sleep, rather than two or three hours before.

Hypnosis

Hypnosis has been known and practiced for thousands of years, but not until the last 200 years has it been studied scientifically. Much more is known about the clinical and practical application of hypnosis than about its true nature. At present, there is some controversy over whether hypnosis is, in fact, a true altered state of consciousness, or whether it is a point along a quantitative continuum that includes the normal waking state. Later on, we will discuss the work of Parrish et al. (1968) which seems to provide evidence that hypnosis is a true altered state. First, we will consider evidence for the other side of the argument. It has been found that only a small percentage of the population can be successfully hypnotized, and that these persons manifest "suggestibility," which can be measured by certain tests devised for that purpose. The suggestible subject attempts to satisfy the demand characteristics of an experimental situation; that is, to do exactly what seems to be expected by the experimenter. In fact, some non-hypnotized, suggestible subjects can be induced to perform in a manner identical to hypnotized subjects when the two groups are given the same experimental instructions. This seems to indicate that hypnosis does not produce a unique altered state. For an interesting discussion of some aspects of this problem, see Orne (1970).

Hypnosis provides a set of training conditions for the suggestible subject that permits a greater than normal degree of generalized relaxation, removal of distracting stimuli, and enhanced concentration upon a given relevant dimension. The hypnotized subject appears capable of ignoring reality and shows an increased responsiveness to a reality created by the hypnotist's words.

A number of studies have investigated how the "altered state of awareness" in hypnosis affects perception. Parrish et al. (1968) determined the effect of hypnotic age-regression on the magnitude of the Ponzo and Poggendorf illusions (see Figure 13-2 a, d). The illusional effect of the Ponzo increases in magnitude from child to adult whereas the Poggendorf decreases. Subjects who were hypnotized and age-regressed to age nine or age five were compared with non-hypnotized and hypnotized, non-regressed controls. The age regression instructions under hypnosis resulted in magnitudes of illusion that were more typical of younger subjects. These results are somewhat controversial and are the subject of continued research.

Hypnotized subjects frequently report modification of time awareness or tempo. If subjects are told that they have a certain number of minutes to complete a task, but are actually given only a few seconds in clock time, they report experiencing the appropriate amount of time. However, the question remains whether this is the result of an alteration in the actual perception of time or simply the subjects' suggestibility. A series of experiments seem to confirm the former (Zimbardo, Marshall and Maslach, 1971). Subjects were trained to press a key at a certain rate in order to maintain illumination of a light. Hypnotized and non-hypnotized subjects were then instructed either to experience time as slowing down or as speeding up, but to continue to press the key at a rate sufficient to keep the light on, even though the light was not illuminated during these trials. Hypnotized subjects were significantly more successful in changing their responding in the direction of the distortion suggestion. It therefore appears that time awareness can be altered and the change seen in behavior, but this modification of time sense requires the hypnotic state of relaxation, concentration, and imaginative involvement.

Meditation

Meditation may be considered a state of awareness which, in its simplest form, results from practice in the skill of relaxing, being quiet, and paying attention. The attention may be concentrated on another person, breathing, a part of the body, or an object, but the goal is to become aware of small cues, details, or beauty that have previously gone unnoticed. The contemplation is done in a nonanalytic, nonintellectual manner.

With training and practice, there are changes in visual perception; for example, a vase may become more vivid in color, luminous, change shape, etc. Time passes quickly, and there is an increased ability to ignore distracting stimuli. Meditation has some relationship to hypnosis in its physical setting, the importance of the expectation of the subject, and the relationship of the experimenter to the subject, especially the naive subject. The striking finding, however, has been the ease and rapidity with which naive subjects have been able to experience the altered perceptual phenomena similar to the mystic experience of those who are highly trained in meditation as part of religious practice.

Yogis practicing meditation have been studied by means of recorded EEG activity. During meditation, Yogis claim that they are oblivious to external and internal environmental stimuli and the brain remains in an awake state called "ecstasy." The EEG shows persistent slow alpha activity during meditation; no alpha blocking occurs when external stimuli are presented (light, noise, heat), as it would in the normal awake condition. In Yogis who have developed increased pain thresholds to cold, there is persistent alpha EEG activity when a hand is immersed in $4°C$ water for a long period of time. This would be very painful to the non-Yogi. These results suggest that these individuals are able to block sensory afferents from activating the reticular formation through some influence between that structure and the cortex, and thereby remain in alpha activity during such stimulation.

Drugs

Drugs are the most popular external agents for altering awareness. There is an extensive literature reporting various psychic effects from both marihuana and the hallucinogens, but the reports are predominately literary rather than scientific. The perceptual experience from any drug seems to depend upon the situation in which the drug is taken, the persons present, and the personality of the drug user.

With marihuana, sensory experiences of those stimuli attended to appear to be enhanced. Some have suggested that most sensory effects are learned and not spontaneous; a person unfamiliar with marihuana must have it pointed out that things may be perceived in a different way. Perhaps the sensory enhancement results from stimulus dimensions being attended to *without* those interpretations, memories, and meanings usually present. There are fewer objects attended to and the person is thus more strongly aware of one individual object; music may be the center of attention as opposed to a normal state in which one focuses on two or more things, such as reading a book while listening to music. Attention is focused differently; it is as though a portion of a photograph were blown up to the size of the original, while the other portions were kept photograph size.

Marihuana brings about feelings of brilliant and clear thought, sometimes euphoria. Time is distorted; it feels as if external time has slowed down and internal experience has continued at the same rate.

The hallucinogens, also called psychotomimetic or psychedelic drugs are powerful agents for altering awareness. The distinctive changes in perception produced by these drugs are frequently called hallucinations but, since the person can usually distinguish such perceptions from reality, they are rarely true hallucinations. Vivid glowing colors, sharply defined detail, and an awareness of beauty are frequently reported. With the eyes closed, abstract or realistic images may be seen. However, the visual perceptions are not always pleasant, but may be distortions of color or shape. Auditory sensations include hallucinated conversations, music, and foreign languages. Odors and tastes may also be imagined. As with marihuana, time is slowed. One of the basic constancies in perception is also affected: the awareness of self or self-identity; there is a feeling of being completely undifferentiated from the ouside world.

Split Brain

The cerebral cortex is composed of two hemispheres that are connected by a number of bundles of nerve fibers called commissures, the most prominent of which is the massive bridge of tissue called the corpus callosum (see Figure 8-1). About 20 years ago, it was discovered in experiments with animals that, when the corpus callosum was cut, the two hemispheres could function independently. Each half of the brain has a full set of centers for the sensory and motor activities of the body: vision, hearing, muscular movement, etc. Each

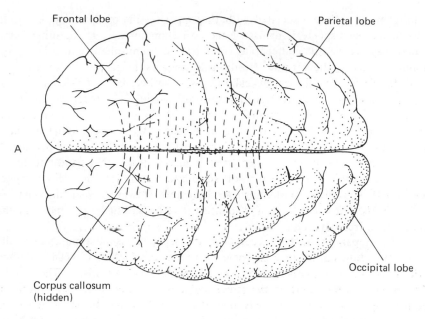

Frontal lobe
Parietal lobe

A

Corpus callosum
(hidden)

Occipital lobe

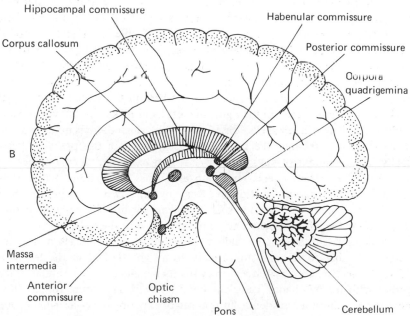

Hippocampal commissure
Habenular commissure

Corpus callosum
Posterior commissure

Corpora
quadrigemina

B

Massa
intermedia

Anterior
commissure
Optic
chiasm
Pons
Cerebellum

Figure 8-1 Two views of the human brain. Top view of the cerebral cortex. The corpus callosum is hidden deep in the brain, although there is a midline fissure that allows one to reach the corpus callosum without going through any nerve tissue. Side view of a midline slice through the brain. Those structures that allow for communication between the two cerebral hemispheres are indicated. Note that the corpus callosum is by far the largest of these.

163

hemisphere is mainly associated with the opposite side of the body; but if an area in one hemisphere is damaged, the corresponding area in the other hemisphere can frequently compensate. In man, one hemisphere is nearly always dominant, usually the left side, and this side contains the centers for speech.

In the human, the corpus callosum is sometimes cut for medical reasons or, in rare cases, an individual may be born lacking the structure. Although such persons seem quite normal in everyday situations, experiments point out the various perceptual problems of having "two brains." That which is learned by one side of the brain is not transferred to the other side. When such a person is asked to name an object that is placed in his right hand but out of sight, he can easily give a verbal report since information from his right side goes to the left hemisphere containing speech centers. However, when the object is placed in the left hand, he cannot identify it verbally, but he can pick out the same object from an array.

The apparatus used to accomplish the separate visual stimulation of the two eyes is shown in Figure 8-2. There is a screen on which images can be flashed briefly so that no compensatory eye movements can be made. The subject fixates on a central point on the screen and stimuli can be directed by means of positioning on the screen to only one of the hemispheres. Because the speech centers are in the left hemisphere, verbal reports of perceptions by that hemisphere are easy to obtain. In order to obtain a report of the right hemisphere's experiences it is necessary to provide a series of objects or pictures for the subject to point to. When different symbols or words are presented to each hemisphere separately by means of this apparatus, Gazzaniga (1967) has demonstrated the independent experience and perception of each hemisphere. When, for example, the word "keycase" is flashed on the screen, "key" to the left visual field and "case" to the right, the left hand picks out a key as a matching object, and right hand spells "case." However, since there is no communication between hemispheres, the subject probably will not use the word "case" verbally in the context of keys, but may say, for example, "a case of beer" or "in case of fire." The subjects report no awareness of separate images or any conflict between the information received by the two hemispheres. Some subjects report compensating for such problems by literally talking to themselves to allow the left hemisphere to communicate with the right.

Perception and abstractive ability are about equal with each hemisphere. A subject is able to respond nonverbally to a light flashed in the left visual field (right hemisphere), match a word with its meaning, or put similar objects together with his left hand. The right hemisphere is also equal to the left in generating an emotional response. In one set of experiments (Gazzaniga, 1967), a set of ordinary objects was flashed on the screen interspersed with the picture of a nude person. When the picture was flashed to the right hemisphere, the patient laughed and seemed embarrassed but could not describe what had been seen even though the sight had evoked an emotional response. The minor (nonspeaking) hemisphere is superior to the dominant one in the perception of certain spatial relationships, recognition of faces, and tonal memory.

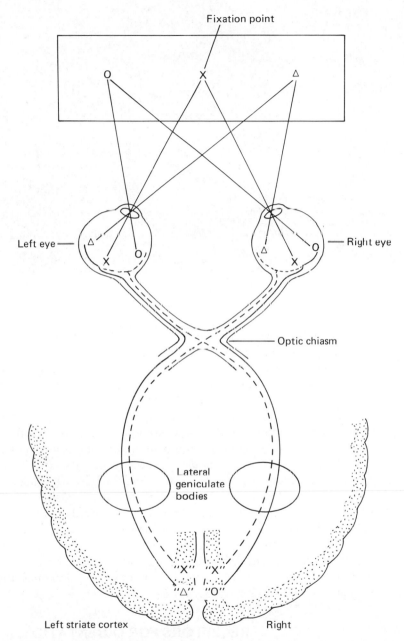

Fixation point

Left eye —

Right eye

Optic chiasm

Lateral
geniculate
bodies

"X" "X"
"Δ" "O"

Left striate cortex   Right

Figure 8-2 Schematic diagram of method of stimulating the left and right hemispheres separately. The eyes are fixated on the X. Because of the nature of the projection pathways of the eyes to the striate (visual) cortex, information to the left of the fixation point on the screen winds up in the right hemisphere and vice versa. (Information that falls on the fovea is projected to both hemispheres.) [After Gazzaniga, M. S. The split brain in man. *Scientific American,* 1967, *217* (2), 24–29.]

9
Orientation
to the World

Maintaining body orientation with respect to the world is perhaps the most basic perceptual problem facing an organism. Except for stationary animals and those that rely on chemotaxis to keep them near their food source, all behaviors of the organism assume that the world is stable. The problem that this presents to the student of perception is considerable. Gravity is perhaps the only physical energy to which earth-bound man is sensitive that never varies independent of his motion. The gravity receptors control largely reflexive behavior and thus give rise to sensations primarily under abnormal conditions, e.g., motion sickness. For this reason the importance of these receptors is ordinarily grasped among laymen only by those who are unfortunate enough to suffer damage to them. It may then become very difficult to stand with the eyes closed, let alone walk. Other disorders may make it literally impossible to roll over in bed without nausea. Orientation to the world presents other problems. Anyone who has followed a trail through the woods or driven as a stranger through a city where the roads follow the terrain rather than a block pattern has an idea of the problems involved in maintenance of geographical orientation (see, for example, Howard and Templeton, 1966).

RECEPTORS FOR ORIENTATION

The number of candidates for position and motion receptors is large. Any tissue of the body that is differentially affected by gravity or movement is a potential orientation receptor. These include the skin, joints and muscles of the limbs, trunk, and neck. The eye muscles are a source of information about the position of the body with respect to the visual world. The vestibular apparatus of the ear is sensitive to acceleration. The major problem in identifying other position and motion receptors is that the potential receptors are imbedded in body tissues, and some of them in the same tissue, so that it is impossible to stimulate one potential receptor independently of the others. This fact should suggest to us at the outset that orientation normally is a function of many receptors in many parts of the body acting together. We will also discover that it is impossible to determine to what degree orientation is accomplished solely by reflexes or how much sensations we are commonly aware of contribute. To complicate matters, we must ask ourselves to what degree these sensations themselves are products of reflex activity.

VESTIBULAR SYSTEM

The vestibular apparatus consists of the inner ear exclusive of the cochlea, namely, the semicircular canals, the utricle, and the saccule. The function of the saccule is unknown and thus will not be discussed further. The semicircular canals consist of three tubes lying approximately at right angles to one another and oriented roughly in the horizontal, vertical, and sagittal (straight ahead) planes of the head. The horizontal canal is oriented about 30° down from the horizontal plane and the superior canal about 45° to the side of straight ahead so that the left posterior is at right angles to the right superior canal (see Figure 9-1). The term semicircular is somewhat misleading because the canals actually communicate through the utricle, thus forming a complete circle. Each canal thus has a partner on the other side. One member of the pair will be stimulated by a given rotation and the other will be inhibited, thereby signaling direction of rotation. Each semicircular canal has a swelling, the ampulla, in which lies the sensory epithelium, the crista ampularis. Hair cells pass from the crista into the cupula, which is a gelatinous mass that seals the ampulla and swings back and forth with movements of the fluid of the canal (see Figure 9-2a). In this manner the semicircular canal is sensitive to angular movement of the canal (rotation of the head). The movement of the cupula and the behaviors that it controls follow the equation describing the behavior of a spring-loaded pendulum, which it is. The canal may be stimulated by irrigating the external auditory meatus (the place you were taught not to stick things into) with warm or cold water. This sets up convection currents in the canals and mimics the effects of adequate (normal) stimulation. Presenting electrical current to the ear produces similar responses by directly stimulating the vestibular nerve.

The utricle lies at the junction of the three semicircular canals. The receptor organ is the macula which contains a sensory epithelium (Figure 9-2b). Cilia project from this epithelium upward into a gelatinous mass containing small stones of calcium carbonate known as otoliths. When the head is upright

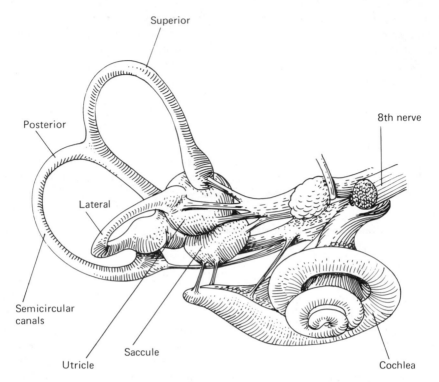

Figure 9-1 The inner ear shown in relation to the orientation of the head. [From Hardy, M. Observations on the innervation of the macula sacula in man. *Anatom. Rec.,* 1934, *59,* 403–18.]

the macula is horizontal and the otoliths lie on the hair cells. Linear acceleration of the head produces a shearing force on the hair cells which is believed to be the method of stimulation, as in the hair cells of the basilar membrane of the cochlea.

PROPRIOCEPTION

Proprioception is the perception of movement and position of the limbs and other structures of the body. A muscle sense is sometimes included along with proprioception. However, present evidence favors the view that the muscle receptors do not contribute directly to sensation but act in a reflex manner to control muscle tone.

There are three types of sensory nerve endings in and around the joint, the most important of which is known as the "spray-type." The initial transient response of these endings signals direction, rate, and extent of movement and the steady response signals the location of the joint. They are known as slowly

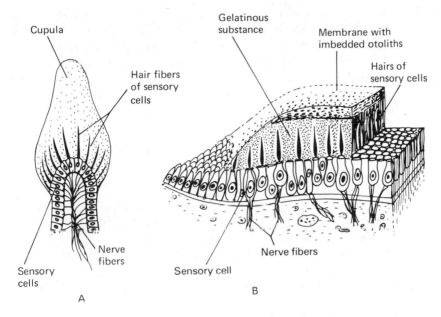

Figure 9-2 The receptors proper of the semicircular canals (a) and the utricle (b). a. Showing the crista projecting into the ampulla and being deflected by the movement of the fluid in the semicircular canal. b. The macula, the receptor proper of the utricle. Both systems contain hair cells similar to those of the basilar membrane. [From Geldard, F. A. *The human senses* (2nd Ed.). New York: Wiley, 1972.]

adapting receptors. However, they do adapt eventually. Anyone who has worn a cast that immobilized a joint has probably noticed a loss of the sense of its position after a while. Sometimes when the entire hand is in a cast the patient will report that his fingers feel like they are crossed or in other unusual positions. Such reports support the notion that the muscles do not contribute to the sense of position.

THE EYES AS POSITION RECEPTORS

The eyes obviously have an important role in orientation. The various functions that eye position plays in orientation will be discussed in a later section but it should be noted here that the eyes provide information about the position of an object with respect to the head by virtue of a correlation between the visual input to the retina and perception of the eye position. If the eye muscles signal position (i.e., are proprioceptive) we have an exception to the statement above that muscles do not signal position. It appears, however, that the eye muscles accomplish this, not by receptors in the muscles themselves, but because of neural activation of the muscles, which is itself a stimulus for perception of movement and eye position (see section on reafference in Chapter 11). The eye is capable of one type of motion that may not be familiar to most readers and so needs to be mentioned. This is an involuntary torsional motion (a rotation about the visual axis) such that the eye tends to keep an object fixed on the retina even though it is rotated about the visual axis or the head is tilted. In the latter case the torsion is a utricular reflex and has a maximum extent of about $10°$

ORIENTATION TO GRAVITY

Normal Posture

The maintenance of posture in the normal organism depends on the combined functioning of all systems described above. Proprioceptive function is sufficient for the maintenance of posture in the absence of visual information since persons with bilateral labyrinthine damage are still able to stand upright in the dark, although with difficulty. Unilateral damage causes a person to fall to one side because of the imbalance in the control of postural reflexes. Normal persons sway a certain amount while standing still. This motion provides stimuli to the proprioceptive, and possibly the vestibular, system for the maintenance of posture. The importance of visual input may be gauged by viewing a pendulum or other moving visual object. Even the suggestion that one is swaying will cause sway and even falling. This has been used as a test for suggestibility.

Perception of the Upright

That the utricles contribute to the perception of the upright is demonstrated by the fact that persons underwater and with the eyes closed, where visual and kinesthetic cues are practically eliminated, are able to point to the vertical with an accuracy better than chance. There is a very large amount of literature on the ability to set the body to the vertical in the titling chair situation. In the absence of visual cues, persons are able to do this from any starting position with an error of one degree or less. The same receptors are involved in the perception of the vertical as in the maintenance of posture, with the possible addition of a contribution from the "seat of the pants."

On a merry-go-round the perceived vertical is altered such that the floor of the merry-go-round appears to slope down toward the riders. The horse seems to lean out and the objects to the inside that were at eye level when the rider was stopped appear to be above eye level. This is an example of the oculogravic effect and is explainable simply by the fact that the apparent vertical is the resultant of the force of gravity and the centrifugal force on the rider (see Figure 9-3). This will be the case in any situation where the body experiences centrifugal force.

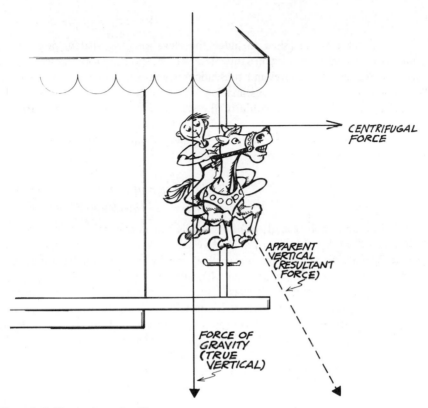

CENTRIFUGAL FORCE

APPARENT VERTICAL (RESULTANT FORCE)

FORCE OF GRAVITY (TRUE VERTICAL)

Figure 9-3 The oculogravic effect.

PERCEPTION OF OBJECT ORIENTATION

Perception of Object Inclination, Visual
Context Normal or Absent

When the body is in the normal upright position, the judgment of the upright is accurate to about one degree. When the body is tilted, the apparent vertical may be shifted but the degree and direction of the shift seems to differ among subjects.

Perception of the horizontal is about as accurate as perception of the vertical but other angles are more difficult to judge. Lines at 45° inclination are perceived with greater accuracy than other positions except for the vertical and horizontal.

Perception of Elevation

When subjects are asked to judge the elevation of a distant point in re-lation to eye level (the horizon) they tend to see points at the objective eye level as being above eye level and thus underestimate the location of eye level. This would explain the underestimation of the steepness of downward slop-ing surfaces and the overestimation of the steepness of upward sloping surfaces. It is a familiar observation that a level place at the bottom of a hill when viewed from the top of the hill seems to slope up away from the foot of the hill and the height of a hill beyond is overestimated.

Perception of Object Inclination,
Visual Context Altered

Witkin and Asch (e.g., 1948) have studied extensively the effect described by Kofka and by Wertheimer of altered visual context on the perception of the upright. When a person judges the verticality of a line surrounded by a frame in an otherwise dark room or when the subject sees the line within a tilted room, the perceived upright is biased in the direction of the visual context. The effect is greater when the subject is also tilted from the vertical. The same effect obtains when the subject is seated in a tilted chair and is instructed to set the chair to the upright. When the room is tilted as much as $30°$ from the vertical the subject may be influenced entirely by the context of the room and say that he is upright when he is actually $30°$ from the vertical. There are wide differences among subjects. Some are heavily dependent on the visual context and are designated by Witkin as "field dependent." Those that rely on gravity are designated "field independent." Witkin et al. (1954) find this classification to correlate with other perceptual capacities such as recognition of embedded figures and various personality characteristics.

Responses to Acceleration

The preceding section was limited somewhat arbitrarily to orientation when the organism is relatively static. Acceleration of the body gives rise to a number of responses that allow the organism to maintain its posture and/or contribute to its locomotion. We will not consider all of the various reflexes involved in the maintenance of posture and locomotion because they involve principles that are beyond the scope of this book. However, the reflexes known as nystagmic reflexes are intimately involved in the judgment of acceleration.

Nystagmus is a rapid movement of the eyes in one direction followed by a slow drift in the opposite direction. The direction of the nystagmus may be horizontal, vertical, or torsional (rotary about the visual axis). There are several types of nystagmus. *Optokinetic nystagmus* is elicited by movement of the visual field past the organism. The slow phase of the nystagmus is in the direction of

How do we know which way is up? How do you tell if a picture is hanging straight on the wall? These are the kinds of questions which motivated the research of Herman Witkin.

There are two types of information that an individual can use to perceive the upright. He can use cues from his own body as a result of the pull of gravity, or he can depend on environmental cues such as corners of rooms, doors, etc. Witkin (1959) decided to investigate how these cues are used and whether everyone uses both cues. In one of his experiments, he seated a blindfolded subject in a chair in a small room. The room was so constructed that the experimenter could rotate it or the chair independently to either side. Once the chair and the room were both tilted, the subject was instructed to remove his blindfold and to direct the experimenter in moving the chair to an upright position. It was found that some people were able to return the chair to its true upright position independent of the slant of the walls of the room; they were using bodily cues to the upright. Other people felt the chair was in a true upright position when it was in fact in line with the slanted walls of the room. There were considerable individual differences in setting the chair to the upright, but most persons fit one of these two categories.

In another experiment, the rod and frame test was used. The subject, seated in a dark room, could see only a luminous square frame surrounding a luminous rod. The rod and frame were each tilted to a different angle. The subject was asked to direct the experimenter how to move the rod to place it in a vertical position. The degree to which the tilt of the frame influenced the judgment of the verticality of the rod could then be determined. Some subjects set the rod so that it was more in line with the tilted frame, while others lined the rod up with their own bodies. Witkin has called the former subjects "field dependent" and the latter "field independent." Field-dependent subjects tend to pay more attention to external environmental cues to perception whereas field independent subjects depend on bodily sensations. Most subjects use the same strategy in each of these experimental situations, the tilted room and the rod and frame test.

Witkin and his associates wondered how these two modes of perceiving would relate to subjects' solutions of other perceptual problems. They tested subjects on finding hidden figures embedded in complex geometrical designs. It was expected that field-dependent persons would take more time to find a hidden figure than would field-independent persons. The field-dependent group would presumably be more influenced by the background or surrounding design, whereas the second group's judgments would be independent of the appearance of the field. This prediction proved to be true.

Consistent sex differences have been found on these tests, with men being more field independent and women more field dependent. Witken et al. (1962) found field dependency to be correlated with social dependency, conformity, and other personality characteristics.

the movement and the fast phase is in the opposite direction. This reflex has the effect of keeping the same part of the visual field fixated on the retina as long as possible, then rapidly switching to a new fixation point. In organisms which lack substantial eye movement, e.g., reptiles and birds, the whole head shows the nystagmic response. *Vestibular nystagmus* is a response to rotary acceleration of the head. The slow phase is opposite to the direction of rotation, and the fast phase is in the same direction. Considering the relative motion of the stable world with respect to the rotating head it can be seen that the result of vestibular nystagmus is also to keep the eyes fixated on the world as much as possible. Vestibular nystagmus, unlike optokinetic nystagmus, can occur in the dark. When a subject in a dark room is first accelerated to a given rate of rotation which is temporarily held constant and is then decelerated to a stop, there are basically two phases of nystagmic response. When the acceleration reaches threshold (stage 1), there is a nystagmus with the fast phase in the same direction as the rotation. This is a response of the semicircular canals and, due to the lag in the deflection of the cupula, continues for a time after the acceleration has stopped and the subject is rotating at a constant rate. Then it reverses for a time and ceases. When the deceleration reaches threshold (stage 2), nystagmus occurs in the direction opposite to the original nystagmus and continues for a time after the subject has stopped rotating, then reverses for a period of time. Within limits, the nystagmus is predictable from the behavior of the cupula of the semicircular canals.

Visual and vestibular stimuli generally operate together to determine the nystagmic responses but they are sometimes in conflict, as when the subject has stopped accelerating but the cupula is still deflected, or when the visual field is caused to rotate with the subject. In these cases vision is generally dominant over vestibular input.

The *oculogyric illusion* refers to the apparent movement of an object in situations where the vestibular stimulation is sufficiently strong to override the visual input. When the body is rotated in one direction and then stopped, the illusion of movement is predictable from the direction of the nystagmic eye movements. Consider the case of rotation to the left in the dark except for a light that is fixed relative to the body. When the acceleration begins, the nystagmus will have the slow phase to the right and the fast phase to the left. Vision is suppressed during the fast phase and need not be considered. During the slow drift of the eye to the right the light is moving to the left relative to the eye and is thus seen as moving left. When the acceleration ceases and there is a constant rate of rotation, the direction of the nystagmus and the apparent movement reverse for a time and then cease. Upon rapid deceleration the situation is exactly reversed. The light that is stationary relative to the body first seems to move to the right opposite to the direction of the previous rotation and then reverses. (Graybiel et al., 1946).

Although the oculogyric illusion is explainable in terms of nystagmus, there are some differences between the duration and degree of illusion and the duration and rate of the nystagmus. The same problem exists for other correlations between nystagmus and subjective movement.

Sensations of Movement

The sensation of movement generally depends on the semicircular canals and the otoliths, rather than either movement or acceleration of the body itself. Motion of the body is sensed only during acceleration. When the body is rotating at a constant rate, as mentioned above, there is no sensation of rotation as long as the eyes are closed. When the acceleration is below the vestibular threshold and there is vision present, the visual input will dominate, and it will appear that the world is moving. This is the explanation for the observation, once commonplace, that when a train begins to pull out of the station the world appears to be moving past the stopped train. Nowadays, what trains there are generally accelerate too fast for this illusion to be seen very often. The relations between sensation and nystagmus and other reflexes of acceleration are complex and not completely worked out. It is clear that sensation is dependent on the reflexes but not in a simple manner. The vestibular system constitutes an interesting example of the difficulty of defining perception in terms of conscious sensations, because perception of acceleration, accomplished by the various righting and postural reflexes, is largely incapable of verbalization. All of the senses give rise to reflexes as well as sensations but the vestibular sense probably relies most heavily on reflexes and might even be termed "nonsensory."

Vestibular Adaptation

Both nystagmus and the oculogyric illusion decrease with repeated exposure to acceleration. The decreases take place both within short sessions and over many sessions and last for long periods of time. Effects found within sessions are sometimes labelled adaptation and those found over sessions called habituation, but this is quite arbitrary. It is a good example of the impossibility of separating (sensory) adaptation from habituation on the basis of the time course of the effect.

Dancers and skaters have the ability to control the aftereffects of rotation. Dancers fixate a point in space as long as possible while they spin and then pick up another fixation point by a rapid head movement. In this way, they inhibit both pre-rotary and post-rotary nystagmus. Skaters, on the other hand, rotate at 250 rpm which is much too fast for this to be possible. They close their eyes during the spin and then when they stop they fixate some object like the foot lights, usually with their hand in the field of view. Collins (1966) has shown that the inhibition of the normal vestibular responses to spinning is specific to the presence of vision upon stopping. When professional skaters were instructed to close their eyes when they had stopped spinning, to their great surprise they immediately lost their balance and fell.

MOTION SICKNESS

It is a rare and fortunate reader who has not experienced motion sickness. This malady is characterized by pallor, cold sweating, nausea, and vomiting. It is caused by certain motions typical of some of mankind's means of transportation including camels, ships, automobiles, airplanes, and spacecraft. Susceptibility to motion sickness is shared with a wide variety of other organisms including, interestingly, fish and birds. The necessary characteristic of motion that will cause sickness is a condition of varying acceleration, either linear acceleration as with a vertical oscillation or angular acceleration as with rotation about a horizontal axis. Any movement of the head relative to the body that is undergoing acceleration will accentuate the motion sickness. Persons who are unusually susceptible show more movement of the head relative to the body during motion than less susceptible individuals. Not all motions involving varying acceleration produce motion sickness since horseback riding does not produce sickness but riding camels and elephants does.

It is not certain what the essential conditions of motion sickness are. A functional vestibular system is necessary since persons who have defective vestibular apparatus are not susceptible to motion sickness. However, vestibular stimulation is not necessary for sickness to occur because situations where the visual field is undergoing motion such as the phantom swing produce sickness. One widely held theory is that sickness is the result of conflict between visual and vestibular input. This helps to explain why looking out of a car or boat at the stable world may alleviate sickness because the visual input will then be consistent with vestibular input. Other ways of reducing the sickness are reclining, restricting head movements, and the use of drugs such as dramamine. Motion sickness generally habituates, although the improvement is specific to the kind of motion and may even show negative transfer to the stable world or a different kind of motion (Money, 1970).

Why Does Alcohol Cause Dizziness?

Many persons have no doubt wondered why drinking alcohol produces sensations of dizziness. Most of these have probably concluded that the effect is a neural one. However, Money and Myles (1975) have recently provided evidence that it has nothing directly to do with the nervous system. They gave people heavy water (deuterium oxide) to drink and studied its effect on vestibular reflexes. They found that the heavy water caused a certain type of nystagmus in response to tilting the head. The effect of heavy water can be predicted from its density. The heavy water will diffuse throughout the body but, owing to the structure of the labyrinth, the heavy water reaches various parts of the labyrinth at different rates. Specifically, the diffusion takes place into the cupula sooner than into the rest of the semicircular canal. As a result, the cupula becomes heavier than the fluid of the canal and therefore responds anomalously when the head is tilted.

What does this have to do with alcohol? Alcohol is lighter than water and causes a nystagmus that is exactly opposite of that produced by heavy water. In addition, calculations based on the specific gravities of alcohol and heavy water showed that their effects were entirely predictable by their physical characteristics without necessitating any neural effect.

In case you should have the idea that you could mix a cocktail with heavy water in order to balance out the effect of the alcohol, the amount of heavy water necessary to do the job would cost about $10 per shot of whiskey. The most practical suggestion is to keep your head still and level. Or not to drink.

10

Perception
of Objects and Space

In the introductory chapter we listed several characteristics of perception. Two of them are particularly appropriate to recall as we begin this section. The first is that perception is objective. We respond to the world "as it really is" to a very large degree. This is such an everyday fact that it may seem surprising to make a point of it. However, such a reaction only reinforces the point. Actually, it is to an animal's advantage to respond to the world "as it really is" since survival is a good deal more probable for an animal that can recognize the edge of a cliff and the fact that the air will not support its weight. The visual properties of water are similar to air and we generalize our avoidance of stepping on nothing but air to stepping onto water. Unfortunately, we also see glass in the same way and sometimes try to walk through glass doors. The application of stickers and other "visible" objects onto glass doors is intended to call our attention to the fact that the visual and tactile properties of glass are incongruent. Another aspect of this "objective" nature of perception is the tendency to see a thing, or object, in the sensory input (i.e., to categorize or give it a form). It is as if the perceptual system were given a problem to solve and it actively seeks an answer. The person who looks at non-representational art and tries to discover "what it is supposed to be" is simply reacting on the basis of a very strong tendency to see the piece of art as representing some thing. Look at Figure 10-1. Until you hit upon what the sketcher intended, there is a strong tendency to try out various hypotheses until the correct one is found. Sometimes the hypotheses lead to impossible solutions as in Figure 10-2. It is significant that the perceptual system does not go "tilt" but tries to solve the problem. Sometimes it takes a considerable amount of analysis to find out what is wrong

Figure 10-1 Boring's "wife and mother-in-law." This picture contains two women, one young and attractive and the other an old hag. Some people experience difficulty in seeing both women. If you have trouble finding the young woman, her head is turned away to your left. The old woman's nose is formed by the same line as the young woman's chin.

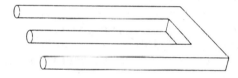

Figure 10-2 The 'two pronged trident.' This is one of a number of familiar impossible figures.

with the solution and why it does not "work." These examples also illustrate that other characteristic of perception mentioned in our introductory chapter: that perception is active. This is most obvious when there is a paucity of stimuli. Anyone who has driven long distances at night has probably had the experience of "seeing" something and then realizing that it could not have been real. The fact that perception is always an active reconstruction of the world based on the sensory input means that there is no sharp dividing line between perception and hallucination.

PERCEPTION OF FORM

The perception of form involves some of the same principles of pattern perception already discussed in Chapter 7. What we are considering now is the perception of objects, including patterns.

A discussion of form perception necessarily brings up the subject of Gestalt psychology. This school of psychological thought developed in Germany in the early 1900's as a reaction to the psychology of Wundt and Titchener. When the major Gestalt psychologists left Germany, it found acceptance in the United States as a counterweight to behaviorism. The Gestalt theory was an approach to the whole field of psychology, but its greatest impact was on the field of perception. It is not possible for us to do justice to Gestalt theory in this book; its hallmark, however, is conveyed by the expression "the whole is greater than the sum of its parts." A perceiver does not organize elemental sensations into a percept, but rather responds directly to a Gestalt. (The German word has no exact English equivalent, but conveys the idea of form, or whole.) A familiar example of the operation of Gestalt is our recognition of a tune as the *same* even if it is played in a different key. There is, according to Gestalt theory, an isomorphism, or correspondence, between the object that is perceived and the response that occurs in the brain. This concept of isomorphism led to some ideas concerning brain functioning that have been shown to be false and seem rather naive in the light of our present knowledge of neurophysiology. However, much of what we do know about the functioning of the nervous system, as, for example, in the work of Hubel and Wiesel, vindicated the Gestalt position by demonstrating that the nervous system responds to patterns, rather than stimulus elements, at a very early stage of analysis.

It is sometimes said that Gestalt psychology no longer exists as a school and that its major points have been incorporated into psychology proper. This is true to some extent, but it is more accurate to say that, as evidenced by this book, psychology has adopted some of the principles of Gestalt theory where they are the most obvious and ignored the rest—Gestalt theory has been co-opted, in the present parlance. The following discussion of form perception is largely based on Gestalt principles of perception.

Contour

The most basic concept in form perception is that of contour. There must be a contour before there can be perception of a figure. Some examples of contours are lines and edges between bright and dark areas. It is simplest to define a contour mathematically as the second derivative of brightness, although this will not be meaningful to all readers. Recall that a gradient is a constant rate of *change* in brightness over distance (a gradient is the first derivative of. brightness). A contour is a change in the rate of change, or an acceleration of the change in brightness. A contour produces the sensation of an edge but a gradient does not. It is possible to measure the minimum amount of acceleration of brightness necessary to produce a contour. Recall Figure 7-15, which was used to illustrate the effects of stabilized images without special apparatus. There is, in this figure, acceleration of brightness change but it falls below threshold for perception of contours and the figure therefore disappears when the eye is fixated on it. Although contour is necessary for the perception of shape, it is not identical with shape. A puzzle piece shares the same contour with the hole that it fits, but the two do not have the same shape (see Figure 10-3). This fact and the effects of the color and pattern of the piece are what

Figure 10-3 Illustration of the distinction between shape and contour in the case of a puzzle piece and the hole that it fits.

makes working a puzzle fun to a puzzle fan. A contour need not be continuous to be perceived. A row of dots or other broken contours will be perceived as a contour as illustrated by Figure 10–4. This is sometimes known as a subjective contour. As we have seen in Chapter 7, the eye is particularly sensitive to con-

A

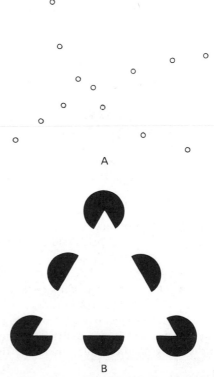

Figure 10-4 Illustrations of subjective contour. In the case of b the contour is so compelling that the triangle even seems brighter than the rest of the paper.

B

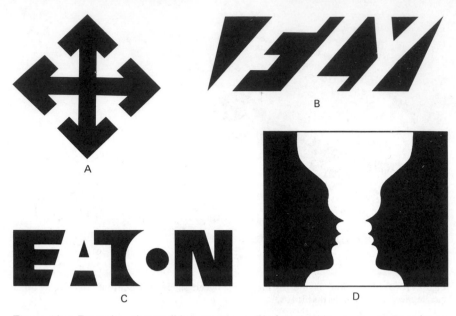

Figure 10-5 Examples of reversible contours. a. Black and white arrows. b. In order to perceive the word, reverse the usual relations of figure and ground. c. The company apparently feels that the attention-getting value of the reversal of figure and ground in some of the letters overcomes the difficulty of perceiving all letters of the word "Eaton" at one time. [Used by permission of the Eaton Corporation, Cleveland, Ohio.]

tours. This explains why cartoons, which contain only the basic contours and ignore shading, can represent something as complex as a face without the slightest difficulty.

Figure and Ground

When one views a pattern, part of the pattern organizes itself into a figure and the rest becomes ground. This happens even before the pattern is recognized, as can be seen in Figure 10-5. In illustration b the organization into figure and ground, on the basis of principles we will discuss below, interferes with the perception of the word "FLY" even though the patterns perceived as figure were not recognized as any particular objects. It was thus necessary to reverse figure and ground in order to perceive the meaningful figure. Illustration d, which is probably included in every book on perception, has a certain undocumented story attached to it. A prince, whose subjects were forbidden to make a likeness of him commissioned a psychologist to discover the principles of figure and ground. This is said to be one of the first cases of public support of science!

The differentiation into figure and ground is the most primitive and basic process in the perception of form. Rubin (see Hochberg, 1971) has summarized a number of facts about figure and ground: (1) The contour seems to belong to the figure rather than to the ground; (2) the figure has form, while the background seems to be formless; (3) the figure seems to be in front of the ground whereas the ground extends behind the figure; (4) the figure has the nature of a thing, as contrasted with the ground which does not; and (5) the figure is better remembered. Thus whichever version of a reversible contour, as for example in Figure 10-5d, is seen as figure is remembered better than the other. It is worth pointing out here that many of these principles of form perception are true not only for vision but for other senses as well. The reader will have had the experience of listening to a single instrument (the figure) from an orchestral group (the ground) or a single voice in a group of voices (the cocktail party effect).

Principles of Grouping

When we have a number of elements in a visual field it is often possible to group them in different ways and to see different figures. The Gestalt psychologists have developed a number of rules to predict what will be seen. The following rules are illustrated in Figure 10-6. (1) *Proximity.* Those elements that are closer together will be seen as units. In illustrations a and b, the O's are seen in rows or columns depending on their proximity. (2) *Similarity.* Similar ele-

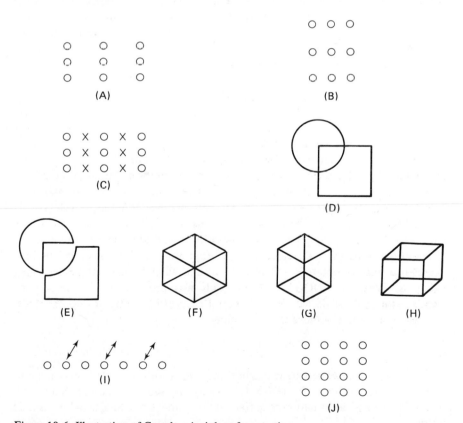

Figure 10-6 Illustration of Gestalt principles of perception.

Figure 10-7 Examples of natural camouflage. Any pattern that disrupts the contour of the animal's body will be effective. Note, for instance, the difference between 1 and 2. Optimal camouflage is provided when patches of the same color exist in the surround as in 3.

ments are grouped together. The O's and X's may be seen as rows or as columns, illustrating the competition between the principles of similarity (columns) and proximity (rows) (sketch c). (3) *Good continuation and simplicity.* When there are several ways that an array can be organized into a figure the simplest one will be seen. Diagram d is perceived as a circle and a square overlapping, rather than a circle with a wedge cut out and a square with a circular piece cut out of one corner as in e, because the former is simpler. Another interesting corollary is that the seen figure is more easily verbalized than its alternate. This is predictable from information theory which has been applied to these principles of grouping with some success (Attneave, 1954). The fewer bits of information a figure contains the better a Gestalt it is.

The principle of good continuation is used extensively in camouflage. Irregular shapes enclosing differing patches of colors are used to "break up" the pattern of the object to be camouflaged. Figure 10-7 shows an example of natural camouflage. Going back to the previous figure, the pattern shown in f forms a good Gestalt in two dimensions, but h is simpler when seen in three. The figure in g is intermediate between the two. (4) *Common fate.* This principle cannot be adequately demonstrated without motion, but if some of the dots move as indicated in diagram i, they will tend to be seen as belonging together. This is sometimes used in TV commercials and special effects. (5) *Set and past experience.* The observer can bias the organization of a set of elements such as the array of dots in illustration j, and see them in a number of different patterns even disregarding the other rules of organization. His past experience and expectation will also determine what is seen in the following string of letters: THEDOGATEMEAT. This was probably read "the dog ate meat" although "the do gate me at" is another possible string of English words. The first is more likely and also has meaning.

Depth Perception

The fact that we see the world in three dimensions may never have puzzled you, but consider that the retina is a two-dimensional structure. Somehow, three-dimensional information is extracted from the input to a two-dimensional retina.

184

What is there about these retinal images that allows us to see in depth? There are three classes of possible depth cues: muscular, monocular, and binocular cues.

Muscular cues. The potential muscular cues are those from the muscles that control position of the eyes as they converge in looking at objects at various distances. The invariant separation of the two eyes and the fact that the fovea is always the center of fixation presents a possible cue to depth by means of triangulation. Related to convergence is the accommodation produced by the ciliary muscles that control the shape of the lens and thus the focus of the eye. These possible cues are related in that they normally vary together. When the eyes fixate on a very near object, the longitudinal axes of the eyes cross and the ciliary muscles simultaneously contract, producing a thickening of the lens that focuses the image of the near object on the retina. You can easily demonstrate this to yourself by crossing your eyes. If you did not practice this dubious skill as a youngster, you can achieve the result by fixating on the end of a pencil and bringing it toward the bridge of your nose. You will notice that as the pencil comes closer and your eyes converge more and more, objects in the distance will go out of focus. It is difficult, if not impossible, to cross your eyes without this occurring. For this reason it is very difficult to study these two potential cues (convergence and focus) in isolation. Nevertheless, it has been determined from a number of different studies that accommodation is an insignificant cue to depth.

However, going back to the eye crossing demonstration, notice that as your eyes cross, objects in the distance appear to become smaller (which is not simply because the image blurs). It clearly demonstrates that convergence is a cue to size perception. Now, since there is a relationship between apparent size and distance (which we will discuss later), it also implies that convergence is a cue to depth. Together, accommodation and convergence provide a powerful cue to depth at distances up to one meter. But they are relatively ineffectual beyond that point.

Binocular disparity. The stereoscope shown in Figure 10-8 is a device that produces apparent depth by making use of binocular disparity. These devices were as common around the turn of the century as TV's are today,

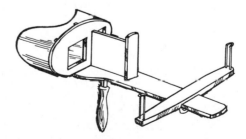

Figure 10-8 An example of a stereoscope. If there is one of these in your attic, don't throw it away. It is worth money. You could also learn a great deal about binocular cues to depth from it.

but today they have become collectors' items. The same principle is used in the popular View Master device and the stereo cameras that are sometimes seen. There are a number of other ways of producing stereoscopic pictures, all of which have some arrangement that presents a different picture to each eye. (The Cinerama movies produce a depth effect that does not rely on retinal disparity but on monocular cues to depth that we will discuss later.) The stereoscopic depth effect results from the fact that our two eyes see slightly different views of the world. Take the pencil again that you used to help you cross your eyes and hold it vertically as close to the bridge of your nose as will allow you to continue to see it in focus. (This distance, incidentally, is called the near point of vision and it increases markedly with age.) Closing one eye at a time, you will notice that the view of the pencil is quite different from each eye. Now refer to Figure 10-9 which shows the visual input to the two eyes

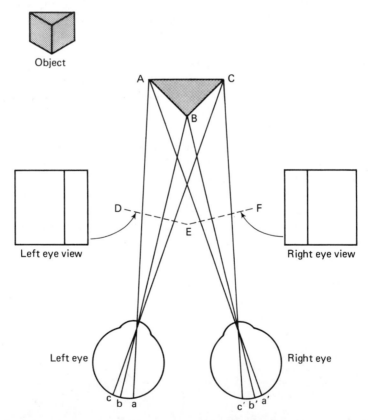

Figure 10-9 Illustration of how a stereoscopic picture is constructed. Although this is the way the pictures are taken, they are presented in the stereoscope by means of lenses that have the effect of relaxing the eyes by causing them to focus on infinity (i.e., no convergence). (An exaggeration of depth will result when the pictures reveal a more extreme separation.)

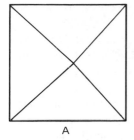 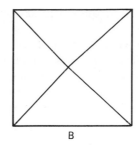 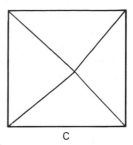

A   B   C

Figure 10-10 Binocular depth perception from flat objects without a stereoscope. Fusing one of the pairs (a and b or b and c) will produce a pyramid that appears concave; the other pair will seem convex. Can you predict which will be which?

from an object having a triangular cross section. The points on each retina that are stimulated by the points labelled A, B, and C on the object are indicated by a, b, and c for the left eye and a', b', and c' for the right eye. Notice the positions of b and b' on the two retinas in relation to the other two points. Both retinal points correspond to B on the object, which is the point that is closer to the observer than either A or C. The non-correspondence of the locations of a, b, c, and a', b' c' on the two retinas is known as retinal disparity. By intersecting the lines from A to a and from A to a' and so forth as shown by DE and EF, respectively, we have a two-dimensional representation of the stimulus to each eye. When a drawing is made of the lines that intersect a plane surface located at DE from all of the points on the object, and the left half is presented to the left eye and the right half to the right eye, the figure appears in depth in the same way that the object does.

The effect of depth is believed by many to be produced by the cortical fusion of the disparate information from the two eyes. If the amount of retinal disparity is too great, the images will not fuse and other effects will result (see below). It is possible to make line drawings such as those in Figure 10-10 and look at them with the eyes crossed so as to fuse them into one and get a depth effect. The fusing of the two pictures (the third must be covered) will produce an in-depth but out of focus image. However, this is fairly difficult and takes a certain amount of practice. A somewhat easier method is to put a piece of paper or cardboard between the two pictures and hold it so that each of your eyes looks down one side only. Now relax your gaze as if daydreaming so that the two eyes will be looking in parallel as if at infinity. The easiest way to study this effect, of course, is to use an old-fashioned stereoscope.

Retinal disparity is a very powerful cue to relative depth. It is often employed to discriminate between objects that are very similar but not identical, such as a counterfeit dollar and a real one. When the two bills are presented separately to the two eyes, any parts of the two bills that differ literally appear to stand out. In aerial reconnaissance, two pictures are taken of a camouflaged target from cameras separated by many feet. When the two are presented to the eyes stereoscopically the depth effect may be strong enough to override the effect of the camouflage.

Some very interesting work in stereopsis has been done by Julesz (e.g., 1964) employing random dot patterns as stimuli instead of line drawings or pictures. One eye is shown a pattern of random dots. The other eye is shown the same pattern of random dots except that the center of the pattern has been shifted to one side (and the rest filled in with more random dots). When one looks at either pattern alone a field of randomly positioned dots is seen having no apparent regularity. When the two are viewed stereoscopically, however, the center portion that has been shifted is seen in depth just as if it were a line drawing having retinal disparity. This clearly illustrates that it is not necessary for a pattern to be perceived prior to the perception of depth. Fusion of the non-corresponding elements in the cortex occurs independently of pattern perception by either eye (see Figure 10-11).

Monocular Depth Cues

The monocular cues to depth are perhaps more interesting because they are less obvious than binocular disparity. They are the ones we must rely on when we use only one eye or when we look at a picture. That these cues are very effective is illustrated by the perceived depth in many photographs and paintings. Another more mundane example is given by the fact that persons who are blind in one eye are able to drive without difficulty. In reading the list of monocular cues below, you may be tempted to dispute our statement

Figure 10-11 Random dot stereogram. If you are not particularly good at fusing stereograms, you can photocopy this figure, paste it on a card, and place it in a stereoscope. Alignment is tricky so you may not succeed without some effort. [From Julesz, B. Binocular depth perception without familiarity cues. *Science,* 1964, *145,* 356–62. © 1964 by the American Association for the Advancement of Science.]

Although we can state the cues for depth fairly concisely, and everyone who has taken an elementary art course has learned the rules of perspective, they have not always been as obvious to artists as they may seem to us. You have probably noticed the lack of depth in medieval European art. Why did the medieval artists not portray depth in their work? Were the rules that are so obvious to us unknown to them? There is good evidence that the Greek and Roman artists of classical antiquity were familiar with the rules of linear perspective and were able to create convincing depth in their work. It appears that the theologically motivated de-emphasis of the natural world during the Middle Ages led to the loss of depth in medieval painting. Thus the ability to produce the illusion of depth in paintings was lost. The rules of perspective were rediscovered during the Renaissance through the work of a number of artists, especially Brunelleschi (1377–1446). The theory of linear perspective developed during the course of the fifteenth century, but it was not until Leonardo Da Vinci (1452–1519) that linear and aerial perspective can be said to have been well understood.

It is perilous to conclude that the absence of perspective in the work of an artist or period indicates an ignorance of it, as a study of the work of a Cezanne or Picasso will amply illustrate. Traditional oriental art does not employ linear perspective but indicates depth by size, elevation, and aerial perspective. However, Chinese artists occasionally used linear perspective convincingly as early as the tenth century (Encyclopedia of World Art, 1966).

that the monocular cues are not obvious; anyone who has studied art has heard of most of these cues. However, it is noteworthy that artists did not discover these cues for many centuries. It was Leonardo DaVinci who first formulated the rules of monocular perspective. The perception of depth in a painting is interesting because the monocular cues to depth must override the binocular cue to flatness resulting from the absence of retinal disparity.

Relative size. The relative distance or depth of two objects can be determined by their relative size. If two similar objects of unknown size are placed at the same distance in an environment lacking cues to distance, the larger object appears to be closer. For this reason, the relative-size cue to distance is ambiguous, as the following demonstration will show. Two white balloons are uniformly illuminated so that they appear as white circles at an indeterminate distance in an otherwise dark room. The balloons are mounted in such a way that they can be inflated or deflated to change their size. As they are alternately inflated or deflated the subject perceives the larger one as moving closer to him and the smaller one as moving away, although actually they remain at the constant original distance.

Familiar size. Whereas the use of relative size as a cue requires comparison of two similar objects, the use of familiar size requires some past experience with a specific object. Even though two objects have the same retinal image. if a person knows that one is in fact larger, then he will correctly judge them to be at different distances. For example, a small boy standing nearby and a man some distance away may project the same image on your retina but, because you know that the man is larger, you will judge him to be farther away. In an experimental test of the use of this cue, subjects were given different instructions as to the nature of an ambiguous stimulus and asked to judge its distance. A disc of light was viewed by subjects under reduced light conditions. They were told it was either a ping pong ball or a billiard ball. The subjects judged it to be closer when told it was a ping pong ball indicating that, in the absence of definite distance cues, subjects perceive distance relative to familiar size.

The relation of apparent size and apparent distance is stated by *Emmert's law*, which says rather simply that, for an object subtending a certain fixed retinal angle, apparent size is proportional to apparent distance. This relationship is shown in Figure 10-12. Emmert proposed this law to account for the fact that afterimages do not have a fixed size but that their apparent size depends on the surface against which they are seen. This is very easy to demonstrate to yourself. Look at a bright window or other surface long enough to develop an afterimage. Then when you look at near and far surfaces you will find that the afterimage changes apparent size according to Emmert's law. Ob-

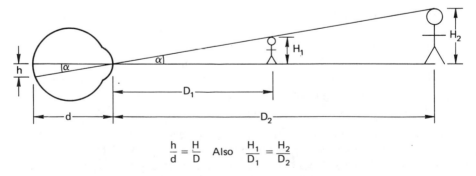

$$\frac{h}{d} = \frac{H}{D} \quad \text{Also} \quad \frac{H_1}{D_1} = \frac{H_2}{D_2}$$

Figure 10-12 Illustration of Emmert's law. Since d (the length of the eyeball) is fixed. H (Height) can be calculated knowing h (the height of the image on the retina) and D (distance). Or, D may be found from h and H. Similarly, for any two objects it is possible to calculate relative size from relative distance and vice versa.

Figure 10-13 Shading and depth. Patterns of light and shade have a profound effect on the perception of depth. Such effects are well known to people who apply make-up to faces and make horror movies. Interestingly, although the reversal of the usual direction of the light alters the appearance of depth it does not cause the face to look like the inside of a mask. Faces seem to be more resistant to such effects than other objects.

viously, the afterimage does not physically change size because it resides in the retina. Emmert's law can be generalized to account for apparent size and distance of any object, but as you might expect, this cue can be an ambiguous one. The size of a familiar object is a cue to depth and the depth of an unfamiliar object can be a cue to size.

Shadows and shading. Shading is frequently used by the artist to indicate rounded or angular surfaces. Shadows indicate the direction of the light falling on an object. We are so accustomed to having illumination come from above that when the light source is beneath the object, we see reversed depth. This results because concavities are now shaded on the upper part and convexities on their lower portion. A good example of this effect is shown in the ghostly aspect of Figure 10-13, which you can approximate by taking any highly shaded picture and looking at it upside down. Shadows also reveal depth when one object shades or partly shades another. They are extremely powerful depth cues and can evoke the perception of an object even when no object is present. An example is shown in Figure 10-14, where merely from the shadows cast by the letters you can easily read the word.

Figure 10-14 SHADING

Figure 10-15 Aerial perspective. Notice the effect of the haze on the apparent distance of the objects in the pictures.

Aerial perspective. Aerial perspective is a cue for distance that depends on the changes in contrast, brightness, saturation, and hue, and the blurring of detail that occur with distance. This particular cue has not been the object of much experimental study, but the nature of its effects is shown in the pictures in Figure 10-15. The buildings in a city appear distant on a hazy day when the air is full of pollution; in contrast, on a clear day, they appear to be quite near. You have probably also noticed that on a clear day distant mountains appear much closer than usual. Besides having less contrast, objects in the distance have a bluish cast. The differential scattering of various wavelengths by particles in the air results in more red wavelengths being dispersed than blue ones.

Interposition. Interposition (also called occlusion) is another powerful cue to distance: nearer objects cover and hide more-distant objects. When a distant object is only partially covered by a nearer one, their common contour usually gives a good idea of which one is in front (Figure 10-16). J. J. Gibson (1950a) reported one of the classic experiments demonstrating this effect. He made up a set of several cards that looked as though they were ordinary cards arranged at various locations in space when they were viewed monocularly from a fixed perspective. However, by cutting out appropriate sections of the cards and making them the right sizes, he was able to reverse the apparent depth from the true depth.

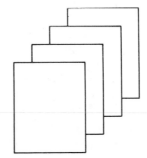

Figure 10-16 Interposition.

Linear perspective. The most common example of this cue is the appearance of railroad tracks or telephone poles as they recede into the distance. Even though the tracks are parallel, they appear to meet at the horizon (Figure 10-17a). As an object approaches the eye, the angle it subtends and the image it projects to the retina increase. One who has studied art knows that all parallel lines appear to converge on a single point at the horizon. This convergence can be strikingly illustrated by looking down a long hallway or between the stacks

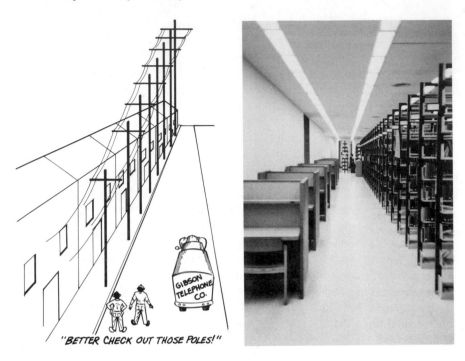

"BETTER CHECK OUT THOSE POLES!"

Figure 10-17 a. (left) Linear perspective. b. (right) Linear perspective in library stacks.

of a library (Figure 10-17b). The fact that linear perspective would normally produce foreshortening and convergence between near and far edges in a perspective view of an object means that figures such as the Necker cube (Figure 10-18) are ambiguous in perspective. As you look at them for a while, the depth reverses direction.

Motion parallax. As you move your head relative to the world, near objects change position rapidly while far objects remain still or move less. Also, objects nearer to you than the point on which your gaze is fixed appear to move in a direction opposite to yours, while objects farther away than your fixation point appear to move along with you. Each velocity is a graded function of the object's real distance from the subject. You have probably noticed these two indications of motion parallax while riding in a car: telephone poles along the roadside seem to move very quickly in the opposite direction, whereas the more distant hills seem to be moving more slowly along with you.

Texture gradient. Many surfaces in the physical world have texture or some type of structural unit repeated over the entire surface. These units, large or small, are part of the depth information presented to the retina. If all parts of the surface are equidistant from the subject, then all the textural units will be the same size in the retinal projection. However, in the real world, surfaces are usually at a slant to our line of sight and the texture is projected onto the retina according to the rules of perspective.

If, for example, we look at a surface made up of square elements such as a tile floor, there is a gradient, or change in the texture density, in the retinal image with distance. Texture size decreases with distance and there is also a change in outline shape—the squares will project as trapezoids because the projections of their far edges are smaller than the projections of their near edges. The sides, although physically parallel, are projected as converging with distance. In addition, the heights of the trapezoids are shortened or compressed with distance.

The subject uses the gradient of texture as projected on his retina as a source of information about the structure of space. J. J. Gibson (1950b) has pointed out the importance of texture gradient and how it provides a perceptual

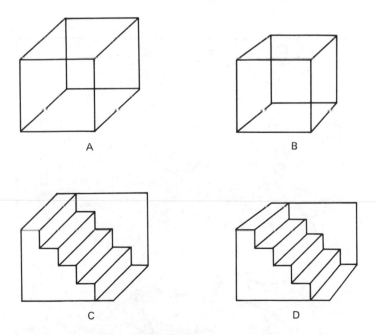

Figure 10-18 Ambiguous figures. a. The Necker cube, shown without linear perspective, not only reverses in depth spontaneously but whichever face appears closer seems too small. b. In linear perspective the cube has less tendency to reverse itself. c. The Schroder staircase is another famous example of a reversing figure. d. The same figure drawn in linear perspective shows a diminished tendency to reverse.

scale for the visual world; many of the monocular depth cues we have previously discussed can be derived from it. Gibson has shown that the textural gradient carries information about the slant of a surface, the sizes and distances of objects on the textural surface, the shapes of objects in the field and the existence of edges or cliffs between surfaces. These points about texture gradients are illustrated in Figure 10-19. Experiments have shown that although texture gradients do provide potentially useful information, subjects do not necessarily utilize them fully without other cues. In addition to the texture gradient, Gibson considers motion parallax an important means by which the visual system responds directly to features of the changing environment and thus obtains information about the world. Gibson believes that the keystone in studying perception is to consider real situations in an actual environment. To him, it is not appropriate to speak of cues; instead, using Gestalt-like phraseology, he experiences depth in the organization of a visual field either as a result of learned rules or because of some innate perceptual organization.

"Flatness" cues. Schlosberg (1941) pointed out that pictures contain cues not only for depth but also for flatness. It is true that pictures as a rule

Figure 10-19 Texture gradient. This figure produces an in-depth effect even though texture is the major depth cue.

do not convey the same impression of depth as does the original scene. A single picture viewed binocularly conveys depth by means of all the monocular cues discussed above except one: motion parallax. Most important, however, is the absence of binocular disparity, so the stereoscopic cues indicate flatness. The additional presence of a border around the picture would also accentuate flatness. These cues can be minimized by looking at a picture with one eye, holding the head steady, and blocking out the border. When we look into a portable, hand-size slide viewer we accomplish all three things. The picture will have better depth than when projected onto a screen.

AUDITORY SPACE PERCEPTION

We have discussed the role of the visual system in the perception of objects and space; the auditory system is also involved in spatial orientation and localization. The function of the auditory system is not merely "hearing" auditory sensations, but perceiving the direction and the nature of an event for orientation and identification. The mechanisms of auditory localization and the importance of the binaural system were discussed in Chapter 6. In this section, we will consider further aspects of perception of the auditory space.

Sound pressure (intensity) is an important cue in determining the distance of a sound source. This cue is easiest to use if we are familiar with the source of the sound and can thus estimate the distance from experience. As the intensity of a sound such as speech decreases we generally judge the distance to be greater. Békésy (1960) determined that, in free space, there was a loss of 6 db (i.e., sound pressure was reduced by three quarters) for each doubling of distance. This is based on the inverse square law, by which the sound pressure decreases inversely with the square of the distance of the sound source. Another factor that plays a part in distance perception is that the frequency composition of sounds varies with distance, low-frequency sounds carrying farther.

In enclosed spaces, reverberation is an important consideration. More reverberant sound sources are judged to be farther away. This has been used to advantage in radio broadcasting since the amount of reverberation increases as the speaker moves away from the microphone and this enhances the perception of distance by the listener.

It is interesting at this point to consider briefly the problem of room acoustics; Békésy studied this area in some detail (e.g., 1967). A sound wave passing over the heads of a seated audience is greatly absorbed by the clothing and bodies of the people and the furniture. To help alleviate this problem of damping, a concert hall must be designed so that sound waves reach the audience at large as well as at small angles. Thus, some sound waves must come directly

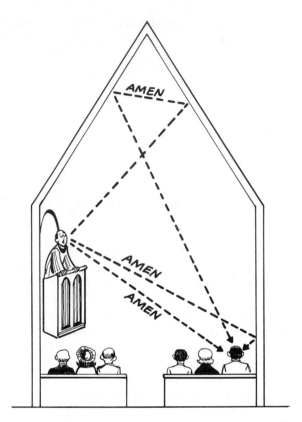

Figure 10-20 Paths of sound waves in a room. Echoes will be heard if the length of the paths differ by more than a certain amount unless the sounds taking the longer paths are greatly attenuated.

from the sound source and others must be reflected from upper parts of the walls and the ceiling as shown in Figure 10-20. However, the reflected sound must not separate too much from the direct sound or else it will be heard later as an echo. To eliminate echo, the length of the path of the reflected sound must not be more than a certain amount greater than that of the direct sound: in other words, the ceiling must not be too high. At the same time, the sound energy of the reflected sound must not be too attenuated to be heard. The time relation of the direct sound and the reflected sound must be such that there is an enhancement of the loudness of the direct sound. The reflected sounds and the direct sound must both be perceived as coming from the same location.

Echoes are undesirable in situations such as the concert hall, but they are used by man and other animals in numerous ways for perception of objects and space. The Navy's "sonar" is a system for detecting underwater objects. A high-frequency sound is sent out and the sound waves reflected back from the object are analyzed at the sound source. This analysis gives information about the object's size, composition, and location. Bats likewise emit high-frequency sound pulses and use their echoes to avoid colliding with obstacles in flight and also to locate flying insects for food. Porpoises also use an "echo-ranging" technique to avoid obstacles and to detect food and other objects in the water. They deliver trains of short pulses of high-frequency sound in order to produce a continuous series of echoes.

The ability of the blind to avoid obstacles has been the subject of experimentation and theorizing over a number of years. The blind person "senses" the wall in front of him without being aware of which sensory system is utilized. It was once thought that "facial vision," a sensation of air on the face or hands, was responsible for the "obstacle sense." However, this theory was ruled out by the demonstration that blind persons wearing gloves and a heavy veil over their heads could still detect an obstacle as well as usual (Supa, et al., 1944). If their ears were plugged, however, blind subjects were no longer able to locate the barrier, thus proving that auditory cues were the basis of obstacle detection. Noises from their shoes or from tapping a cane while walking provided the sounds that echoed from an obstacle and thus served as cues. Persons who are deaf and blind, or deaf persons who are blindfolded subjects in an experiment, are unable to perceive barriers. The ability of the blind to detect objects is indeed remarkable; one blind boy has been known to avoid obstacles while riding a bicycle (Kellogg, 1962).

In addition, various characteristics of objects can be discriminated by means of echoes as Kellogg has shown in a series of tests with blind and sighted subjects. Blind subjects were very successful at discriminating depth, size, and degree of reflectivity of surfaces (whether of metal, cloth, etc.). They could also detect a change in position of a disc, 30 cm in diameter placed 60 cm away when it was moved closer or farther away by 10 cm. Sighted subjects, although not as efficient in using these cues as blind subjects, could improve their performances with practice, indicating that the blind do not have a unique "sixth sense."

HAPTIC SPACE

The term "haptic perception" refers to an active, exploratory process with *obtained* and not *imposed* stimulation. The whole body, most of its parts and all of its surfaces, are for feeling and doing as opposed to passively receiving stimulation as do the ears. The skin and the extremities, especially the hands, are used to obtain information about an object such as shape, surface, weight, rigidity, temperature, and so on. The hand itself, rather than the minute receptors in the skin, is the organ of haptic perception. In the following section we will be discussing the concept of the haptic system as developed in the research of J. J. Gibson (1966); many of the points also reflect the work of David Katz (1884–1953) (Krueger, 1970).

The visual system is usually predominant in our awareness, but the haptic system is not so inferior to the optic system in its abilities. The blind use the haptic system for much of their realm of perception. We become aware of the haptic system on those occasions when it is more acute than vision. For example, when you want to test the smoothness of the surface you are sanding, or if you need to test the sharpness of a knife, haptics predominate over vision. This is also true when you must identify something in the dark, for example, your house key, by its shape or texture.

Gibson (1962) had subjects feel irregularly shaped objects with their hands, using random movements in order to obtain a set of "touch postures." Gibson stresses that the form of the object is always what is perceived, never the form of the skin indentation, analogous to the perception of the figure and not the ground. In a short time, subjects can readily identify the objects by touch and even describe them without ever having seen them.

Katz has shown that surface texture can be learned haptically in much the same way. Subjects studied 12 kinds of paper by touch—rough and smooth—from blotting paper to writing paper—and were able to learn to identify each one if allowed to rub the fingers over the surface. There has to be mechanical friction of the skin to obtain a perception of the surface. Also, as mentioned previously, the stimulus information has to be actively *obtained.* Fine to coarse sandpaper and grades of slipperiness can be distinguished in the same way with some experience. Binns (1937) studied wool graders who performed their jobs by pulling fiber strands through their hands and looking at the strands, and then assigning them a grade. Binns discovered that when these people looked at the wool and felt it separately, their tactual and visual ratings were highly correlated.

It is easier to discriminate weight, surface texture, and structure by lifting an object than by having the object rest passively in your hand. In addition, wielding an object (tossing, catching, shaking, passing from hand to hand) seems to be important in making judgments about material composition and consistency. In this mode of haptic perception, information is obtained not only from the skin but also from joints, muscles, and tendons. "Effortful touch" (squeezing, pushing, stretching) helps to detect rigidity, elasticity, and viscosity of an object. Firmness or softness is an attribute that can be measured only when forces are exerted on an object as by a hand. The physician relies on the haptic information obtained in percussion and palpation of the body to aid in diagnosis.

The hands are not the only organs of the haptic system. The feet and mouth are also important. The feet attain special importance in those people who have no arms or have lost the use of their arms and hands; in these persons the discriminations we have discussed become well developed with practice in using the feet. Most of us, however, perceive at least the difference in the feel of two pairs of shoes, or the variations in texture when going barefoot on sand, gravel, grass, and so forth.

The mouth, and especially the tongue, is very sensitive to size, shape, texture, and temperature. Much of the information we obtain about food is based on its consistency and texture as determined by the tongue and jaws. In one experiment subjects had a randomly shaped object placed in the mouth and attempted to match it with a visually mounted copy. If the objects were not too similar, they performed very well on this demonstration of the haptics of the mouth. It is thought that active manipulation by the tongue is probably necessary for this discrimination.

PERCEPTUAL CONSTANCY

We perceive an object in an environment as a stable and permanent thing regardless of the illumination, the position from which we view it, or the distance at which it appears. The tendencies to recognize an object as the same despite changes in light and shadow are called color and brightness constancy respectively. The tendency to see it as an invariant shape regardless of viewing angle is shape constancy and, as its usual measurable size, regardless of distance, is called size constancy. The term "constancy" may be somewhat of an exaggeration, but it does express our relatively stable perception of objects. We will discuss these types of perceptual constancy in the sections that follow.

Brightness Constancy

White paper looks white and black paper looks black whether seen under indoor lighting or outside sunlight. The white paper may reflect 90% of the light, and the black only 10%. When the papers are moved from room illumination to sunlight, the incident illumination, and therefore the reflected light intensity, may increase 1000 times; yet the papers will appear to have the same brightness as they had indoors. Outside the black paper reflects more light (0.10 $\times$ 1000 = 100 units) than the white paper inside (0.9 $\times$ 1 = 0.9 units); but the black paper outside still looks darker than the white paper inside.

The classical experimental situation for the measurement of brightness constancy consists of presenting a subject with a standard grey paper viewed under normal room illumination and a graded series of comparison papers (black through grey to white) viewed under the same illumination. His task is to pick out the comparison grey that matches the standard grey in brightness. This is a simple task when the illumination is the same on both greys. The subject picks out the comparison grey with the same reflectance (ratio of reflected to incident light) as the standard grey. However, the critical tests occur when the illumination on the standard grey is changed (keeping the illumination on the comparisons constant); for example, suppose the intensity of the light on the standard grey is cut in half. If the subject were making his choices on the basis of the physical intensities of light reflected from the standard and comparison greys, he would now choose a comparison grey with a reflectance half of the standard. However, usually the subject picks a comparison grey that is physically identical to the standard—that is, one with the same reflectance as the standard, just as he did in the first experiment. The subject tends always to make the same choice, regardless of the illumination of the standard; that is, he is showing brightness constancy.

It would appear that the subject is responding to the reflectance of the grey surfaces rather than to the actual amount of light reflected (luminance). In other words, he seems to be responding to a property of the object itself, independent of the intensity of the retinal image of that object. How could the subject know about the reflectances of the surface? Only from prior experience with the actual reflectances, or with a knowledge of the actual illumination. But the experiments described above work when the subject has no prior knowledge of the surfaces being judged, so past experience is not necessary; also, knowledge of actual illumination levels has been found to be irrelevant to demonstration of the phenomenon.

There is another source of information available to the subject concerning the reflectance of the standard grey. When the illumination on the standard is changed, it is also changed on the background against which the standard is seen. If the standard reflects 80% of the 100 units of illumination and its background reflects 10% of these units, the respective luminances will be 80 and 10. If the illumination is doubled, the luminances will be 160 and 20, respectively. The ratios of the luminances (80/10 = 160/20) have remained constant under changing illumination. This constant ratio tells the subject that the reflectance of the standard grey did not change.

Cornsweet (1970) has offered an explanation of why these constant ratios of the intensities of images produce brightness constancy. First, he reviews evidence that the output of visual receptors is probably a logarithmic function of the intensity of the input. These data come from the work of Rushton (1961) in the horseshoe crab, and Brown, Watanabe, and Murakami (1965) and Cone (1965) in the mammalian retina. Cornsweet assumes that this log transformation occurs earlier in the visual system than the stages involving lateral inhibition. (This is not to say that brightness is necessarily a log function of intensity, but that there may be a log transformation at one stage in the processing of visual information.) Such a transformation means that, when the over-all illumination is increased, the effect of such a change is to add an equal amount of excitation to all parts affected by the illumination change. In the experiment just described, we had illumination (I) of 100 units, and reflectances (R) of 80% and 10% for the standard and the background, respectively. If the input (e) to the lateral inhibitory system is proportional to the log of the intensities of the standard and background, then:

$$e = k \log (\text{IR}) \qquad k = \text{constant}$$

$$e_{\text{std.}} = k \log (100 \times 0.80) = 1.9 \, k$$

$$e_{\text{bgd.}} = k \log (100 \times 0.10) = 1.0 \, k$$

when the illumination is doubled,

$$e_{\text{std.}} = k \log (160) = 2.2 \, k$$

$$e_{\text{bgd.}} = k \log (20) = 1.3 \, k$$

Therefore, doubling the illumination results in adding an equal amount of excitation ($0.3k$, for example) to all points of the input to the lateral inhibitory system. The difference between the standard and the background remains constant. Adding a small uniform increment to the input of a system with strong lateral inhibition results in a negligible change in the output because the increase in inhibition cancels out the increase in excitation.

However, it is important that the light be added to the entire scene and not just the standard, because otherwise the inhibition would not be equal and a brightness difference would be produced.

Another sort of brightness constancy not often discussed is that involving a surface of uniform reflectance but nonuniform illumination, such as we experience when viewing a wall painted a single color lighted by one lamp at the far side of the wall. Illumination varies markedly, following the inverse square law, but brightness varies only a little. To demonstrate the degree of the constancy, take a sheet of paper and make two holes in it in such a way that when you hold the sheet up toward the wall you can see widely separated parts of the wall through the two holes. This simple device serves to break down one's perception of brightness constancy, revealing that the two parts of the wall have very different brightnesses indeed. This effect is predictable from the transfer function. Recall that the eye is relatively insensitive to very low spatial frequencies—in this case, the wall. Thus we respond to the wall as if it were uniform.

The physiological mechanism is almost certainly that of lateral inhibition (discussed in Chapter 7).

As Cornsweet (1970) points out, brightness constancy is essentially a loss of absolute intensity information by the visual system. But this is not very useful to us anyway. It is more important to be able to recognize and distinguish different objects under varying conditions of illumination. If the absolute intensity information were not lost, we would be like walking light meters, having to take a reading before attempting to identify an object.

Color Constancy

Color constancy is a phenomenon analogous to brightness constancy in which the perceived hue of a surface does not change even if the wavelengths of the illumination on the surface change. As with brightness constancy it is critical that any change in illumination include the background as well as the object being judged. Color constancy is responsible for the fact that a red apple looks essentially the same in sunlight as in a room illuminated by incandescent light, even though the spectral compositions of the lights reflected from the apple are quite different. Cornsweet (1970) has proposed that the physiological mechanisms, a log transformation and lateral inhibition, which may account for brightness constancy can also predict the occurrence of color constancy. The one additional requirement is that the lateral inhibition be greater among like color receptors than among unlike ones. Then, for example, if a moderate amount of green light were added uniformly over a field, the green receptors would undergo very little change in output. The relative output of the color systems would not be changed, and hence the perceived color would remain the same. Another factor that may enter into color constancy is "memory color." The remembered color of familiar objects helps to determine what we see, especially under conditions of reduced visibility where colors may be somewhat ambiguous. However, this factor has been shown to be of only limited use in color constancy, since experimental results suggest that our memory colors are usually considerably different from the natural colors of the objects we are remembering.

Size Constancy

Size constancy refers to the tendency of the perceptual system to compensate for changes in the retinal image with viewing distance. The image (height and width) of an object doubles whenever its distance from you is halved, but the object will still look almost the same size. You can demonstrate for yourself how compelling a phenomenon size constancy is. Look around a room where several persons are seated at various distances from you, and note that their heads appear about the same size, because of size constancy. Now, with your thumb and forefinger, bracket the head of one of the persons sitting close to you and then do the same for a person sitting farther away, keeping your hand the same distance from your face. The distant head will be found to subtend a much smaller visual angle.

Because the camera does not have size constancy, a photograph represents the unaltered retinal image, unaffected by constancy. If you compare a drawing with a photograph taken from exactly the same position, you can determine how closely the artist draws the world as he sees it after retinal images are scaled by constancy. In general, distant objects look too small in photographs: your friend standing at the base of the large monument may be barely recognizable in a snapshot.

Size constancy does not hold under all circumstances, even though distance cues may be available. When the object is viewed at a great distance or from an unusual angle (as in looking at the streets below from the top of the Washington Monument), then its apparent size "regresses" to retinal size. Cars look like toys and people like ants. This comes as a surprise to most people when they have their first experience viewing the world from a great height, but to children it is not. A child watching cars on a road below a lookout point may express a desire to "have one to play with"; likewise, he may say that the toy airplanes he plays with are larger than the 747 he sees just after it takes off at the airport. This may reflect cognitive rather than perceptual differences, since size constancy has failed for both the adults and children. Size constancy of objects at distances of everyday experience, however, develops fairly early in life and the child of eight or nine is about as adept as an adult.

Various theories have been proposed to account for size constancy. The size-distance theory assumes that the visual system makes a response to the size of the retinal image and then modifies that response based on distance information and any other cues that are present. Gibson, on the other hand, has suggested (1950a) a relational theory in which the sizes of objects are determined as a function of the amount of environmental texture the objects hide. This follows directly from the normal visual world in which objects usually stand on a ground and their intersection with the texture gradient of the ground gives information about distance. A given object would cover a constant number of textural elements and thus would look the same size at any distance in spite of changes in the size of its retinal image. Both points of view have considerable supporting data, but are still at present incomplete and unsatisfactory for providing an explanation for size constancy. These theories are also applicable to shape constancy which will be discussed in the next section.

Shape Constancy

When a door swings open toward you, the retinal projection of its rectangular shape goes through a series of distortions (see Figure 10-21). It becomes a trapezoid with the edge toward you looking wider than the hinged edge; then, the trapezoid grows thinner until finally all that you see is a vertical line the thickness of the door. You can distinguish these changes, but you perceive the door as a rectangle swinging on its hinges. The fact that the door does not change shape demonstrates shape constancy.

Many figures drawn in isolation on a flat surface are ambiguous since they could represent a number of different objects seen in different orientations. If the figure, however, is a familiar object in a picture, we can readily identify it no matter what its orientation. Thus, an ellipse at an angle might be a boy's hoop, but at another angle, it might represent a circular man-hole cover in the street. We have no difficulty identifying the ellipse as a different object, as long as it is in the context of a drawing.

Figure 10–21 Example of shape constancy.

The distortions that occur when a familiar object rotates are used by us as cues to its rotation rather than as indications that the object is changing; this shows the strength of shape constancy. The Ames (1951) window illusion is a well-known demonstration of this (see Figure 10–22). When a flat, trapezoidal window-like object is made to rotate slowly by means of a small motor. a complex series of illusions results. The direction of rotation is ambiguous, seeming to change spontaneously. (This apparent reversal in direction of rotation also occurs when a rotating windmill is seen angled against the sky.) No matter what the actual position of the window, edge *a* always seems closer than edge *b* due to shape constancy. Therefore, as the window rotates, it gives the illusion of oscillating. To Ames, the phenomenon was based on the subject's

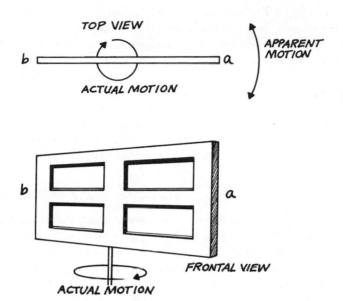

Figure 10-22 The Ames window. There is an optimal viewing distance and the effect is best when viewed monocularly.

continuing to see the window as the familiar rectangle and basing his perception on that. However, some recent experiments have produced the same effect from other unfamiliar shapes, and many questions remain as to the mechanisms of the illusion. It has turned out to be a very dramatic demonstration, but a very complex research tool.

MOTION PERCEPTION

The perception of motion is obviously of critical importance for the survival of most species. However, in spite of its importance and the extensive study that has been done in the area, it is still difficult to organize the experimental and theoretical data into a cohesive whole. One problem is reconciling the phenomenal characteristics of the motion perception with the physical characteristics of the stimulus. The retinal image by itself is ambiguous as to the location and motion of objects in space. For example, an image moving on the retina may mean that the object is moving or that the eye is moving. In Chapter 9 we discussed the sensory systems that give a person information about his bodily position and movement and thus aid in perceiving motion and location. In the absence of such kinesthetic feedback, it would seem that perhaps motion could be accounted for by successive stimulation of retinal loci. However, it is not quite that simple, since physical displacement and perceived movement are not always correlated. The hour hand of a clock or the shadow of a fixed object in the sun will be displaced in space over time, but you cannot report having seen them "move," only that they are in new positions. It appears that the movement experience requires a perceptible rate of change in the position of some stimulus element with respect to another; for example, figure with respect to ground, to another figure, or to the boundaries of the visual field. This is complicated by the existence of induced and apparent motion; we will consider these phenomena after our discussion of real movement.

Real Movement

Movement is perceived if an image moves across the retina while the eye is stationary or if the image is made to remain stationary on the retina by the eye's pursuing the object. Ask someone to wave a lighted cigarette around slowly in a dark room, and follow it with your eyes. The movement of the light will be seen even though no image is moving across the retina. The periphery of the retina is the area most sensitive to movement, but it is very difficult to identify an object at the far periphery of the visual field. As you have probably noticed, movement in the periphery of the eye is what usually initiates the movement of the eye in pursuit of an object so that it can be brought to focus on the fovea. Movement may also be perceived, however, when both eye and retinal image are stationary (afterimages).

The velocity threshold is influenced by a number of factors. It varies inversely with luminance (Leibowitz, 1955) and duration (Brown, 1955). As the velocity of a moving target increases, acuity decreases, presumably because the eye cannot follow the motion of the target (Ludvigh, 1965). The velocity threshold for a single object is much lower if a stationary reference stimulus is present than when the stationary framework is not present. It has thus been suggested that different mechanisms may be involved in judging absolute as opposed to relative (to other objects) motion. The minimum distance (angular excursion) over which movement can be detected is the displacement threshold. Displacement thresholds also appear to be lower when the target is surrounded by a stationary framework than without one, even for very short exposures. Also, Henderson (1971) has shown that, given a constant stimulus luminance, the motion (displacement) threshold is characterized by a tradeoff (see Chapter 4) or inverse power relationship between exposure duration and the distance of movement. This relationship is shown in Figure 10-23. Under optimal conditions a minimum displacement threshold approaches the resolution acuity for the stimulus itself; in other words, if a stimulus with lines of a certain width in minutes of arc is displaced by that amount, the perceiver will say that the

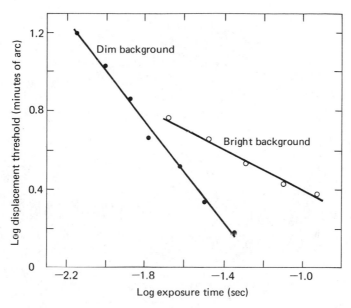

Figure 10-23 The tradeoff between duration and displacement for the threshold of motion perception. The two curves are for different background luminances. The brighter background renders the movement less visible and changes the slope of the function. The target was more intense than the background so the dimmer background would give more contrast. [From Henderson, D. C. The relationships among time, distance, and intensity as determinants of motion discrimination. *Perception and Psychophysics*, 1971, *10*, 313-20.]

stimulus has been moved. He will not necessarily say that he sees it moving, but only that it is in a new position. Whether he sees it moving will depend on many other factors: its size, illumination, contrast, texture of the field, and so on. Increases in all of these factors except for size will lower the motion threshold; it is easier to see small objects in motion than larger ones.

Movement aftereffects. After viewing certain stimulus configurations in motion, we see illusions of movement commonly called movement aftereffects. The most marked of these phenomena is the "waterfall effect." If you look at a nearby waterfall for several minutes and then direct your eyes to the bank or any fixed object, it will seem to move in a direction opposite to the flow of the water. A similar effect may be obtained from a rotating spiral as shown in Figure 10-24. This will seem to expand while rotating and contract as an aftereffect once the motion has ceased (or vice versa, depending on the direction of rotation). The "waterfall effect" occurs only if there is relative movement in different parts of the retina, not if the moving field covers the entire retina and moves as a whole (Gregory, 1973). It has been shown that the motion

Figure 10-24 The spiral aftereffect.

aftereffect requires the actual movement of images across the retina and operates independently of eye movements. However, the physiological origin of the aftereffect has still to be determined. Anstis and Moulden (1970) have shown that both peripherally and centrally operating components are involved. In their experiments, when the left eye was adapted to the opposite rotating motion from the right eye, the resulting monocular motion aftereffect was specific to the eye viewing the stationary pattern afterwards. This evidence suggests a retinal locus. However, when each eye was separately adapted to a clockwise rotation, but the two eyes together saw a counterclockwise rotation, then a clockwise motion would be the binocular aftereffect. This effect seems to suggest a central functioning mechanism, since the peripheral motion aftereffects from each eye on its own would have been counterclockwise.

Apparent Motion

The visual system can be "fooled" into seeing motion when what it actually sees is only a series of still pictures. Although a movie film presents us with 24 still scenes per second, we perceive them as continuous motion. This depends on two visual phenomena: the fusion of a rapidly flickering light and stroboscopic movement. We perceive a light as flashing up to the critical fusion frequency (cff), above which point it looks like a steady light. The cff varies from around 30 to 50 flashes per second, depending on its intensity (see Chapter 7). Since the pictures in a movie are projected at less than cff, one would surmise a very flickering picture. This was of course true of the early "flicks," but modern projectors have a special shutter that shows each picture three times in rapid succession, yielding an actual flicker rate of over 72/sec. Flicker is thus perceived only when the brightest parts of the picture fall on the peripheral retina.

Stroboscopic movement has been the object of a great deal of research. It can be studied by using a very simple setup: two lights that can be switched on sequentially. If the distance between the lights and the time interval between their flashes is right, then what is seen is a single light moving from the position of the first light to the second. This is the basis for the motion seen in flashing lights on theater marquees or on "animated" signs. Stroboscopic movement is also experienced by the cutaneous senses with vibratory stimuli on the skin. Interestingly, the optimal interstimulus interval and stimulus duration are quite similar for the two senses, suggesting similar mechanisms. There are a number of types of apparent movement, such as that evoked by the change in size of an object or the appearance of movement from one place to another. It has been shown that eye movements are not necessary for the perception of apparent motion. It is also clear that the retina is not actually stimulated between the two points, since apparent movement occurs if one light is presented to the left eye and the other to the right eye. Consequently, theories have been proposed involving cortical spread of excitation between the region excited by the first stimulus and the region stimulated by the second. This spread of excitation has even been generalized to code the sensation of motion. Although there is abundant evidence against such an hypothesis, an adequate theory has yet to be proposed to explain apparent motion. One explanation posits cortical motion detector cells which would fire if a light falls on one region of the retina and then on another without crossing the space between the two points, as in the stroboscopic movement phenomenon (Frisby, 1972). We will discuss the evidence for central motion detector systems later in this chapter.

Several types of stroboscopic movement have been distinguished based on the temporal relationship and shape of the stimuli. What we have been discussing is optimal movement which, as the name implies, is the perception of the stimulus as moving smoothly from its first to its second position. Another interesting type of apparent movement has been called "pure phi" movement. This occurs when the interval between the two stimuli is longer than that for optimal movement. Instead of seeing the first stimulus move through space to the location of the second stimulus, the appearance is that of "pure movement" or a perception of movement without seeing an object itself move. It is not uncommon for all types of apparent movement to be lumped together under the phi phenomenon in textbook discussions of movement perception.

Induced Movement

Most perceptual research is conducted with a stationary observer, who looks through an apparatus that presents him with flashing lights or pictures. However, in real life, the observer must frequently make perceptual decisions when he is in motion. It is difficult to investigate the real-life situation, but such research in motion perception has important implications for activities such as driving and flying, as well as space travel. We have mentioned the problems involved in deciding what is moving. When you are walking or running, you get feedback from your body telling you about your position. When you are riding, the only information you receive is from your eyes and some from the vestibular apparatus when you accelerate or decelerate. In an airplane, vestibular and visual input concerning the upright is often in conflict with reality, causing pilots to have to rely on instruments for navigation and passengers to walk about firmly holding on to fixed objects.

You may have had the experience of sitting in your car at a traffic light when the car next to yours drives off and it appears that your car is moving backward when, in fact, it is standing still. In this phenomenon of induced movement we find that, when movement is known only by vision, we make the "best bet" about that movement based on the evidence that we have. For example, the Gestalt psychologist Duncker (1929) showed that, when using only visual cues, we tend to accept that the largest objects are stationary and the smaller objects moving; or, in some cases, we perceive those things to be

Why Do the Wagon Wheels Sometimes Go Backwards in Western Movies?

This question is often raised when apparent movement is under discussion. This is a special case of stroboscopic movement and is predictable fairly simply from the rate at which the successive frames of the movie were shot and the rate of rotation of the wagon wheel. If the wagon is moving at a speed such that the wheel has rotated through exactly the angle between the spokes of the wheel (or some multiple of the angle) during the interval between frames, then each frame will show exactly the same picture of the wheel and the wheel will appear to be stationary. If, however, the wheel has moved through slightly less than the angle between spokes in the interval between frames, each frame will catch a spoke at a position just slightly behind that in the frame before and the wheel will appear to be moving backwards. Similar reasoning will explain a wheel that appears to rotate slowly forward.

Stroboscopic movement is often used to study periodic motion of objects that are moving far too fast to be seen with the eye under steady illumination. When the movement is "caught" by a light that is flashing at a slightly slower or faster rate than the period of the movement, the object will be seen in slow motion. You may have seen a drummer in a discotheque playing under flashing light and have seen his hands appear suspended in the air or to be moving very slowly. This is another example of stroboscopic movement and its explanation is the same in principle as the wagon wheel example.

moving that we know from past experience are mobile, as opposed to neutral objects. Thus if a spot of light is projected onto a screen or some background, and the screen is moved, the stationary spot of light is seen to move rather than the background. This happens even though the information at the eye shows the image of the frame and not the light moving across the retina. It appears that, with incomplete information from relative displacement, the decision is based on the rule that it is generally small rather than large objects that move. This is especially true if the larger one encloses the smaller one. Wallach (1959) stressed the importance of the relationship of the surrounded object to the surrounding object (see Figure 10–25). For example, he presented the viewer with a dot surrounded by a circle. No matter which object was moved, the viewer saw the dot move and the circle remain stationary. This is a rather invariant rule. If the dot is surrounded by a rectangle that is in turn surrounded by a ring, and the rectangle is moved, the viewer sees motion in both the dot and the rectangle. The ring is seen to remain stationary. The perceived motion of the rectangle is in the direction of its objective motion, while the dot seems to move in the opposite direction. The dot appears to move and the ring does not, even though there is no relative displacement between the two. This happens because of the two relative displacements: the dot is surrounded by the moving rectangle, and the rectangle is in turn surrounded by the ring. This effect is produced when you look through wind-swept broken clouds (rectangle) framed in the tops of trees (ring) and see the moon (dot)

213

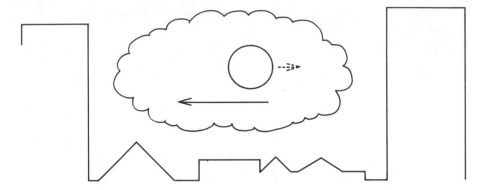

Figure 10-25 Induced movement.

appear to sail across the sky against the motion of the clouds. Another real-life example is presented when one tries to stand or walk in rapidly moving shallow water. You will do all right if you look at the shore but when you look at your feet you begin to fall. The moving water is the large part of the visual field, which is taken perceptually as the stationary frame. Your feet are seen to move relative to the water and you compensate and begin to fall.

Mechanisms of Movement Perception

A question still unresolved is whether perceived motion perceptions caused by real movement, by apparent movement, and as aftereffects are due to the same visual mechanism. In the following section, we will discuss the physiological evidence that supports the concept of a motion detection system. Hubel and Wiesel (1962) found cortical cells in the cat that responded to displacement in the retinal projection of a stimulus. These cells had relatively large receptive fields and did not respond to a stationary bar of light. Some cells were specific in responding to stimuli of a certain length, width, orientation, or direction and velocity of motion.

The evidence for motion detection systems in humans is based, for obvious reasons, primarily on psychological studies of motion aftereffects. Retinal cells have been discovered in the rabbit that respond only to downward motion and are inhibited by upward motion, and vice versa (Barlow and Levick, 1965). These appear to be similar to the direction-specific cortical cells in the cat. Earlier, Sekuler and Ganz (1963) argued that, if motion is perceived in the human by means of such motion detectors, then viewing motion in one direction should decrease the sensitivity of that motion detector. Consequently the threshold for motion in that direction should be higher than for motion in the opposite direction. Sekuler and Ganz had subjects view stripes that moved in one direction for five seconds. They then tested the luminance threshold for the movement of stripes in both the original and the opposite direction. Their findings confirmed that the threshold was elevated for motion in the same direction as the previously viewed pattern. This argues for a unitary motion detection system that is modified by stimulation.

11

Plasticity
of Perception

If you wear eyeglasses (or have tried on someone else's) you may have noticed that the world appeared distorted when you first put them on. The distortion may cause you problems in motor coordination as in judging the height of the curb, for example, or in being uncertain when reaching out to touch something. However, in a few hours or maybe a day, the distortion disappears. Evidently your central nervous system makes some adjustment so that the world looks normal again and you are able to move around without hesitation. This "plasticity" is demonstrated vividly by the adjustment of the nervous system to the growth of the body. The proportions of the body change rapidly and radically in the course of development. The newborn baby has a disproportionately large head and very short legs; his head makes up a quarter of his total height and is already 60 percent of its adult size. From birth on, the head grows less than the rest of the body and becomes about a tenth of the individual's total height in adulthood. The legs, however, change from one-third of the newborn's height to around one-half of the adult's total height. The nervous system which provides sensory-motor control in the 75 cm long infant must also be able to maintain that control in the adult who may be three times as tall.

The phenomenon of plasticity, then, has important implications both for perceptual-motor functioning in the adult and for the course of development in the young animal. The factors involved in development, and particularly its dependence on environmental interactions, will be discussed in the next chapter. In this chapter we will consider what effects various transformations in the sensory input to the central nervous system have on perceptual-motor functioning.

REARRANGEMENT OF INPUT

Rearrangement, or distortion, of sensory input has been studied for several sensory systems and various animals, including humans. The earliest work, and the most extensive, has involved the visual modality. You will recall from our discussion of motion perception in the last chapter that visual information by itself is often ambiguous. Nonvisual information, for example, about the relation of the various parts of your body to the world, is therefore necessary to make perceptual decisions. In order to determine how these sources of visual and nonvisual information work together, it is instructive to disrupt their normal relationship. Lenses producing various types of distortion may be used to alter the visual information reaching the eye. The information received by the other senses (tactile, auditory, etc.) remains unchanged, and we can study how the observer reacts to such discrepancies between the testimony of the various senses.

Early interest in the problem of optical transformation grew out of the knowledge that the image of the world was inverted on the retina. The question at that time was whether an optically right-side-up image would appear inverted. At the end of the nineteenth century, Stratton experimented with wearing an inverting lens system on one eye (1896). His other eye was covered. He reported that the world did look inverted at first, but that after a few days of wearing the lens, it sometimes appeared "right side up" or appeared to be in "normal position." Many people have concluded from these statements that an actual change took place in Stratton's visual perceptions. Others have suggested that his descriptions were "metaphorical" and he actually only became "familiar" with seeing his visual world in a certain way. A number of more recent studies have concluded that, although subjects' ability to get around improves with time spent wearing such lenses, no changes occur in how the world actually looks. In fact, one subject who had worn the lenses for a month was puzzled when asked how the world appeared and found it very difficult to answer.

The Innsbruck studies of Erismann and Kohler (Kohler, 1962) repeated and extended the Stratton studies. This extensive work provided information concerning the initial reaction to distortion, gradual changes in ability to function with distortion, and perceptual aftereffects experienced when the distorting instruments were removed. In some of these investigations mirrors replaced lenses, and the subject viewed the scene through a system of mirrors placed under the visor of his cap, with direct vision blocked. The mirrored image was thus inverted (but not reversed left to right). Subjects were tested for periods ranging from six days to two weeks. At first, the subjects had difficulty walking around and needed help. Errors were made in trying to touch objects. However, after about three days a subject was able to ride a bicycle, and after a week, to ski! Subjects reported that they experienced the world as upright at times, but only sporadically. For example, simultaneously viewing and touching an object, such as a hand-held plumb line, or observing smoke rise from a cigarette both had the effect of suddenly causing the inverted scene to appear upright. Thus, perceptual adaptation seemed to depend on touch, alignment with gravity, and familiarity. Subjects who achieved this righting of the world reported that when the mirrors were removed objects reverted to an upside-down position, but that in less than an hour the aftereffects started to go away.

Another sort of distortion of visual input is caused by prisms. A prism refracts (bends) light waves in such a way that the location of objects seen through the prism seems to be shifted in the direction of the apex of the prism. This shift is known as the deviation of the prism. The deviation angle is about half the angle between the faces of the prism, and since the angle is independent of the object's distance, farther objects seem to be shifted through a greater distance than those close by. The prism also produces color fringes at contours. Color fringes result because short wavelength light (e.g., blue) is bent more than a long wavelength (e.g., red) light. This effect is known as chromatic aberration and is a property of prisms and other simple lenses. The result is that a light square on a dark background viewed through prisms having the base to the right will appear to have a blue fringe on its left-hand edge and a red fringe on the right border. The most obvious effect of a prism, however, is the distortion of contour. Vertical lines appear to be curved with the concave side to the left. This occurs because light entering the prism at oblique angles is bent more than light that enters more perpendicularly.

To a subject wearing prism glasses, the world is shifted in the direction of the apex of the prism, there are colored fringes at the left and right sides of objects, and vertical lines appear curved. However, things get more complicated when the subject moves his head—the world then appears to be made of rubber. Objects expand and contract when the head is moved from side to side; they seem to slant one way and then the other when the head is moved up and down, producing a "rocking chair" effect.

Despite all these distortions, Kohler (1962) found that perceptual-motor adaptation to the prisms occurred rather quickly. Errors in reaching for objects disappeared within one day. In two days, the apparent visual motion disappeared. After about ten days, surfaces began to straighten out and appear undistorted. As Kohler points out, this adaptation is quite amazing when one considers the extremely complex relationship between the prisms and the eye. The eye moves with respect to the prism goggles and thus each point on the retina receives different amounts and types of distortions as a result of eye and head movement. Nevertheless, adaptation does take place.

J. J. Gibson (1933) was the first to discover the curvature aftereffects of prism lenses in experiments with subjects who wore them for only a few days at a time. Kohler himself wore the prisms as long as 124 days. When he removed them, it was as if he were looking for the first time through prisms with orientation opposite to those he had been wearing for so long: all of the distortions appeared in reverse. The general aftereffects were noted for as long as 23 days.

Color fringes were generally no longer perceived after a few days of wearing the prisms. When the lenses were removed, however, a complementary aftereffect appeared: the blue fringe became red and vice versa. A similar result was obtained when goggles were used in which the left half of each lens was blue and the right half yellow. When the subject began wearing the glasses, he saw blue when he looked to the left and yellow when he looked to the right. The effect of wearing these glasses was measured by having the subject adjust the color of a target until it looked neutral grey. On the first day, when the subject looked at the window through the yellow half of the glasses, he had to add an extra measure of blue in order to achieve the neutral hue. When he looked through the blue half of the glasses, he needed to add yellow. (Recall that mixing complementary colors yields grey; see Chapter 3.) Finally, he viewed the window without glasses and with his eyes turned first to the right and then to the left; this control situation enabled the investigator to establish the subject's pre-experimental adjustments to neutral grey. After the goggles had been worn for 60 days, adaptation was tested and confirmed: the adjustments needed to compensate for the colors in the glasses were not as great. Moreover, when the glasses were removed, there were complementary aftereffects. The target had to be adjusted to yellow in order to look neutral grey on the side where the yellow lens had been, and the formerly blue side had to be made blue.

Following these early discoveries, various types of optical rearrangements were devised for the experimental study of plasticity. Mirrors and lenses can be used to invert, to reverse, tilt, displace laterally, distort (curve), magnify, or minify the retinal image produced by a given stimulus array. Answers to a number of questions have been sought by studying such visual rearrangements. We have already asked whether visual appearance change takes place, causing the subject to see the world "normally" after wearing such devices for a period of time. As we have mentioned (and will further explore), adaptation to the distortion does occur in that a subject can walk, turn, reach, and make other movements accurately after some experience with the distortion. These results will define adaptation to distortion.

There are a number of ways to study the adaptation to distortion of visual input. In the colored lens experiment just discussed this was done by measuring a change in the setting of a neutral color. Another way is to measure the decrease in the error made in pointing toward an object while wearing prisms. When a subject newly fitted with prism lenses points "instinctively" to an object, he will miss by an angle equal to the deviation of the prism. After a while his aim will improve considerably, and when he takes the lenses off there will be an error in the opposite direction.

The nature of the change that takes place with adaptation to distortion has been of interest to many investigators. But before we can discuss the research on this question it is necessary that we digress a while to discuss the concept of "reafference."

Reafference and Exafference

Reafference is a term coined by the German physiologists von Holst and Mittelstaedt (1950) to refer to a distinction between sensory input that is the result of some movement of the animal and that input which occurs independently of him. It is largely based on a distinction between actively and passively obtained sensory input as the following example illustrates. They studied the optokinetic reflex in the fly. This reflex is a movement of the fly in response to movement of the visual world; its result is to compensate for that external movement. As a result of the optokinetic reflex the fly's eye is looking at the same part of the world as before. It is similar to optokinetic nystagmus discussed in Chapter 9.

The experimental situation consists of a fly that is free to turn around on a surface inside a cylinder having vertical stripes on the inside wall. When the cylinder rotates to the left, the fly does the same and so the movement of the world is compensated for by the optokinetic reflex. However, if the fly turns spontaneously, he is able to do so without being hindered by the reflex even though the input to the eye is exactly the same whether the cylinder moves to the left or the fly moves to the right. One might suggest that the optokinetic reflex is simply inhibited during self-produced movement. However, Mittelstaedt demonstrated that this is not the case by rotating the head of a fly 180° with respect to his body, essentially interchanging the positon of the two eyes. Now when the cylinder moved to the left the fly moved to the right, as you might predict from the reversed positions of the two eyes. But the key question now is, "What happens when the fly initiates a movement?" If the reflex were simply inhibited, the response should not differ from that of the normal fly. However, once the fly moves the optokinetic reflex is triggered and he circles continuously in the direction that he first turned until exhausted. This is conceptualized in the following way (see Figure 11-1). A command from a higher center causes an efferent message to be sent to the effector, which would be a muscle in this case. In addition, an efference copy is left at some place in the central nervous system. The effector, activated by the efferent message has some effect on the stimulation that enters the receptor. The afferent, or sensory message, is compared to the efference copy and if they match, the efference copy is nullified. If the afference matches the efference copy it is called reafference. Stimulation that does not match an efference copy is called exafference. In the case of the fly, the motor command is the decision to move left, say. This

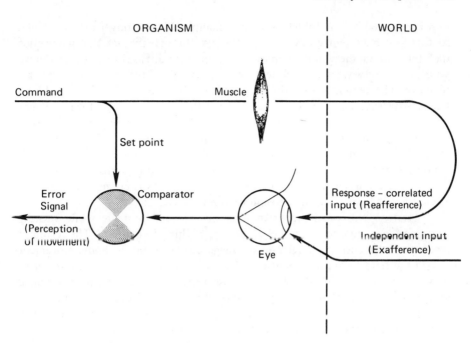

Figure 11-1 Diagram of the reafference system.

command goes to the muscles involved with moving left and also is stored as an efference copy in the fly's brain. Now the result of the motor command is to cause the world to move across the fly's eye at a certain rate. When this happens, it is known as reafference because the movement across the eye matches what is stored in the efference copy. When the fly's head has been rotated 180° the motor command tells the fly to move left and that it is the message that is stored in the efference copy. However, because the fly's eyes are reversed, the world seems to have moved to the right. This input is considered exafference because it does not match the efference copy. The input to the eye in the case of the normal fly when the cylinder is rotated is also exafference because there was no efference copy for movement at all. Exafference requires the fly to correct for the input in order to nullify the mismatch between the efference copy and the afference. In the normal fly the optokinetic reflex takes care of this nicely. However, when the fly's eye has been rotated, the reflex correction only adds to the mismatch and the poor fly spins faster and faster in the wrong direction. The more he spins the greater the mismatch.

   Reafference theory is an example of the application of control systems thinking to behavior. For those familiar with control systems, the mismatch between the afference and the motor copy results in an error signal that, in the normal fly, is corrected by negative feedback. When the fly's head is rotated, the error signal becomes positive feedback, producing an unstable system.

   A clear example of reafference, or feedback if you will, in human perception is provided by the following simple example. Place a finger on your eyelid so that you may gently push or tap your eye through the lid. You will notice that this caused the world to appear to jump around. However, you can move your eye many ways with your neck or eye muscles and the world never appears to move. The reason is that the neck and eye muscles are involved in the ef- ference-afference feedback loop that involves the efference copy for movement of the eyes. However, when you move your eye with your finger no efference copy for eye movement is left in the central nervous system. Then, when the afference comes in saying that the visual input is jumping around the retina, this is interpreted as movement of the world. This is a result of a mismatch between the efference copy which says that no eye movement was commanded and the afference which says that the visual input is moving.

Stratton and others reported that any movement made while wearing inverting lenses caused the world to swing or whirl about them. The left-right reversal of the customary relation of image displacement to body movement caused the field to appear to move in the direction of the person's movements, only faster. As with the fly, there is a positive rather than a negative feedback loop involving the efference copy. Humans, however, can cope with this. Also, they adapt so that the world eventually appears stationary during head move- ments. The fly does not adapt, but circles to exhaustion.

ADAPTATION IN ACTIVE AND PASSIVE CONDITIONS

In the Innsbruck studies, the subject wearing the goggles was allowed self-initiated free movement. Is this movement necessary for adaptation to take place or is it necessary only that altered visual information be available to the subject? Held and Hein (1958) compared the performance of a subject before and after looking through a displacing prism under three conditions. In the first, he looked at his hand while it was stationary; in the second, he watched his hand being passively moved back and forth by the experimenter; in the third, he watched while he actively moved his hand around. Before and after this treatment, the subject marked the apparent location of the corners of a square which, along with his hand, he saw only as a reflection in a mirror. Comparison of the results from the three groups showed that only a few minutes of active movement produced substantial compensatory shifts. Most of the active' subjects showed complete adaptation or compensation for the shift caused by the prism in about one-half hour. The subjects in the passive groups, however, showed no adaptation. The eye had received the same input in the active and passive groups, but evidently the link between motor output and sensory input (reafference) was the essential factor missing for the passive group. Similar results were found when the whole body was in- volved in the movement (Held and Bossom, 1961). The subjects, sitting in a

Why Can't You Tickle Yourself?

Perhaps most readers will have wondered why it is impossible to tickle oneself. Exactly the same physical stimulus applied to the bottom of the foot, on the ribs, or elsewhere will be intensely "ticklish" when someone else does it but will feel like an ordinary touch sensation when one does it himself. Or, is it the same stimulus?

The principle of reafference provides an explanation of this puzzle. When you touch yourself, there is an efference copy of the motor command left in the brain to which the afference is compared. A command to touch yourself on the ribcage is compared to the afference of being touched on the ribcage. The result is an interpretation of the input by the brain of your touching yourself. However, when someone else touches you there is no efference copy to compare the input and the interpretation is of being touched. In the first, or active, case the input was reafference and in the second, passive, case it was exafference. To a ticklish person the passive, exafferent situation is interpreted as tickle and the active, reafferent situation is interpreted as touch. You may object that it is possible to tickle yourself with a feather or a hair held in your hand. However, the feather introduces a certain lack of correlation between your movements and the movements of the tip of the feather. This is sufficient to break down the match between the efference copy and the afferent message, resulting in the sensation of tickle.

Physicians often have the problem of examining a ticklish patient. The method that has been developed to get around the problem is to have the patient place his/her hand on the physician's hand. There is apparently enough active movement in this situation that the patient receives reafferent instead of exafferent stimulation and the physician still receives his information about the appendix or whatever. Weiskrantz, Elliot and Darlington (1971) tested the reafference explanation experimentally. They built a special tickle device that could administer stimuli to the sole of the foot. Stimuli could be presented by the experimenter, by the subject, or by the experimenter with the subject's arm resting passively on the control. They found, as expected, that experimenter-administered stimuli were the most ticklish, self-administered the least, and stimuli in the passive situation were intermediate in ticklishness.

chair that could rotate, were asked to position themselves so that a randomly placed target (dimly illuminated slit of light) appeared directly in front of them. After several trials on this task, they put on prism goggles, and the first group went for a walk along an outside path, while the second sat in a wheel-chair that was pushed along the same path for the same length of time. The subjects then removed the prisms and were retested on the target-finding appa-ratus. The first group (active) showed far greater adaptation to the distortion than did the second (passive).

There have been some studies in which passive subjects adapted to dis-placement as well as active subjects, and so apparently movement is not uncon-ditionally necessary. Wallach, Kravitz and Lindauer (1963) tested subjects both on pointing toward a target and on pointing straight ahead. On both tasks, subjects showed adaptation even though they stood passively while wear-ing the prisms during the training period. A large amount of adaptation was also observed in the straight-ahead pointing task even when subjects lay on their backs with their heads propped up to passively view their feet during the training period. It may not be the activity per se that is important for adapta-tion, but that the subject, when he is active, derives greater information about the distortion produced by the prisms. Howard, Craske, and Templeton (1965) have suggested that the subjects in Held's procedures (Held and Bossom, 1961) were provided little exafferent or reafferent information in the passive condi-tion. Subjects who were pushed around in a wheelchair saw only the moving visual display through the prisms and were not given any indication as to the extent of the visual displacement; they were not allowed, for example, to view their own bodies. Howard et al. (1965) had subjects point to a target light seen by means of a displacing mirror. After this pretraining, some subjects were touched on the lips with a rod which they watched from a distance of 36 cm. A second group differed only in that the rod approached but did not touch them. All subjects were inactive during the experiment. The group that was touched showed significantly more adaptation to the displacement. Howard et al. conclude that "discordant exafferent stimulation" which gives a subject information regarding optical distortion can lead to adaptation. Similarly, Kravitz and Wallach (1966) reported that adaptation would occur if a subject's arm was passively vibrated while the subject watched it through a prism. This is in contrast to Held's experiment in which no adaptation occurred when a subject viewed the passive arm.

Moulden (1971) suggests that the necessary antecedent condition for adaptation is "salient" or "powerful" information, regardless of its source, about the non-correspondence between the location of objects perceived visually and their location via some other modality. Moulden tested this hypothesis by removing all information about the movement of the limb from the situation and providing visual information only about the instantaneous arm position. The subject wearing displacing prisms viewed his hand as it held a moving lever only at one and the same place on each of its excursions back and forth (a light flash occurred at this point in a dark room). Subjects in this group showed as much adaptation as did subjects who viewed the complete movements of their arms in a fully lighted room. This suggests that the continuous relation between self-produced movement and its sensory feedback as hypothesized by Held may not be necessary. Rather, self-produced movement may provide more information to the subject in visual rearrangement studies. This is an area of continuing study. The few reports presented here do show that there may be some question concerning the necessity of applying the reafference principle to the problem. It is possible that reafferent stimulation is a sufficient basis for adaptation to distorted input, but it may not be a necessary condition.

WHAT IS THE NATURE OF THE CHANGE TO ALTERED INPUT?

It is of interest to consider not only the mechanism and conditions necessary for adapting to visual distortions, but also the end product of the adaptation. What change does the adaptation produce in the subject? Some investigators have suggested that adaptation results in a change in visual perception; others claim that it consists of learning new, specific motor responses. Proponents of the reafference theory say that adaptation consists of newly correlated information derived from the correlation between movement and its sensory feedback. On the other hand, Harris (1965) has proposed that adaptation consists of a change in the felt position of various parts of the body. When a person first puts on displacing prisms, he is surprised to see, for example, that his hand does not appear to be where he felt it was, and this discrepancy must be resolved. According to Harris' "proprioceptive change" hypothesis, the subject comes to feel his hand to be where he sees it through the prisms. If this is true, then the subject's judgment of that arm's position relative to any other part of the body will be incorrect. Harris has tested his hypothesis in a number of studies and has found that most data in this area are consistent with such an explanation. In one study, subjects adapted to laterally displacing prisms by repeatedly pointing straight ahead at a target for several minutes. They showed significant adaptation when tested, but adaptation affected pointing only with the hand used during practice. The fact that the unexposed arm was not affected has been cited by Harris as supporting the view that the felt position of the hand, and not the apparent visual position of the target, was changed by the adaptation. However, Taub and Goldberg (1973) have shown that intermanual transfer will occur in this experimental situation if subjects are given spaced practice (practice trials interspersed with rest periods) rather than one continuous massed practice as in Harris' study. This evidence does not contradict the proprioceptive change theory, but it does negate one particular aspect of Harris' argument.

The proprioceptive change interpretation also implies that a subject should make errors in judging how far his adapted hand is from other parts of his body. Subjects adapted their right arms by pointing at a target seen through prisms and then were asked to place their unexposed hands specified distances from their adapted hands while blindfolded (Harris, 1963). After seeing their right hands shifted to the right by the prisms, subjects felt their hands to be farther apart than they really were. Other interesting supporting evidence comes from experiments with split-brain monkeys. Bossom and Hamilton (1963) found that adaptation to displaced vision showed complete interocular transfer but no intermanual transfer in these animals; thus, the adaptation is specific to the arm, not the eye.

VISUAL CAPTURE

One very interesting result of the experiments with distorting prisms deserves special comment. Early students of perception were interested in how we *learn* to perceive the world, if perception is indeed a learning task. This problem will be discussed more fully in the next chapter. However, one aspect of the question is relevant here. One school of thought held that we learn to see things as they appear to the proprioceptive and cutaneous senses. After all, visual input is often ambiguous but touch is more "immediate" or "real." The other school of thought held that vision is preeminent and we learn to associate the feel of an object with its appearance. Even though the first position has a certain intuitive appeal, there is considerable evidence of the primacy of vision, at least in the adult case. A powerful illustration is to grasp a straight vertical stick while looking at it through prism lenses. As long as one is looking at the stick it definitely feels curved when one runs the hand up and down it. When the eyes are closed the feeling of curvature disappears only to return when the eyes are opened again. This is known as visual capture or visual dominance. You may have had a similar experience if you ever looked at your feet through binoculars held backwards. Your feet *felt* small and/or far away and you had trouble walking. The difficulty in walking was caused by the dominance of visual input that told you that you were not moving your feet as much as you normally do; you tried to compensate by producing exaggerated movements which then conflicted with the proprioceptive and vestibular input needed to maintain an upright position.

Rock (1966) made an experimental study of the effect of distortion of size and shape on visual perception. A minifying lens was used to make the stimulus smaller and another optical device made the object appear narrower. In the first part of the experiment on size, the subject looked at a plastic square through the minifying lens but did not touch it. Here, perception was governed totally by the distorted visual appearance, and the square was judged as reduced in size. Various methods were used to measure what the subject perceived—how accurately was he able to draw a corresponding square; how well could he match the square with visually presented figures; what comparisons did he make with objects perceived only tactually? In a second condition, the subject grasped the square under a thin cloth and looked at it through the lens. In this case, judgment of its size was still governed by its visual appearance. Parallel experiments with optical distortion of shape yielded similar results. All consistently indicated the dominance of vision.

OTHER TYPES OF DISTORTIONS

There are limitations to the distortions possible by simple optical means so a different technique has been used by K. U. Smith (e.g., Smith, 1962). Smith uses a television camera so that the subject can watch his own hand on a monitor which can be connected electronically to the camera to give any desired change such as left-right or up-down reversal of the image, displacement in space, or distortion in size. The subject's hand is behind a barrier so that he sees only the image of his hand on the television monitor. This advantage is counterbalanced, however, by the fact that these studies are limited to short-term adaptation. Despite this limitation there have been several interesting findings. An up-down reversal disturbs a subject's ability to write or draw more than a left-right reversal does. Changes in size have very little effect.

The television technique has been used by Smith and Smith (1962) to displace retinal images in time as well as space. The television camera and monitor are used as described, but a video tape recorder is introduced between them so that there can be time delay between recording and playback. The subject watching the monitor sees everything in the past. Even a short delay (around 0.5 sec) makes movements jerky and uncoordinated. Drawing (tracing a star) is almost impossible and writing so difficult that it is largely illegible. Practice does not produce much improvement. These experiments are of practical interest because the controls used to operate many machines cause this delayed action phenomenon. Obviously a delay that upsets a person's performance could be quite serious. This is particularly true of the remote control of vehicles in space, as in landing and docking maneuvers.

Skilled behaviors depend on a complexity of feedback through a variety of sensory modalities. As we have seen throughout our discussion, the importance of feedback becomes most apparent when it is eliminated or distorted in some way. Studies in the monitoring of singing and speech provide further illustration of this point. Deutsch (1960) found that although singers attempt to produce a steady tone, the sound actually oscillates slightly. Deutsch amplified the voice sound and delayed its reception by the singer. It was found that the singer maintains the constant note by continually making corrections based on the auditory feedback that he receives. These corrections are toward a standard or "target value" and are disrupted by an auditory feedback delay. Speech is monitored in the same way by our ears. If there is a delay between speaking and hearing, speech rapidly becomes incoherent. Frequency and amplitude fluctuate and words are jumbled. In short, we are monitoring the feedback that is no longer appropriate.

As you will recall from Chapter 6, the sound from a localized source reaches the listener's nearer ear a fraction of a second earlier than it reaches his farther ear. This difference in time of arrival of the sound at the two ears is used by the listener to locate the direction of the sound source. What would happen if the listener's ears could be displaced around the vertical axis of his head by some amount? This would be a means of distorting the input to the auditory system in a way analogous to the use of displacing prisms in the visual system. The questions to be answered by such a manipulation would be similar to those considered relative to the visual system: how does the distortion affect the subsequent behavior of the subject, and what factors influence the behavioral change that takes place?

The original pseudophone, an instrument designed by Thompson in 1876 was a device something like a pair of ear trumpets, which picked up sound waves at different locations and fed them to the two ears. For example, the normal relations of the ears could be reversed by locating the input to the right ear on the left side of the head and vice versa (see Figure 11-2). Most experiments today substitute earphones for the tubes, and the signals from the two sides are separately amplified and fed into a pair of stereophonic headphones. Such an apparatus permits rearrangement of the subject's accustomed relationships between interaural time, phase, and intensity differences and bodily orientation.

Held (1965) reported that a subject wearing a pseudophone for the first time was inaccurate in sound localization by an angle equivalent to the angle of displacement of his ears. After wearing the pseudophone in a reasonably noisy environment for several hours, subjects showed compensatory shifts in localizing sounds. However, this adaptation occurred only if the subjects were allowed to move freely during the time they wore the pseudophone. On the other hand, Kalil and Freedman (1967) have shown that compensation for auditory rearrangement can occur in the absence of subject movement. Their subject wore a pseudophone which rotated the interaural axis 15° either left or right and watched the sound source (microphone) while moving it by means of a rope in his hand. He was allowed no other movement during this fifteen-minute exposure period. The extent of the adaptation to the pseudophone was determined by measuring the difference in error in placing the sound source in a straight ahead location (in the dark) before and after the exposure period. Subjects showed significant adaptation (i.e., decrease in error) despite the lack of active movement of the body and head and the short exposure period. Similar results have been reported from studies in which subjects were tested by having them point at a concealed auditory target while listening through a pseudophone (Freedman, Wilson, and Rekosh, 1967). The exposure condition here consisted of listening through pseudophones to a sound source held in one hand while moving that hand about. Subjects adapted as a result of this experience.

Figure 11-2 The pseudophone.

ANIMAL WORK

In addition to the human studies of plasticity, there have been a number of animal studies. Various manipulations have been used to alter the normal patterns of sensory input to the central nervous system. The point of interest, of course, is the compensation or adaptation process by which the animals deal with these transformations in the normal peripheral-central relations. The following approach has provided clues to the nature of the mechanisms that are basic to the compensation process. If, as has been hypothesized, one factor or a group of several closely related factors is responsible for the ability to compensate for various types of distortions in sensory input, then as Taub (1968) has suggested, it should be possible to trace the phylogenetic development of that factor. In the following discussion, we will use that framework to consider various procedures with animals such as tendon crossing, nerve transposition, limb reversal, and prismatic transformation of the visual world.

Visual Transformations

Sperry (1956) surgically altered the visual system of the newt by rotating the eyeball 180° (upside down) leaving the optic nerve and blood vessels intact. The animals' responses showed clearly that their vision was reversed. When bait was held above the newt's head, it would begin digging in the sand rather than looking up. If something was presented in front of the head, it would turn around and look behind it, and vice versa. The animals also conformed in color to the brightness above rather than to that under them, as would normally be the case. The newts never reacted normally, even after as long as two years. If their rotated eyes were turned back to the original position, they immediately resumed normal behavior. In other experiments, the optic nerves to the two eyes were cut and their connections to the brain were switched. Normally each nerve crosses to the opposite side of the brain. When the nerves were connected to the same side of the brain and were allowed to regenerate, the newts acted as if the left and right halves of the visual field were reversed. For example, when a fly appeared on the right, the animal would strike on the left. Frogs and toads responded in the same way as the newts in Sperry's experiments, and in all cases the animals failed to make any correction after experience with the rearrangements. Von Holst and Mittelstaedt (1950) found that fish fitted with inverting prisms never showed motor adaptation.

There is conflicting evidence as to whether chickens show any correction in their misdirected pecking at grain while wearing displacing prisms. Hess (1956) found that chickens wearing prisms that shifted the image to the right or left by 7° would always peck about 7° to the side of the grain; they never adapted to the shift of the visual image. Pfister (1955) put reversing prisms on hens and they showed no improvement in pecking accuracy after as long as three months. However, Rossi (1968) reported that newly hatched chicks wearing prisms significantly reduced pecking errors over four days.

The story is different when it comes to mammals. Foley (1940) fitted a binocular inverting lens system on a rhesus monkey and observed him for eight days. Initially the monkey was very disturbed and refused to move at all. The first movements were backing away from objects (inverting lenses tend to re-verse depth perception) and viewing the world from between its legs. In a few days, however, the animal was able to move around and localize objects effec-tively. Similarly Bishop (1959) showed that kittens reared in the dark until two months of age and then fitted with inverting prisms seemed to get around in their environment as well as controls treated identically except for the ab-sence of prisms. Control kittens improved more than prism-wearing kittens on locomotion tasks, but the latter did improve steadily over time.

Other Peripheral Arrangements

Weiss (1937) reversed the normal orientation of amphibians' limbs by interchanging a pair of right and left limbs. The grossly inappropriate movements were never corrected by the animals, and they were thus unable to walk since the forelimb and hindlimb continually pushed in opposite directions.

The muscles at a given joint can be made to work in reverse either by crossing the tendons or the nerves of the flexors and extensors. In amphibia (Taylor, 1944) such procedures caused reversed movements that were never corrected. Rats with similar rearrangement showed only partial compensation (Sperry, 1943). In contrast, monkeys displayed excellent compensation for nerve crosses; in fact, Sperry has reported that in time such monkeys cannot be distinguished from intact monkeys in a colony.

A similar phenomenon in the cutaneous sense has been reported by Sperry (1951). Two corresponding skin flaps from opposite sides of a tadpole's back were exchanged without cutting the nerve supply to the flaps. When the tadpoles became frogs, stimulation of either patch of skin resulted in defensive reactions directed toward the wrong side of the body.

In summary, animals below the class mammalia are unable to compensate behaviorally for transformations in sensory input such as visual inversion or reversal of the direction of action exerted by limb muscles. Higher mammals are able to compensate for these arrangements. The rat shows a transitional amount of compensation for nerve and muscle transposition, and perhaps for retinal inversion. We might conclude that in lower animals the sensory-motor aspects of behavior are "wired in" and thus the plasticity shown in the higher mammals is lacking.

12

Development
of Perception

The question of perceptual development typically takes two forms. First, how do animals that come from different phyla differ in the perception of their environment? This may be called the phylogenesis of perception. Second—the ontogenetic question—how does an individual's perceptual ability change with age and physical maturation? We will look first at the phylogenetic development of perceptual systems.

PHYLOGENETIC TRENDS

Although it has been common to look for trends in perception that correspond to the "phylogenetic scale," and there are certain trends that we will examine below, a great deal of the variation in perceptual ability among animals is unaccounted for if we ignore the fact that an organism's perceptual abilities are adapted to his ecological niche and his way of life. The German biologist J. von Uexkull suggested that perception is a symbolic process involving those features of the environment that have adaptive significance to the organism; that is, *the organism perceives only those features of the environment that it needs.* Von Uexkull (1934) defined the term *Umwelt* as the unique world of the organism. The *Umwelt* has two parts: the *Merkwelt* (perceptual world) and the *Wirkwelt* (behavioral world). These two parts are linked together in a functional cycle of detection and triggered motor responses. For example, the *Merkwelt* of a tick consists solely of butyric acid, warmth, and light, the only stimuli relevant to it. The mated female tick climbs to the top of a bush and clings there, for months or even years, unresponsive to sounds, smells, or other stimuli changes until she detects butyric acid, a breakdown product of mammalian sweat. The detection of this odor triggers the motor response of dropping from the bush. The tactual cue of landing causes the tick to move until it detects warmth and can bore through the skin and suck blood. Out of the hundreds of events in its environment to which it might respond, the tick selects only butyric acid.

A number of other examples illustrate the adaptedness of each animal's perceptual system. The arthropods (e.g., insects, ants, and spiders) have small bodies, in which there can be only a limited number of receptors. These receptors are also simplified in that they combine the function of primary reception and the conduction of impulses to the central nervous system in a single neuron. The only human receptor that consists of a single neuron rather than a chain of neurons is the olfactory receptor. Since the arthropod's body maintains so few neurons, each one responds to rather specialized aspects of a stimulus. This, combined with the fact that its motor system is made up of a small number of fast-conducting elements, yields a sensory-motor system that concentrates on speed at the expense of information. For this reason a fly is annoyingly hard to swat but also has rather crude taste preferences.

It has been determined experimentally that bees have great difficulty learning to distinguish simple geometric shapes. These insects, however, visit flowers with the most complex contour and can readily discriminate figures that are broken up into black and white areas from geometrical shapes. Since bees apparently prefer figures with uneven outlines, researchers have theorized that the alternations in visual stimulation as the bee passes over ("flicker") make the stimulus effective. Flicker is also thought to be important in the courtship behaviors of a number of insects.

Lettvin and his colleagues have described certain visual mechanisms that operate in the frog. Retinal ganglion cells are specialized to detect, among other things, the movement of small dark objects across the visual field (see Chapter 7). These mechanisms are particularly suited to the frog's prey-catching and predator-escaping existence.

Another example of sensory mechanisms performing necessary tasks of an individual species is provided by the behavior of the bat. Bats do their food gathering at night, catching flying insects. They use the echoes from their short high-intensity, frequency-modulated pulsed cues to avoid hitting walls and to catch insects in the dark.

You may have heard the expression "going to bed with the chickens" (or conversely, "getting up with the chickens"), meaning going to bed at dusk (or getting up at dawn). The reason for the chickens' habits is that they have all-cone eyes and thus cannot see under conditions of low illumination. Their behavior directly follows from the range of light intensities they are able to see.

You may think that as humans we are aware of most information in our

Why Don't Cats Like Candy?

It is well known that, whereas most animals can be trained to perform tricks for a candy reward, cats are uninterested in sugar. This difference between cats and other animals follows directly from the physiology of their taste system. It has been known for some time that the taste system of the cat responds very weakly to sucrose (Pfaffmann, 1941). This makes good sense when one considers that the cat is a carnivore. In fact, sugar is a poison for cats because they are deficient in the enzyme, sucrase, that is necessary to metabolize sucrose. But their taste nerve does respond to sucrose a little. Why don't they react to concentrated sucrose? The cat, along with certain other animals, has what is called a "water response"; water will cause a discharge of the taste nerve. We now know that the water response actually occurs only after the tongue is adapted to certain substances such as salt. The amount of salt in saliva is sufficient to produce the water response.

The water response is quite large in the cat and might serve to mask the weak response to the sugar. Bartoshuk et al. (1971) reasoned that cats might go for sugar if they could prevent the water response. They presented the cats with sugar in a salt solution strong enough to prevent the water response but weak enough not to stimulate the salt fibers. They drank this solution avidly, indicating that they like the taste of sucrose but cannot taste it as it is normally combined in substances. In fact, the cats had to be limited in the amount of sucrose they could drink because they became sick.

we emphasized the effect of different types of experience. Now we raise the environment. It is probably true that we respond to a wider range of stimuli than any other creature, yet there is information in the environment to which we are not responsive and other species are. The high-frequency sound pulses used by bats in echolocation are two to three octaves above our upper limit of hearing. The pit viper uses its sensitivity to infrared radiation to locate prey. Certain fish (Lissmann, 1963) generate electric fields around themselves and detect their prey in the darkness by sensing changes in their self-generated fields. The bee can see ultraviolet light that we cannot.

We could give many examples of specialized perceptual mechanisms that enable organisms to survive in their particular environment. However, another characteristic of perceptual development warrants our attention in considering phylogenetic differences, and that is the shift toward greater plasticity in stimulus-response relationships in higher forms of animals (see the detailed discussion in Chapter 11). In studying the effects of adaptation to distorted sensory input,

They Don't Call Him Hawkeye For Nothing.

It has long been suspected that the visual acuity of certain birds of prey must exceed that of humans. Most people have seen hawks soaring at high altitudes from which they swoop down to seize small animals from the ground. Certain features of the anatomy of the eye of hawks and falcons support the likelihood of great visual acuity, especially the very densely packed cones in the fovea. R. Shlaer (1972) recently made the observations of the retinal image quality in a live African serpent eagle and concluded that this bird should have a visual acuity between 2 and 2.4 times as great as the human. This was confirmed behaviorally in an experiment by Fox et al. (1976) on the American kestrel, a small falcon. They trained a kestrel to fly from a perch to one of two windows. One of the windows contained a fine square wave grating, the other a uniform field. Using an adaptive method of choosing the size of the grating for a particular trial (see chapter 2) they measured his ability to detect gratings as a function of the width of the bars. They found that the kestral was able to detect a grating of 160 cycles per degree of visual angle 50% of the time. They concluded that the kestrel's acuity was 2.6 times that of a human. This means that an insect 1mm long would be threshold size to a kestrel sitting in a treetop 18 meters above the ground. They suggest that the acuity of the hawks and falcons is as great as would be advantageous to the bird, considering the energy spent in flying down to seize the prey and returning to the starting place compared to the caloric value of the prey.

question to what extent the development of perceptual abilities depends on experience, or, reversing the coin, what aspects of perceptual ability are innate.

ONTOGENETIC TRENDS

The nature-nurture question has been a controversial one in the study of psychology. As you can imagine, an experimental attack on the problem is quite difficult. Ideally, we should test infants as soon as possible after birth, before they have much perceptual experience. However, human infants are too poorly coordinated at birth for most of the methods available for perceptual testing. Some of the most important advances in this area have been the result of ingenious utilization of the limited behavioral capacities of infants. Ethical considerations preclude depriving them of normal stimulation until they mature sufficiently to be tested. However, there have been a number of experiments in which the effect of different types of experience or the lack of early experience has been studied on nonhuman animals. We will review these in the next section and also discuss that small number of cases where naturally occurring deprivation modified human infants' early perceptual experience.

Light Deprivation/Restriction

Are animals able to perform visually guided tasks without having any previous visual experience? One of the earliest studies to address this problem was done by Riesen (1947). Two chimpanzees were reared in darkness for the first six months of their lives. They were then exposed to light periodically until twenty-one months of age. At this age, severe deficits were observed; reaching responses were grossly inaccurate and blinking to an approaching object did not appear until they had spent one and a half months in the light.

The visual cliff, an apparatus designed by Gibson and Walk (1960) has been used to study depth perception, including the effects of restricted early experience. Briefly, the cliff consists of a board laid flat across a large sheet of heavy glass which is supported several feet above the floor (see Figure 12-1). To one side of the board a sheet of patterned material is placed flush against the under-surface of the glass, making the glass appear, as well as feel, solid. On the other side a sheet of the same patterned material is laid on the floor and this side becomes a visual cliff. The experimenter places the young animal (or human infant) on the center board and observes whether it refuses to move out onto the cliff, an indication of depth perception. In their 1961 experiment Walk and Gibson reared kittens in the dark from the time before their eyes opened until twenty-six days of age. After this deprivation, the kittens were tested on the visual cliff. They descended with equal frequency to either side of the apparatus, showing no preference for the "shallow" side, and thus failing to distinguish the two depths. Fantz (1965) found similar results with infant

Figure 12-1 The visual cliff. [After Gibson, E. J. and Walk, R. D. The visual cliff. *Scientific American*, 1960, *202* (4), 64–71.]

rhesus monkeys. Animals deprived for as long as two months showed no preference for the shallow side. The most obvious interpretation of these results is that early light deprivation prevents an animal from acquiring certain perceptual abilities; that perceptual development is arrested at some early level.

However, a number of studies have shown that early dark-rearing does much more than just interfere with perceptual development. Light deprivation causes actual physical degeneration of the visual system. The length of time necessary to cause damage and the type of damage to the system appear to vary with the animal tested. There may be morphological changes such as a reduction in the number of retinal ganglion cells (Chow, Riesen, and Newell, 1957), or biochemical changes in the retina (Brattgard, 1952; Riesen, 1966). More centrally, cells in the lateral geniculate receiving input from a deprived eye are smaller, and fewer cells in the striate cortex respond to stimulation of the deprived eye (Hubel and Wiesel, 1970). Some changes are seen after only a few months of deprivation and others do not occur until there has been lengthy (1 to 3 years) deprivation.

Modified deprivation procedures have been devised in order to assess the contribution of visual-motor experience to perceptual development without such deterioration. One such study was performed by Riesen and Aarons (1959). Kittens were reared in the dark for their first sixteen weeks of life, and then provided various kinds of visual experience. Group 1 was exposed to light through diffusing goggles that prevented patterned vision for 1 hour per day, but was not allowed to move during this exposure. Group 2 was also restrained but received normal visual experience for 1 hour per day. Group 3 was unrestrained and was given normal visual experience for 1 hour per day, and Group 4 (controls) moved freely in a normal visual environment all the time. The animals were then trained to respond differentially to a moving or stable pattern by pushing open the correct door to obtain a food reward. The first two groups were unable to solve the discrimination problem in the training period, whereas Groups 3 and 4 had no difficulty with the task. The restrained animals also appeared to have problems in coordinating their movements in the test apparatus. Other experimenters have reported that such animals are unable to avoid obstacles, jump from a platform, and perform other similar tasks. The fact that the animals had difficulty in learning a discrimination problem requiring them to locomote, combined with their reported coordination problems, suggested that restricted visual experience may not have affected the ability to perceive motion, but may have kept the animals from distinguishing objective from self-produced motion. Meyer (1964) tested that hypothesis by having the animals learn the same discrimination as in the Riesen and Aarons (1959) study, but they responded with leg flexion rather than some locomotor response. In this situation, the animals showed no impairment of learning as a result of patterned light deprivation. This suggests that to ensure development of the visual control of behavior, early visual experience must include self-produced changes in stimulation.

Held and Hein (1963) have suggested that the visual feedback resulting from movement, reafference, is important in the development of motor co-ordination in the young animal as well as perceptual adaptation to distorted input. These researchers devised the apparatus shown in Figure 12-2, in which one kitten moving around normally would pull another around in a gondola. The passive kitten would receive the same amount of visual stimulation as the active kitten, except that, for the passive kitten, changes in visual stimulation would be independent of any movement it made within the gondola. Both kittens were kept in the dark with other animals except when they were in the apparatus. After a number of daily sessions, the active kitten showed normal visually guided behavior. It blinked to an approaching object, put out its paws to avoid collisions if carried toward a surface, and it avoided the deep side of the visual cliff. The passive kitten did not show these behaviors, but they developed after several days of normal experience. Held and Hein emphasize that these results indicate the importance of sensory-motor feedback or reafference.

An alternate explanation tested by Hein, Held, and Gower (1970) was that the passive kittens learned that their actions would have no effect on their environment. Serving as its own control in the gondola experiment, each animal participated in the active condition with one eye open and in the passive condition with the other eye open. When the kittens were later tested on the visual cliff, they performed normally when using the "active" eye, but they readily ventured out on the deep side of the cliff when using the "passive" eye. Therefore, it appears that the impaired performance of the passive animals was not caused by their learning the ineffectiveness of their movements, since this would

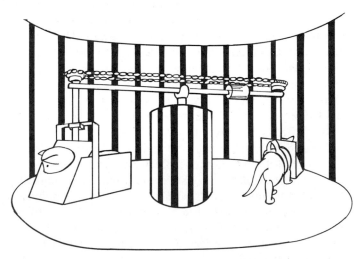

Figure 12-2 The kitten gondola. [From Held, R., & Hein, A. V. Movement produced stimulation in the development of visually guided behavior. *J. Physiol. and Comp. Psych.*, 1963, *56*, 872-76. © 1963 by the American Psychological Association. Reprinted by permission.]

have affected performance with both eyes. Rather, it seems that Held's suggestion of interference with sensory-motor feedback is the best explanation.

We discussed reafference in Chapter 11. You will recall that, in order to distinguish changes in the stimulus array caused by your own movements from those caused by actual movement of the array, you need feedback information about the movement of your own body. If this feedback (reafference) matches the record of motor commands (efference copy) then the objects are seen as stationary. If the two do not match, then the objects are seen as moving. Restrictively reared cats seem to be unable to make the comparison between reafference and efference; they are able to learn a movement discrimination when they themselves are restrained, but not when they must move around. Because the passive kittens did not receive reafferent stimulation in their early experience, they could not distinguish movement of a stimulus object from their own movements. In the visual cliff experiment, the passive kittens could not discriminate between the two sides, then, because without the reafference-efference comparison, they could not use motion parallax information to perceive depth. Why the restricted kittens in the Held and Hein (1963) study did not show a response to impending collision is a more difficult question to answer. Most animals show a loom-avoidance response early in life, but it is possible that restricted rearing could adversely affect the maintenance of existing abilities.

Hein and Diamond (1971) have also shown how specific the calibration of the reafference-efference system is to the conditions and the experience given the animal. Kittens were reared under low levels of illumination and allowed to move around freely. Under these light conditions, only the rod system of the eye would be used and thus only it would receive reafferent information, and not the cone system. When the animals were tested, they showed accurate visual guidance of behavior only when performing under low levels of illumination, and not when placed in normal levels of light.

Other studies have been concerned with the effect of visual deprivation on the learning of form discrimination. Here again some species differences are revealed in the effect of dark rearing. Hebb (1937) found that rats were not affected by such treatment when tested on form discrimination tasks. Riesen (1950), however, showed that an hour and a half of light per day was necessary for chimps to perform normally when tested on differentiating between vertical and horizontal stripes. As with other deprivation experiments, such studies are complicated by the possibility of visual pathology or general retardation. Thus the results of these animal studies do not lead to any firm conclusions regarding the development of form perception.

Obviously, we cannot purposely deprive human infants of visual stimulation for various periods after birth simply to test their perceptual abilities. However, some institutionalized infants and those exhibiting pathology of the visual system do not receive normal stimulation. In a series of studies White and his collaborators (White, et al., 1964; White and Held, 1966; White, 1971) worked with institutionalized infants to determine what effects an enriched environment would have on their perceptual development. White reasoned that the infants' responses to added stimulation would provide information about the contribution of experience to perceptual development. His first step was to gather normative data on their visual-motor coordination. At around 1½ months of age, the children started to watch their hand and finger movements. Swiping at a colorful target occurred at around two months. This activity may seem to indicate the infant's coping with the seen and felt position of the hand. Accurate grasping occurred at about 4 to 5 months of age. White then systematically enriched the environment of the infants and compared their development under the two conditions. Each infant was handled twenty minutes per day and placed on its stomach fifteen minutes each day. Also, colored mobiles were hung over their beds and colored sheets and bumpers were substituted for the usual white ones. Hand watching and swiping were slightly delayed in the enriched group, but directed accurate reaching for a target occurred about 45 days earlier. A second modification added wearing red and white striped mittens to the other enrichment. This resulted in earlier hand watching and accurate reaching. A third modification involved simply mounting two pacifiers on the crib and surrounding them with red and white circles. This change accelerated hand watching, swiping, and accurate target reaching. Interestingly, these modifications, though minor compared to the stimulation a home-reared child receives, produced considerable acceleration of perceptual development.

Von Senden published a monograph in 1932 reviewing all reports up to that time of patients who, when operated on for congenital blindness, were old enough to give a verbal report of what they saw. Most were cases of cataracts which had clouded the lens or cornea. Although these persons would have received no patterned stimulation, the diffused light they did see would prevent retinal deterioration. The oldest of these reports dates to 1020 A.D. but even the more recent lack scientific rigor. However, one facet of the reports is remarkably consistent: the patient's form perception in the immediate postoperative period. Patients immediately perceive unitary figures differentiated from the background but have a great deal of difficulty identifying them. Thus despite perception of the distinctive features of an object, patients remain for a long time unable to attach meaning to the features, to remember them, or to generalize them—that is, to discriminate them visually. This relatively simple task for the haptic system required at least thirty days for the visual system to master. Associations between descriptive terms such as "long" and "short" and between the names of objects and their visual appearance had to be learned. Judgment of distance and depth in these patients was poor, but this may have been a "mechanical" problem and not a true perceptual deficit. These patients generally have difficulty in accommodation and convergence for several weeks postoperatively, and this would make it difficult to interpret the results from any tests requiring adequate focusing. Individual differences in intelligence, age, type of operation, and so on also influenced all the results reported. London (1960) summarized Russian reports which agree well with von Senden's review. He also notes that the two children blinded at ages three and five progressed much more rapidly to restored normal vision than did the congenitally blind.

Gregory and Wallace (1963) report a case of recovery from early blindness through a corneal transplant in adulthood. Unlike von Senden's patients, this man was able in a few days to readily transfer information from the tactual to the visual modality; that is, he could identify by sight letters previously known by touch and also tell time, having previously used a watch without a crystal. However, he never learned to read more than a few words, and remained unable to see several geometric illusions such as the Poggendorff, or experience reversals in figures such as the Necker cube. This extremely well documented clinical case of vision gained in adulthood does not confirm the slow rate of perceptual learning previously reported. Such studies thus remain difficult to interpret, even though they do provide some information about the course of perceptual development in infants. In considering this area of investigation, it is well to question whether comparisons between an immature and a mature nervous system, an intact and a damaged visual system, and an inexperienced infant and an experienced adult will lead to valid conclusions.

It is quite possible that perceptual abilities present in infancy can be lost as a result of deprivation of patterned visual input. We previously discussed the deterioration of the visual system that occurs when an animal is raised in such a way as to deprive it of light stimulation. A related question concerns whether certain types of restricted early experience might modify the structure and/or response of the visual system to stimulation. There is evidence of such an effect. Blakemore and Cooper (1970) placed kittens from two weeks of age to five months in an environment of either all vertical or all horizontal stripes for five hours a day. They could not see their own bodies. At the end of this period, the kittens displayed many of the behaviors previously reported in restricted environments: temporary lack of loom avoidance and placing response, and permanent clumsy movement of head and body. The cats appeared behaviorally blind to contours perpendicular to the orientation they had experienced. For example, a "vertical" kitten would follow and play with a rod held vertically, but it would ignore a rod held horizontally. When it was held horizontally, a "horizontal" kitten would be attracted to it.

Neurophysiological studies were done when the kittens were 7½ months old. Single-unit recordings from the primary visual cortex showed abnormal distributions of preferred orientations of cells. The "horizontal" kittens showed most cells responding to horizontally oriented stimulation and the "vertical" kittens had mostly vertical-responding cells. Most interestingly, the authors found no areas of non-responding cells, indicating that this effect was not caused by passive degeneration of unstimulated cortical neurons. Rather, Blakemore and Cooper suggest that the visual cortex changes during maturation depending on the nature of the visual experience. Other results bearing on this question have been reported by Pettigrew and Freeman (1973). They placed dark-reared kittens in an opaque polyethylene sphere three hours a day for a total of 39 hours. The kittens' only visual experience was a random array of point sources of light. They saw no lines or linear shapes. Most cortical neurons were subsequently found to be sensitive to small dots of light and not to straight lines, as would be true in a normal cat.

Mitchell et al. (1973) extended these studies to ocular astigmatism, in which a person sees lines in one orientation (e.g., the vertical) clearly and another (e.g., the horizontal) as blurred. This condition is the result of a difference in the refractive error of the eye in two different orientations. The subjects, whose task was to resolve gratings of different orientations, were "deprived" of sharp images of contours of certain orientations throughout the time that their astigmatism was uncorrected. Even when fitted with lenses to correct the astigmatism fully, most subjects achieved normal acuity for only one grating orientation, and the acuity for a grating orthogonal (perpendicular) was abnormally depressed.

What conclusions can we draw from these studies? We cannot resolve the nature-nurture question. The results indicate that, if innate, the specialized nature of cortical cells appears to be readily modified by early experience. On the other hand, this specialization may be derived completely from visual experience. It appears that there is a "critical period" during which the visual system is susceptible to modification by its input; in the cat and monkey, this is approximately the first three months of life. For the human, some clinical data indicate that about the first two years may be the critical period for the influence of visual input.

PERCEPTUAL DEVELOPMENT IN THE HUMAN

In the next sections, we will be discussing the normal sequence of perceptual development in the human. We will consider such areas as depth, distance, size, form, and pattern perception. We are interested in several questions: When do certain perceptual abilities appear? How do these abilities change as a function of growth and maturation? What type of experience is necessary for the development of different perceptual abilities? And, we want to know what information is being used in each situation in which some perceptual response is made.

Depth and Distance

We have described the visual cliff and its use with animals. The same apparatus has been frequently used to study perceptual development in human infants. The child is placed on the center board and his mother uses toys to attempt to entice him into coming to her over either the deep or shallow side.

If the child can discriminate between the two sides, he should crawl to his mother over the shallow side only. Walk and Gibson (1961) tested a number of infants from six to fourteen months of age. Most of the children who ventured off the center board crawled to their mothers over the shallow side; very few would go onto the deep side. Walk (1969) has determined how precise the child's discrimination of depth actually is. The child was placed on the center board, which now was tapered so that at the end where the mother stood, it was too narrow for the child to remain on it. Thus the child had to get off the board in order to reach his mother. The deep side was varied from 13 to 102 cm below the glass, and the shallow side was immediately below the glass. Most children showed a preference for the shallow side, even when the deep side was only 13 cm under the glass. The conclusion, then, is that infants who are capable of crawling can discriminate differences in depth of as little as 13 cm.

Other studies have determined that infants can perceive depth even before they can locomote. Campos, Langer, and Krowitz (1970) measured the heart rates of infants when they were placed on the glass over the deep (102 cm) and the shallow side of the cliff. Children approximately 55 days old showed a significant decrease in heart rate when placed on the deep side. The decelerated heart rate, combined with the fact that the infants did not cry or appear afraid, led Campos et al. to suggest that the depth caused an attention response rather than fear which would have accelerated the heart rate. It therefore appears that quite young children can perceive depth. We know from an earlier discussion (Chapter 10) that there are a number of cues that can be used to perceive depth and distance. Which of these cues are children able to use, and at what age?

Binocular Cues—Retinal Disparity.   There is evidence that children at two years of age use disparity information to perceive depth. An apparatus was used with which an image of an object such as a doll could be stereoscopically projected so that the subject with binocular vision would localize the object between himself and the screen. The experimenters (Johnson and Beck, 1941) asked the child if he would like to touch the doll and then noted the point where the child reached in order to touch it. The child's reach and his comments about touching the doll indicated that he was perceiving depth through the use of disparity information. Other studies suggest earlier use of disparity, but these results are inconsistent with data indicating lack of convergence in young infants. Some degree of convergence is necessary for binocular vision. Binocular cues may not be that important for children; several studies have shown that performance on the visual cliff was the same using one eye or two eyes.

Monocular Cues—1. Motion Parallax.   Bower (1965) has demonstrated the use of motion parallax information by infants. His study is an example of how a series of experiments can be used to rule out alternative hypotheses. Bower operantly conditioned a group of two-month-old infants to turn their heads every time a cube was presented 91 cm away. (The reinforcement was the experimenter popping up and saying "peek-a-boo".) After training, children were tested under three conditions: wearing stereoscopic goggles and viewing projected stereograms, with one eye covered, or while looking at a photograph of the test situation. Bower found that the infants made the same number of responses in the monocular and binocular situations, but few responses were made when the photograph was used. Pictorial cues were not effective. However, the infants were not relying solely on binocular disparity information since they made as many responses in the monocular as in the binocular condition. Therefore, these two-month-old infants seem to have been using motion parallax information, at least to some extent.

Monocular Cues—2. Texture Gradient. Wohlwill (1965) had subjects from age six to age 16 look at photographs of three wooden toys on surfaces of different textures and at different distances from a fence. Subjects were to judge which toy was closest to the fence in each picture. Older children were more accurate in making the judgments, but the youngest children were able to perform the task. Accuracy of all subjects increased with the number and regularity of texture elements.

Form and Pattern Perception

A large number of studies have considered the response of infants to patterns. Visual fixation or the visual looking response has been the criterion for preference. Fantz (1956) devised an apparatus to observe reliably and record fixation with infants. Fantz (1961) has shown that infants prefer patterns such as a checkerboard, to a plain surface. Also, black and white patterns (a face, bull's eye, newsprint) are preferred to any solid colored surface. Infants from one day to at least six months prefer to look at patterned rather than plain surfaces.

It is a common observation that infants show a great deal of interest in the human face. The question is what characteristics of the face stimulus are responsible for the infant's interest. Studies comparing normal faces with scrambled versions have reported diverse results. Kagan (1967) concluded that the results depend on the response measure being used. There was no difference in fixation or vocalization, but subjects smiled more to the regular face than to the scrambled one. There are other problems inherent in such studies of response to visual patterns. The preference techniques provide information only if preferences occur and, even if they do occur, there has been no way to determine which aspect of the stimulus attracted the infant's attention. In addition, all of these experiments must operate within the limits of the infant's visual-motor capacities.

Another response that has been used to study pattern perception in the infant is the direction of gaze or visual scanning. This procedure is employed to track the parts of the stimulus that are effective in eliciting attention or orientation. The data from such experiments show us that an infant responds selectively to elements of form (a border or angle, for example) from birth. With age, visual scanning for inspection and recognition becomes much more efficient. Mackworth and Bruner (1970) compared six-year-olds and adults while they scanned photographs presented at three levels of definition: very blurred, blurred, and sharp. With the sharp pictures, children showed shorter tracks than adults and had twice as many small eye movements. Adults were more skillful at visually selecting informative areas in out-of-focus pictures. The investigators suggest that the results were due primarily to the adults' ability to examine details with the central retina and simultaneously monitor the periphery for important information to be scanned later.

Several other studies have considered the factors important in perceptual recognition in older children. Changes in the importance of spatial orientation of stimuli have been investigated by Deich (1971). Seven-, eleven-, and thirteen-year-olds were presented with lists of words either right side up or upside down. The number of children reading the inverted lists as fast as the upright list decreased from fifty percent in seven-year-olds to five percent in thirteen-year-olds. Orientation appeared to play an increasingly important role in recognition with increasing age.

Spitz and Borland (1971) did an analysis of drawing recognition in children. Parts of drawings of familiar objects (bird, apple, man, doll, etc.) were randomly deleted without regard for their information content. It was found that the number of lines required to recognize the drawing of an object decreased with age. Dramatic improvement occurred between the ages of 4½ and 8 years, after which it was gradual. The investigators suggest that the older child becomes sensitive to more distinctive features on which he can base his identification of an object.

A study by Elkind, Koegler, and Koegler (1964) shows that children may first attend to the parts of a pattern before attending to the whole. The drawings used in the study were of common objects formed by putting together other familiar objects. For example, a heart was composed of two giraffes with curved necks; a tricycle of pieces of candy, and an airplane of vegetables. The four- and five-year-olds reported only seeing the parts, but by the age of seven, children would report seeing both parts and whole ("giraffes and a heart"). By eight or nine years of age, most children reported seeing parts and whole simultaneously ("a heart made of giraffes").

OBJECT PERCEPTION

Bower and his colleagues (e.g., 1971) have conducted a number of studies on the perception of objects by the infant. Bower has been concerned primarily with the development of the concepts of solidity and permanence. The expectation of solidity was determined by observing startle responses (facial expression, crying) on the part of the infant subjects to apparent impending collision. A special stereoscopic apparatus made it possible to present a virtual image of an object which looked real and solid to the subject seated before a screen. It was, however, an illusion and intangible. Infants from sixteen to twenty-four weeks old showed startle responses when they reached out to the place where the object was apparently located but were unable to touch it. None of the infants showed surprise when they were able to touch a real object in front of them (Bower et al., 1970).

Based on Bower's observations, the concept of object permanence would also seem to appear early in development. He placed infants in front of an object which was then covered during various intervals (1.5 to 15 seconds) by a moving screen. In half of the trials the object was still there when the screen moved away; in the other half it was no longer there. If the infant knew that the object was still there behind the screen, he should have shown surprise at its absence when the screen moved away. On the other hand, if he thought the object no longer existed behind the screen, he should have been surprised at its still being present. Surprise was determined by a change in heart rate. All of the subjects (aged 20 to 100 days) showed surprise when the object did not appear after being covered for the short period of time. The oldest infants expected the object to reappear after the long period, but the younger ones did not register surprise at its disappearance. Bower suggests that in the 15-second interval they had forgotten about the object. The general conclusion, however, is that very young infants do show object permanence.

You will recall that, in the adult human, vision is dominant over touch (Chapter 11). An area of interest in perceptual development has been determination of whether vision precedes touch or vice versa in providing the infant with information about object size, shape, and hardness. Ontogenetic development has generally held that "touch teaches vision." However, Bower, Broughton, and Moore (1970) have found evidence against this traditional hypothesis. Their results suggest that the visual system is capable of more refined control of the grasping response at an early age than is the touch system. An object was presented to the infant visually (virtual image) or was placed in his hand out of sight. Observations indicated hand shaping (grasping movements as in reaching for an object) was better under the visual conditions for infants. Kaufman, Belmont, Birch, and Zach (1973) looked at interrelations of the visual and somatosensory systems in older children (ages three to nine years). These investigators found developmental changes in the extent to which stimulation in one sensory system affected the reaction time to stimulation in the other modality. In one experiment they examined the effects upon reaction time to a visual stimulus when there was an intervening 3-minute period of tactile stimulation, or vice versa, when visual stimulation intervened with an original tactile stimulus. In a second experiment, presentation was in one sensory system and its effect on reaction time to subsequent stimulation in the other modality was studied. Tactile stimulation was more effective in slowing reaction times to visual stimulation in younger children; in older children (over six or seven),

Jean Piaget's study of cognitive and perceptual development began with observations of his own three children as they grew. He listened to the children's sayings and found that they revealed certain beliefs about the world. He set up informal experiments to determine how his children perceived objects. From these early ideas evolved the semi-clinical interview that became Piaget's trademark. He trained students in his institute in Switzerland to talk to children and ask them questions without suggesting the answer.

From these studies came Piaget's concept of four stages of human development. Every child passes through these stages in an orderly sequence, but the age at which children attain each level varies. The first level, termed the Sensorimotor Stage, extends from birth until about two years. The child in this period is primarily interested in what can be directly manipulated. At about one year, the concept of object permanence develops (Piaget, 1952). Until this time, the child will not look for an object that is temporarily out of sight, for example, a doll placed under a blanket in front of the child or a ball that rolls behind a chair. Presumably, until the concept of object permanence develops, any object out of sight is thought to cease to exist. This accounts for the surprise and part of the fun in playing "peek-a-boo."

The second stage of development, the Preoperational Stage, includes the development of language. At first, names are believed to be a property of the objects themselves, but later on children come to understand names as symbols which represent things and people. The child in these first two stages is egocentric—that is, he thinks that the world revolves around him. He lacks any social orientation or the ability to view things from another person's perceptual angle. For example, the five-year-old child can easily point out his right and left hands, but if standing facing another person, the child will indicate that the other person's left and right hands are directly opposite his own left and right hands.

The stage of Concrete Operations extends from approximately age seven to age eleven. The child at this stage can organize things that are present; that is, he can classify and serialize objects and also determine relations such as bigger, longer, taller. The concept of conservation of quantity develops during this period. In his studies on conservation, Piaget was interested in whether children would perceive that the quantity of a material might remain the same even though its appearance changed. He presented the child with two identical glasses, each containing the same amount of a colored liquid. In front of the child, Piaget would pour the liquid from one of the glasses into a taller, thinner glass. He would then ask the child if there was the same amount of drink in the two glasses. Until the child develops the conservation concept, he cannot solve this problem. The child would usually say that the tall, thin glass contained the most liquid, because his thought is dominated by a single perception, the height of the glass, rather than the three dimensions determining volume (Inhelder and Piaget, 1958, 1959).

The child attains the Stage of Formal Operations between twelve and fifteen years of age. At this time, he becomes capable of abstract thought and deductive reasoning. He can think about the future and construct ideals and goals. He is also able to perceive the humor in satire (Inhelder and Piaget, 1959).

visual stimulation exerted a greater effect on touch, indicating a change from tactile to visual prepotency with age.

In studies of the interaction of visual and auditory modes of perception, the emphasis has been on determining the origin of the perceptual ability visually to locate a sound source. Aronson and Rosenbloom (1971) designed a study to test whether infants perceive within a common auditory-visual space. A spatial discrepancy between audition and vision was created by having the voice of the infant's mother displaced 90° left or right as she spoke to the infant. The infants (one to two months old) showed various distress reactions to the displaced voice. This result indicates that infants as young as one month perceive auditory and visual information within a common space; the dislocation is a violation of the organization of the infant's perceptual world.

In conclusion, we can say that human perceptual development proceeds in an orderly and predictable fashion. The sequence of events will be essentially the same for all children, but the age at which any given behavior will be attained will vary as a function of both the environment and the child's genetic endowment. We know that an impoverished sensory environment will impede perceptual development. In some extreme cases, even general physical development will be affected by lack of sensory stimulation. Conversely, enriching the surroundings of an institutionalized child, for example, will bring its sensory environment to the level of a child's in a normal family environment. Sensory enrichment even makes it possible for many of these children to attain normal perceptual development. On the other hand, there is as yet no definitive evidence concerning the enriching of an infant's environment beyond a "normal" amount of stimulation. The question remains whether bombarding an infant or child with sensory stimulation will accelerate or expand his perceptual or intellectual ability.

It appears from various studies that infants are able to process perceptual information much earlier in life than was once believed. A general problem in perceptual development, however, continues to be that of designing experiments that are both informative and within the physical capability of the infant.

13

Perceptual
Illusions

Look at the two lines in Figure 13-1a. They look the same length and they are. Now look at the two lines in b. These lines do not appear to be the same length but you can confirm that they are by measuring them. Figure 13-1b is a representation of the Müller-Lyer illusion. You have probably seen this one on the back of a cereal box or on a restaurant placemat along with other well-known perceptual illusions. The Müller-Lyer illusion is a compelling one to most people.

   We must ask what a perceptual illusion is. The obvious answer is to say that an illusion is a distortion of perception. But, a distortion compared to what? Perceptions are influenced by many factors as we have seen in the case of size or shape constancy, but we do not think of these perceptions as illusory. In those situations that we consider to be examples of perceptual constancy, the distortion of perception is of such a nature that the perception remains more faithful to the nature of the object than to the stimulus generated by the object. On the other hand, a perception is generally labelled illusory when the actual percept is in conflict with "objective" reality. But this distinction must not be pushed too far because one theory of illusions holds that they are the result of the same mechanisms that maintain perceptual constancy. Perhaps the best we can do is to say that an illusion is a case in which a perception based on one method of perceiving differs from what another perceptual mode would tell you about the same stimulus. In the case of the Müller-Lyer illusion, looking at the lines directly tells you they are different but comparing each of them to the markings on a ruler tells you that they are equal. We put more faith in the

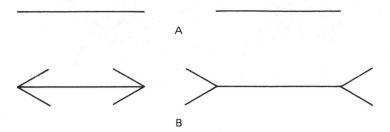

A

B

Figure 13-1 The Müller-Lyer illusion is shown in part b. All of the horizontal lines are the same length.

perception obtained when employing the ruler and so we call the direct estimation illusory. But we should emphasize that many of our perceptions could be called illusory on this basis. Those that we choose to call illusory are simply more extreme or impressive examples of what happens in all perception.

If there is nothing perceptually unique about illusions, why do we have a separate chapter on them? Three reasons. First, there are many intriguing illusions, some of which have puzzled thinkers for millenia. Second, they have historically provided much of the impetus for the study of perception. If one had never seen the Müller-Lyer illusion, it might never occur to ask how we are able to judge the length of anything. Third, although several illusions are still as puzzling as they were a century ago, other illusions have yielded valuable insights into perceptual processes. Perhaps the best example of this is the Mach band phenomenon, which led to an understanding of the importance of lateral inhibition in perceptual processes. We have already discussed certain illusions elsewhere in this book as they pertained to a specific principle of perception—for example the oculogravic effect and apparent movement. We will devote the remainder of this chapter to a discussion of the geometrical illusions and some of the theories they have stimulated. Then we will turn to several illusions we have not previously described but whose explanation seems reasonably clear.

THE GEOMETRICAL OPTICAL ILLUSIONS

This is a class of optical illusions based on the geometrical properties of certain figures (see Figure 13-2a–h). They involve distortion of size as in the Müller-Lyer and Ponzo illusions, or of shape as in the Hering and Poggendorff illusions. Many theories have been proposed to account for geometrical illusions; actually you could probably generate most of them yourself with a little thought. The *eye movement theory* was proposed to account for the Müller-Lyer illusion, the idea being that the tails of the figure either drew the eye out in the "feather" version or prevented them from moving as far in the "arrowhead" version. This kind of unscientific explanation, often used by artists to analyze

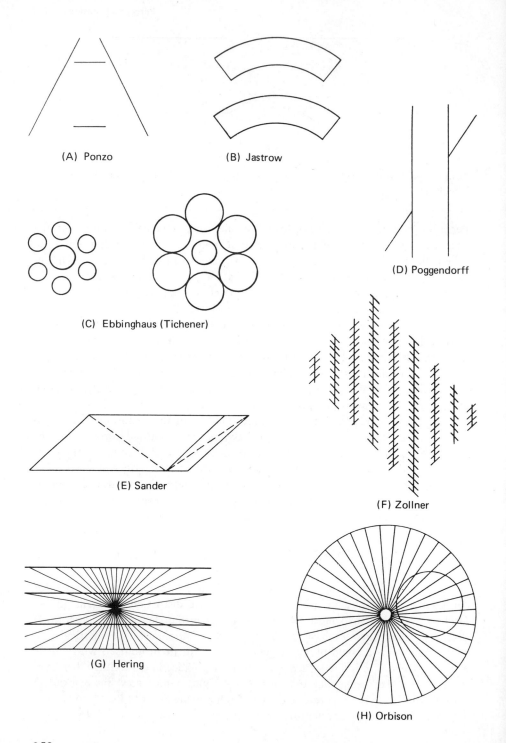

(A) Ponzo

(B) Jastrow

(C) Ebbinghaus (Tichener)

(D) Poggendorff

(E) Sander

(F) Zollner

(G) Hering

(H) Orbison

the esthetic value of a painting, can be rejected because the illusion is still seen when eye movements are prevented, either by tachistoscopic presentation or with stabilized retinal images. The *empathy theory* is similar to the eye movement theory except that the viewer is believed to feel the movement suggested by the lines. In the case of the vertical-horizontal illusion, the reason the vertical line looks longer, according to the empathy theory, is that one imagines the effort required to move along a vertical line to be more than that for horizontal movement. This theory has little to recommend it beyond a certain plausibility and has not been fruitful in generating testable hypotheses.

The *perspective theory* is one that has received considerable attention. Certain illusory figures contain strong cues to depth, especially the Ponzo (railroad track) illusion. The converging lines are seen as parallel lines in depth. Thus, objects that subtend the same visual angle will be perceived as larger when they are seen to be farther away, following the predictions of Emmert's law. Gregory suggests that the Müller-Lyer is seen in depth, with the arrowhead version seen as one would view the corner of a house from the outside. The feather version would be seen as indicating perspective in the manner of a corner of a room (see Figure 13–2i). Since the two subtend the same visual angle, the one that is perceived as being farther away (the inside of the room, or the feather version) will appear bigger. The one that is seen as nearer (outside of house or arrowhead version) must be smaller. This theory seems plausible, because some people do report apparent depth in at least some of these illusions. Gregory (1973) devised a clever apparatus to determine at what distance people saw the versions of the Müller-Lyer illusion by examining convergence of the eyes when they looked at the figure monocularly. He found that, indeed, they tended to see the longer version of the figure as farther away. However, the theory is still controversial. Kaufman (1974), describes experiments showing the existence of the illusion even if the Müller-Lyer figures are presented stereoscopically so that the depth is reversed from what the perspective theory predicts. Such results are difficult to interpret one way or the other; we will encounter the same dilemma with the "apparent distance of the moon" when we attempt to understand the moon illusion.

Although a number of people have suggested theories based on constancy, Day's (1972) theory is the most general explanation. He says that illusions of size, shape, orientation, and movement result when the stimuli that normally preserve perceptual constancy are present but the image of the object is physically constant. In some of the geometrical optical illusions such as the Müller-Lyer, he notes that the cues for distance are varied but the visual image is not.

Figure 13-2a–h Some well known illusions. a. Ponzo: the two parallel lines are equal in length. b. Jastrow: the two figures are identical. c. Ebbinghaus: the inner circles are the same. d. Poggendorff: the slanted lines would meet if continued. e. Sander parallelogram: the dotted lines are the same length. f. Zollner: the verticals are parallel. g. Hering: the horizontal lines are straight. h. Orbison: the inner figure is a true circle.

Figure 13-2i A version of the vertical-horizontal illusion. The Gateway arch in St. Louis. The arch itself is exactly as wide as it is high.

Distortion of size results because constancy mechanisms usually operate when the size of the retinal image is changing.

We have considered only a few of the theories about geometrical illusions, but we have chosen those that are illustrative of the thinking about illusions over the years. We can expect that the work going on in the field of perception will ultimately lead to an understanding of these illusions.

SOME ILLUSIONS THAT ILLUSTRATE GENERAL PRINCIPLES OF PERCEPTION

There are a number of illusions that are well understood because they can be related to accepted principles of perception. We will consider some of these in the sections to follow.

The Moon Illusion

Most readers have probably puzzled over the fact that the moon at the horizon looks much larger than at the zenith. What causes this illusion? The moon subtends the same visual angle in each case so that the retinal image is the same, as various measurements have proved. Yet the horizon moon looks as much as

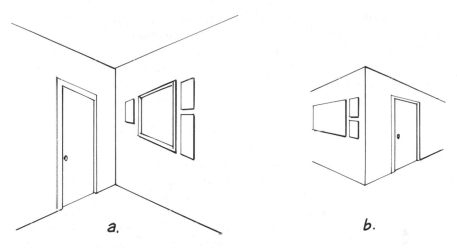

Figure 13-2j Illustration of the perspective theory of the Müller-Lyer illusion.

Figure 13-2k The twisted cord illusion. The spiral is actually a series of concentric circles.

one and one-half times larger than the moon high overhead. This illusion has interested thinkers from antiquity and, although a number of theories have been proposed, only two have been taken seriously.

The oldest theory has been attributed to Ptolemy, a second-century astronomer (Robinson, 1972). His idea was that the horizon moon was assumed to be at least as far away as the most distant objects on the horizon—i.e., farther away than the zenith moon. Thus it will be perceived as large compared to the zenith moon which is nearer—ergo smaller. We would now say that Emmert's law is the reason that the horizon moon appears larger; that is, if the eye receives two images of equal size, the object seen as farther away will be perceived as larger. This theory has been called the apparent distance theory and, as we shall see, it is still a viable theory.

When Boring (1943) asked subjects to judge the apparent distance of the horizon and zenith moons, they said the horizon moon appeared closer. This is the opposite of what the apparent distance theory requires so Boring proposed a theory based on the angle of regard, or the manner in which the subject was viewing the moon. He found that the illusion was present when subjects looked at the moon by raising their eyes. However, if the subjects raised their heads to look straight at the zenith moon, there was no illusion. If subjects were lying on their backs, the illusion was reversed (zenith moon appeared larger), presumably because in such a position they would look straight ahead to see the zenith moon, but would have to raise their eyes to see the horizon moon. Boring therefore attributed the illusion to the elevation of the eyes.

Kaufman and Rock (1962) questioned the methods used by Boring and proposed a more direct test of the illusion. Their apparatus allowed subjects to look through a viewer and see an artificial moon against the sky. One such device was pointed toward the horizon and one toward the zenith. The size of the artificial moon could be varied to enable the subject to match apparent sizes of the two "moons." Using this method, Kaufman and Rock found that the angle of regard produced only a small effect.

Now, Ptolemy had thought that the horizon moon looked larger because it was seen as farther. On the other hand Boring found that subjects perceived the moon as nearer. This is a logical contradiction and, for Boring, that was the end of the apparent distance theory. But, perhaps the subjects saw the moon as nearer, *because* they saw it as larger. This may not seem to be much progress, because it is still logically incompatible with the apparent distance explanation. However, it may not be correct to require logical consistency in this matter. Consider the following. The moon is seen as larger because of Emmert's law. This effect is a direct, perceptual one, not particularly subject to cognitive processes. However, when a person is asked which moon seems nearer, he engages in a more cognitive process. He may reason as follows: "the moon looks bigger. Since bigger appearing things are normally closer, it must be closer." At any rate, it is clear that different sorts of questions are asked of the subject and we should not be surprised if he arrives at logically inconsistent answers.

Why should the zenith moon be seen as nearer? It was known that the sky is seen not as round, but as a flattened dome something like a ceiling that extends to the horizon (see Figure 13-3). This is particularly true when the sky is overcast or cloudy. Rock and Kaufman (1962) found that the moon illusion was greater when the sky was overcast, in accord with the apparent distance

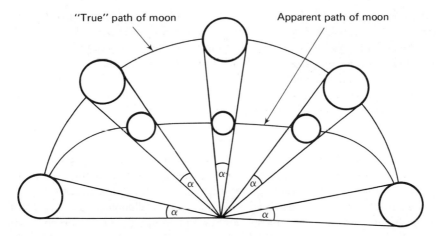

Figure 13-3 Illustration of the apparent shape of the sky and its effect on the apparent size of the moon.

theory. In addition they found that the illusion increased as the horizon was made to appear farther away. You may have noticed yourself that the moon appears larger at the seashore or where the land is very flat as in the "Big Sky Country." If you live in a city you can study the moon illusion by looking out the window from different floors of a building. Those views that present the moon against a more distant horizon will produce a bigger illusion than those in which you see the moon against a nearby building. In summary, the apparent distance theory, suggested so long ago by Ptolemy, is now well supported by the experimental evidence.

The Autokinetic Phenomenon

If you view a stationary lighted flashlight in an otherwise completely dark room, after a few minutes the light will seem to wander in a random manner. Likewise, sometimes a star in a dark sky will appear to move. This movement, called the autokinetic phenomenon, usually follows no pattern; in fact, it will be different for each person looking at the light. There are some situations in which persons are required to make complex perceptual judgments where autokinesis presents a problem. Night flying is one of these situations, the greatest danger coming from having to deal with lights on the ground during takeoff and landing. Some observers have also reported subjects' difficulty in telling when a once moving light actually stops. Geldard (1972) points out the related danger to pilots who must watch the lights of the next aircraft in a formation.

The perceptual experience in autokinesis is particularly susceptible to suggestion and group pressure. The most widely known work in this regard is that of Sherif (1935, 1937). He showed that if instructions were given as to the direction the light should move, subjects tended to see movement in that direction. Subjects in a group often see the same movement. Rechtschaffen and Mednich (1955) told subjects that the light would spell out specific words, and the subjects reported that it did! The words were ones relevant to each subject's personal life and in fact embarrassed some of them. Perhaps this could be a new Rorschach! Toch (1962) found that autokinesis within a light display was influenced by the form of the display. A "running" animal or person as a stationary stimulus was perceived to be moving forward, in the normal direction.

Most explanations of the autokinetic phenomenon have dealt with eye movements. One theory frequently held in the past was that the eyes cannot fixate for a long duration on a spot of light and therefore drift, causing apparent movements of the light. However, Guilford and Dallenbach in 1928 photographed eye movements during autokinesis and compared subjects' reports with the photographs. They found no correlation between the two, and the eye movements were not large enough to account for the autokinetic movement. Other experimenters report that autokinesis can occur without any eye movements. In one case, Matin and MacKinnon (1964) eliminated autokinetic movement by stabilizing the image on the retina. In another, Brosgole (1968) reported that autokinesis of a positive afterimage could be obtained.

The most widely accepted theory at present is that of Gregory and Zangwill (1963). Their theory says that when the eye fixates on a stationary light for a period of time, the eye muscles become fatigued. When this occurs, greater than normal signals must be sent to the eye muscles to maintain the fixation. Since these "supra-normal" signals are usually sent to cause the eyes to follow a moving stimulus, we see movement—although neither the image nor the eye is moving. The autokinetic phenomenon is due, then, to the fact that the system monitoring the outward commands for eye movements is misled by the fact that the eyes have been "told" to move in order to maintain fixation. This is the same perceptual system which enables us to separate movement of a stimulus from movement of our eyes. You will recall that in such a case, it is the absence or presence of a command to move the eyes which determines whether or not we perceive movement in the world around us.

The difficulty with this theory, as Gregory (1973) acknowledges, is the question of why this monitoring system is exact under normal conditions and inexact only in the presence of a single stimulus and in the dark. He suggests that under normal conditions and with large objects we assume the world to be stable. It will be important, however, for any comprehensive theory of autokinesis to consider this problem.

The Pulfrich Phenomenon

You can easily demonstrate this striking effect for yourself. Fasten a weight (a ring will do) to the end of a string about a meter long. You can either have a friend hold this pendulum for you or tape it in a doorway where it can swing freely. After you have caused it to swing from side to side in a direct path, place a dark filter (such as a sunglass lens or a piece of exposed film) over one eye and view the swinging pendulum with both eyes. Now it will appear to be moving in an elliptical path (see Figure 13-4). If the filter is over your left eye, the weight will seem to swing nearer to you as it goes from right to left, and farther away on its swing from left to right. Switch the filter to the other eye and you will get the opposite effect.

What causes the effect? The explanation is based on the difference in intensity of the light reaching the two eyes and the fact of stereoscopic depth. You will recall that the reaction time, along with other aspects of sensory response, is a function of intensity, obeying Bloch's law ($I \times T = K$). The eye that sees the weight through the filter has a longer latency of seeing the weight and so sees its position to be slightly retarded compared to the other eye. At each end of its swing when the weight is stopped both eyes will see it in the same place, but as it swings back the difference in latency occurs again, although the effect is reversed, and the weight therefore describes an elliptical path. Why the movement appears in depth follows directly from the facts of binocular disparity (see Figure 10-9).

A modern variation of the Pulfrich phenomenon was discovered by Enright (1970). He found that a distortion of apparent velocity occurred for a person looking out of the side window of a moving vehicle if the person was wearing a pair of sunglasses with only one lens. When the right lens was intact and he was looking out the right side window, the velocity seemed to be reduced and objects were nearer and smaller. When he looked out the left side window, the velocity appeared to be increased and objects were larger and farther away. In other words, the speed seemed to be decreased when the uncovered eye was in the leading position. The opposite effects were found when the lens was put over the other eye. Enright's explanation for this phenomenon is that if the filtered eye is the following eye it will perceive the environment a few milliseconds after the uncovered eye because of the filter and the motion of the observer. This is analogous to the situation in which the Pulfrich pendulum moves from left to right and the observer has a filter over his right eye; the weight appears closer to the observer. Of course, with the Pulfrich pendulum, the observer is stationary whereas he is moving in the Enright illusion.

The dwarfing in Enright's illusion occurs because although the objects appear to be closer, they still subtend the same visual angle. Therefore, we perceive the roadside objects as small. The altered velocity, according to Enright, can be explained on the same basis. For a given velocity of the observer, there is a reciprocal relationship between distance and apparent angular velocity of an object in the visual field. Therefore, if the objects are seen as being closer while still having the same horizontal angular velocity, they will have a reduced velocity relative to the observer.

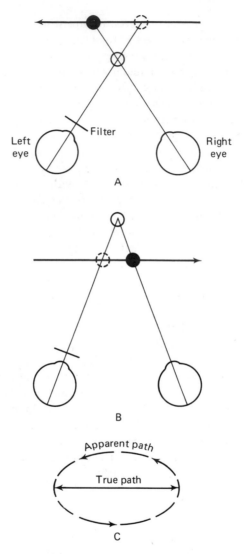

Figure 13-4 Illustration of the Pulfrich effect.

The Size-Weight Illusion

An illusion that involves two sensory systems, haptic and vision, is the size-weight illusion. The illusion is this: the larger the volume over which a given weight is distributed, the lighter that weight will feel. You have no doubt experienced this when lifting an empty box. Stevens and Rubin (1970) studied this illusion and provided a thorough description of the various factors involved.

These investigators had subjects make magnitude estimates of the apparent heaviness of a number of weights. The stimuli varied not only in weight, but also in volume and density. Thus any given weight was presented to the subject a number of times, each time in a bottle of a different size (volume). They found that, for any given volume, apparent heaviness grew as a power function of weight (Figure 13-5). And for any given weight, heaviness decreased as a function of volume, thus indicating the illusion (Figure 13-6). Stevens and Rubin were able to demonstrate several other interesting aspects of the illusion from the same data. Holding volume constant, the *growth* of heaviness with weight was steeper with heavier weights. The functions converge at a point corresponding to the heaviest weight that can be lifted, indicating that (1) the illusion will be greatest with lighter weights, and (2) the weightiest object that can be lifted will have the same heaviness regardless of volume. This experiment is an especially good example of the examination of a perceptual

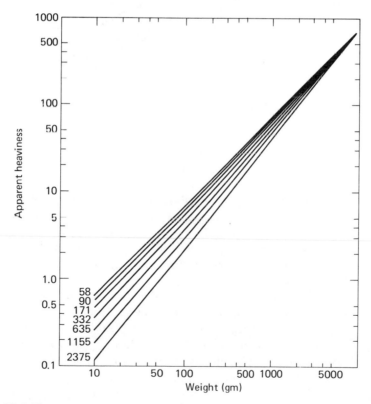

Figure 13-5 The size-weight illusion: Apparent heaviness as a function of weight. Each line is for a different volume of container lifted. The curves are idealized. [From Stevens, J. C., and Rubin, L. L. Psychophysical scales of apparent heaviness and the size weight illusion. *Perception and Psychophysics*, 1970, *8*, 225–30.]

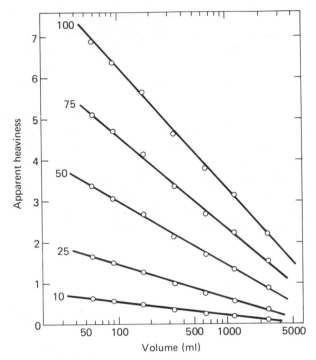

Figure 13-6 Apparent heaviness as a function of volume. These curves are based on Figure 13-5 and are plotted so as to show how heaviness decreases with volume of the container, thereby showing the size-weight illusion directly. Each curve is for a different weight. [From Stevens, J. C., and Rubin, L. L. Psychophysical scales of apparent heaviness and the size weight illusion. *Perception and Psychophysics*, 1970, *8*, 225–30.]

problem by direct psychophysical methods (Chapter 2). These results would have required thousands of tedious comparisons by older psychophysical techniques.

   If you are still questioning the importance of studying such a seemingly impractical topic as illusions, consider the following. As already indicated, the study of illusions has provided the impetus for the discovery of many important ideas—e.g., the lateral inhibitory mechanisms in the retina. By studying "misperception." theorists have been able to achieve a better understanding of "correct" perception. We might even say that the real test of a theory of perception is how it accounts for (or even predicts) illusory phenomena. Hopefully, this brief examination of illusions has spurred your interest in testing some aspects of perceptual theory.

14

The Contribution
of the Observer

Consider the crowd at the football game between Alma Mater and Rival University. To the casual fan the action on the field looks like a chaotic scramble only vaguely related to the location of the football. The knowledgeable fan, however, sees key situations of third and long, draw plays, play-action fakes, and missed blocks. Only after much experience, and perhaps some tutoring from Howard Cosell, does the casual fan begin to grasp what is taking place in front of him. However, not even all knowledgeable fans see the same things. One will perceive the local team as goats even when winning and another as heroes even when losing, the difference being seen as due to good or bad luck. A classic paper of social psychology concerned the differences in the perception of the 1951 Dartmouth-Princeton football game by fans of each school. It was considered a big game by both teams and was a rough one with many penalties and several key injuries. The conduct of the game became a controversial topic and even led to rancorous discussion in the respective local publications. Hastorf and Cantril (1954) conducted a study of those who had seen the game or films of the game. They found that Dartmouth students tended to feel that the game was rough and fair, but Princeton students saw the game as rough and dirty. (Guess who won?) Both sides felt the other team had started the rough play. It was quite clear from the overall responses of the students that two very different games had been seen by the fans of the two schools. Even with instant replay the same sort of thing is commonplace in the reporting of sports events in local newspapers.

Despite the existence of blatant differences in perception, of which many more examples could be given, we have treated the topic of perception as if all normal individuals would perceive the same stimulus in the same way. There are two good reasons for having used this approach. The first is that any good scientist works very hard to eliminate all variables that do not contribute to an understanding of the process under study. By and large, individual differences do not lead to clarification of perceptual phenomena (a notable exception is color blindness).

The second is that the area of individual differences in perception, although of great potential usefulness to personality and social psychology, remains controversial. The various phenomena that we will discuss, although they often seem compelling in their demonstration form, become much less impressive when they are subjected to the controls that are necessary for the scientific study of perception. However, there is a large literature on the role of the observer in perception. Many psychologists define various areas of psychology in perceptual terms; personality, for example, might be roughly defined as differences among people in their perception of the world, or learning as a change in perception, and so forth. This chapter will consider a number of these areas where perception overlaps with personality, social, and learning theory.

EFFECTS OF VALUES AND NEEDS

During the 'forties and early 'fifties there was a great burst of research on the effect of a subject's needs, motivation, and values on his perception. Of the vast literature on this topic we will consider the work of Postman, Bruner and McGinnies because it is typical and has also achieved quite some notice. Postman et al. (1948) first categorized their subjects on the basis of their interests as measured by the Allport-Vernon scale of values. Then they measured the subjects' duration thresholds for recognizing tachistoscopically presented words that related to the various interest categories. They found that subjects' duration thresholds were a function of their interest patterns. For those areas in which the subject's interest was high the thresholds were low and vice versa.

In a similar study McGinnies (1949) had his subjects recognize "taboo" words such as "belly," "bitch," "raped," and the like among a list of neutral words presented tachistoscopically. He found that the thresholds for the "taboo" words were higher than those for the neutral words. The concepts of perceptual defense and perceptual vigilance were invoked to account for these results. It was proposed that perceptual vigilance reduced the thresholds for those words related to the subject's interests and perceptual defense increased the thresholds for those words that were threatening to the subject.

Howes and Solomon (1950, 1951) advanced other explanations, one being the word frequency explanation. We know that words that occur more frequently in the language have lower recognition thresholds. From this it follows that words related to a person's interests would also have lower thresholds, simply because of their familiarity. The other explanation proposed by Howes and Solomon is even more prosaic. Imagine a student who has volunteered to be a subject in an experiment. He is not sure what is expected of him so he is being quite circumspect. Something is flashed on the screen. It is hard to make it out, but it looks like it might be "whore." But would the experimenter put that word on the screen? What would he think if I said "whore" and it was only "where." I'll try "where." (It helps to remember that this experiment was done in the late 'forties before the liberalization of speech mores.) It would not take much of this sort of bias to produce a higher threshold for the "taboo" words.

Eriksen (1963) and others have extended this type of work and related the findings to personality characteristics of the subjects. Using material known to be anxiety arousing to the particular subjects, it was found that some subjects showed lower thresholds for the anxiety-arousing material and others higher thresholds. They were termed sensitizers and repressors, respectively. There has been much debate and research concerning the question of whether the differences in threshold are true perceptual differences or are differences in the subjects' response criteria. Eriksen concludes (1963) that it is only the response occurrence that is affected by the subjects' needs and not the perceptual process per se.

One other aspect of the McGinnies experiment deserves comment. McGinnies measured the subjects' galvanic skin response (GSR) as well as their verbal response. (The GSR is taken to be a measure of anxiety.) He found that the GSR often indicated that the word was perceived one trial previous to its correct detection. (He used the method of ascending limits, so that if the subject said *no* on a given trial the same stimulus was flashed again with longer duration until he recognized it.) McGinnies suggested that the GSR response was an indicator of an unconscious process.

Eriksen (1960) has pointed out certain fallacies of these experiments that are important for an understanding of the relation between perception and verbal report. He showed that the GSR, rather than being prior to or more "objective" than the verbal response, is simply another response to the stimulus that is partially correlated with the verbal response. In other words, sometimes when the verbal response is negative, the GSR will be positive (subception), and at other times the GSR will be negative when the verbal response is positive. One is not necessarily more sensitive than the other. Each is correlated with the stimulus and at the same time is partially correlated with the other. Eriksen concluded (1960) that there is no other more sensitive indicator of perception than the verbal response.

An experiment by Zajonc (1962) confirms Eriksen's conclusion. He had subjects learn a list of "paired associates." In this task a stimulus word is flashed on the screen and the subject's job is to say the correct response word before the correct pair is flashed on the screen. Some of the stimulus words were "taboo" words and others were neutral. The same was true of the response words. Stimulus words were paired with response words in such a way that all possible types of combinations occurred: taboo-taboo, taboo-neutral, neutral-taboo, and neutral-neutral. After the list was learned, Zajonc measured the duration threshold for recognition of the stimulus words by having the subjects respond, not with the stimulus word, but with the response word that they had just learned as its paired associate. Now he was in a position to separate out any perceptual defense effect from a response bias. It turned out that the thresholds for seeing the stimulus words depended only on what the subject had to say and not at all on whether the stimulus word was a taboo word or a neutral word.

You might think that Signal Detection Theory (Chapter 2) would make it possible to separate defense processsess (sensitivity, d') from response biases (β). Some investigators (e.g., Broadbent and Gregory, 1967) have applied SDT to this problem and found differences in sensitivity between emotional and neutral words. Others have found less impressive results. In general, however, the application of SDT to perceptual defense is not straightforward because of the nature of the stimuli and the task involved. Consequently the results that have been obtained are difficult to interpret.

Although the position we have taken probably represents the consensus, Erdelyi (1974) has applied the information-processing approach to the problem of perceptual defense. He argues that since there are many steps in the processing of information by the perceptual system, there are many places at which perceptual selectivity could operate. Erdelyi suggests that perceptual defense can be expected to operate in such a system and that the objections to perceptual defense such as those raised above fail to take the complexity of the perceptual system into account. It remains to be seen whether this approach will finally provide convincing evidence in favor of perceptual defense.

EFFECTS OF CULTURE

There has not been a great deal of work on the effects of culture on perception, no doubt partly because of the difficulty of conducting adequately controlled studies.

Illusions

An extensive and careful study was performed by Segall, Campbell, and Herskovits (1966) comparing a number of Western and non-Western cultures living in varied environments (desert, forest, savanna and urban.) The study consisted of obtaining measures of various common geometrical illusions. It was found that persons from Western cultures were more susceptible to the Müller-Lyer illusion than those from non-Western cultures. This was attributed to the Westerners' greater experience with "carpentered" environments, having many right angles that serve as cues to depth and size. On the other hand, non-

Western cultures showed generally greater susceptibility to the horizontal-vertical illusion than the Western cultures. This was attributed to experiences with open vistas where vertical lines would be interpreted as lines receding toward the horizon and thus overestimated. Leibowitz et al. (1969) found that American students were more susceptible to the Ponzo perspective illusion than students from Guam, where the terrain is hilly and forested, and who therefore had little experience with open vistas. Furthermore they had never seen a railroad track, the most common everyday example of the Ponzo illusion. In this study, the effect of the illusion was about twice as great for the American student as for the Guamanian student. One should not, however, overemphasize the effects of culture on illusions for it has been shown that the Müller-Lyer illusion is seen by pigeons (Malott et al., 1967).

Color

There is considerable evidence that there may be cultural differences in color experience. Most primitive languages lack words for some of the psychologically primary hues, most often the short wavelength, or blue, end of the spectrum. Many cultures do not discriminate between blue and green. Does this indicate a difference in perception per se, or only the use of language? Bornstein (1973) has summarized a large body of evidence indicating that most cultures which fail to distinguish short wavelengths linguistically belong to the more pigmented races. There is a well-known correlation between degree of skin pigmentation and the amount of yellow pigment in the eye. A yellow pigment will pass long wavelengths and filter out short wavelengths. This has two important advantages. First, it protects the retina against ultraviolet light. Second, it improves visual acuity because short wavelengths are more subject to chromatic aberration in a non-color-corrected optical system such as the eye. Bornstein suggests that these advantages have caused eye pigmentation to be selectively adapted at the expense of color vision in the case of peoples living in tropical regions. Although this explanation is plausible, the question remains whether the amount of weakness in the short wavelength region is sufficient to account for the absence of blue and green color words.

Woodworth (1910) suggested many years ago that cultural differences in color names may be accounted for on a utilitarian basis. If color names developed only when it was necessary to label abstract color, as distinct from an object that always has a certain color, then blue and green would be less likely to be developed as names because they are "background" colors. The sky is generally blue and grass green. When it would be necesary to indicate a deviation from those conditions, the sky can be called cloudy and the grass dry. Abstract color is more important when identifying objects such as animals and fruit that have colors in the red end of the spectrum. To this day the English language contains more abstract color names in the red end of the spectrum than in the blue end.

In summary, the question still seems open. More-highly pigmented peoples are less discriminative to colors in the blue end of the spectrum compared to less-pigmented peoples, and this may account for some of the differences—but these peoples are not blue-blind in the usual sense. It seems likely that color names developed only when needed as abstract concepts, and that this occurred first in technological cultures with an assist from the somewhat better blue sensitivity of peoples outside the tropical regions.

Perception of Pictorial Material

There has been considerable work on the question of cultural differences in the perception of pictorial material (e.g. Miller, 1973). There is no doubt that cultural differences in pictorial *representation* do exist. The question here is whether there are cultural differences in the perception of objects, particularly in depth perception in photographs and other pictures with true perspective. One might ask why there should be any differences in picture perception. As discussed in Chapter 10, a picture contains not only depth cues, but also certain cues to the fact that it exists on a flat surface. These flatness cues conflict with the depth cues and may be particularly confusing to persons unfamiliar with pictures. There are a number of reports that people from certain primitive cultures unfamiliar with pictures have difficulty perceiving depth, and some-times even in perceiving objects, in pictures. Many of these studies are difficult to interpret because of ambiguities in the question asked the subject and doubts about the rapport between subject and experimenter. A typical procedure is to present two pictures of an object, one in true perspective and the other in complex frontal view. The first picture conveys the normal retinal projection of the object at one viewpoint; the second picture represents more information about the object but from several different viewpoints simultaneously. African natives generally prefer the complex frontal drawing as a representation of familiar objects, but they could more easily pick out the correct three-dimensional model of an object using a conventional perspective picture than from a complex frontal picture (Deregowski, 1969, 1972). In sum, it seems that a fairly small amount of practice with pictures may be necessary before objects will be recognized, but recognition of unfamiliar objects may be better from true-perspective pictures than from complex-frontal view pictures. However, African natives generally prefer those pictures that present more information about an object even if perspective is not consistent.

The phenomenon of binocular rivalry has been used in studying cultural effects on perception. Recall that if a slightly different scene is presented to each eye, the two scenes will fuse into a single picture having depth. If they are too different, only one or the other will be seen. Bagby (1957) showed pairs of pictures to Mexicans and Americans. One of each pair showed scenes typical of Mexican culture and the other of American culture. They were different enough so that they would not fuse and thus only one could be seen at a time. The subjects tended to report seeing those pictures from their own culture. In this study the presentation time was 15 seconds, making it possible for subjects to see both pictures and selectively report the one that was more familiar to them. A similar study comparing perception of violent scenes by students taking police training and by control students makes this less likely (Toch and Schulte, 1961). In this study, a violent scene was presented to one eye and a neutral scene to the other for 0.5 sec. Advanced police-training students saw over twice as many violent scenes as the control students. The possibility that the difference could be attributed to personality differences between those who become policemen and those who do not was tested by considering a third group that was beginning police training. They saw slightly more violent scenes than the controls but still only about half as many as the advanced police trainees.

EFFECTS OF PERSONALITY

Projective tests such as the Rorschach, Thematic Apperception Test, the Blacky test, and others are considered to be perceptual tests of needs and/or personality. The person viewing the material is believed to project his needs or personality into the ambiguous material. There is an enormous literature on the validity of these various tests, particularly the Rorschach. In general it may be said that, at best, these tests are not very reliable indicators of personality. The more ambiguous the material, the more variable the responses become, which is not surprising, and the greater the opportunity there is for deviant behavior to manifest itself. The problem with the projective test is that other more direct measures of deviance are more reliable and valid. From these and other considerations it does not seem likely that deviance should be conceived to be a distortion of perception. The less ambiguous the perceptual material, the less difference there is between normals and deviates.

There is, however, one line of research that indicates a reliable influence of personality on perceptual behavior. Witkin and his associates (Witkin et al., 1954) find large differences in the perception of the upright among individuals. Some are able to orient themselves in the vertical plane with little interference from conflicting visual cues whereas others are heavily dependent on the visual cues almost to the exclusion of the gravitational cues. The first type, known as field independent, also are able to orient a luminous rod with little influence from the surrounding frame in an otherwise dark room whereas the other group, the field dependent, are influenced largely by the orientation of the frame. Field dependents have more trouble identifying hidden figures such as the hidden cube than do field independents. This, in itself, would not be very interesting except for the fact that field-dependent persons show personality differences from field independents.

Field independents have higher IQ's but this is due to better performance on those parts of the intelligence tests that measure perception. The field independent is more independent in social settings and has a more definite awareness of his role, status, and needs. Boys are more field independent than girls and field independence increases with age. It should not be concluded that one or the other mode of perceiving is evidence of better adjustment. Each group tends to have its own characteristic types of maladjustment when they occur. Interestingly, it has been found that field-independent boys have mothers who tend to foster independence and growth more than those of field-dependent boys. It should be noted, however, that these labels do not constitute exclusive categories but instead a continuum of field dependence.

PERCEPTUAL LEARNING

E. J. Gibson (1953, 1969, Chapter 9) has reviewed a large number of experiments indicating that perception improves with practice. Many experiments on detection and discrimination thresholds and recognition and identification tasks show improvement with practice. Interestingly, it is not necessary for the subject to respond overtly or to be differentially reinforced for the performance to improve. Apparently the perceiver learns to attend to certain aspects of the stimulus with practice and to sort out the identifying features of the stimulus.

In a typical experiment, Gibson and Gibson (1955) had subjects look at a standard scribble and then match identical scribbles presented later. Their performance improved as they went through the series until after a few trials they no longer made errors. This occurred despite the fact that they received neither negative nor positive feedback.

Sexing of newly hatched chicks is a commercially important task that allows farmers to avoid having to spend time and feed raising birds that will not lay eggs. There are slight external differences between the sexes but they are extremely subtle. Nevertheless, it is possible for a chick sexer to obtain nearly 100% discrimination, with practice. Interestingly, the method used in teaching a person to sex chicks is by example rather than by principle (Lunn, 1948, from Gibson, 1969).

Learning to discriminate species of trees is another clear example of perceptual learning. In this case some of the cues are easily learned—for example, fir trees have flat needles attached to the sides of the twig whereas spruces have needles that are diamond shaped in cross section attached at any point around the twig—but other differences are rather difficult to verbalize, such as that between a red and a black oak.

Because perceptual learning does take place, it is advisable to give the subject a certain amount of practice before collecting the "real data" in a perceptual experiment. On the other hand it is worth noting that the vaunted ability of experts to identify wines or perfumes and the like does not exceed by very much what a layman could do with a modest amount of practice.

Other effects that are not attributable to practice alone but are dependent at least in part on developmental changes have been discussed in Chapter 12.

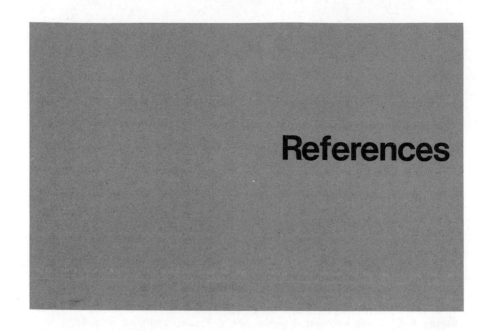

References

Ames, A. Visual perception and the rotating trapezoidal window. *Psych. Monographs,* 1951, *324,* entire issue.

Amoore, J. E. The stereochemical theory of olfaction: 1. Identification of the seven primary odours. *Proceedings of the Scientific Section of the Toilet Goods Association,* 1962a, *37* (Suppl.), 1–12.

Amoore, J. E. The stereochemical theory of olfaction: 2. Elucidation of the stereochemical properties of the olfactory receptor sites. *Proceedings of the Scientific Section of the Toilet Goods Association,* 1962b, *37* (Suppl.), 13–23.

Anstis, S. M., and Moulden, B. P. Aftereffect of seen movement: Evidence for peripheral and central components. *Quart. J. Exp. Psych.,* 1970, *22,* 222–29.

Aronson, E., and Rosenbloom, S. Space perception in early infancy: Perception within a common auditory-visual space. *Science,* 1971, *172,* 1161–63.

Attneave, F. Some informational aspects of visual perception. *Psych. Rev.,* 1954, *61,* 183–93.

Bagby, W. A cross-cultural study of perceptual predominance in binocular rivalry. *J. Abnormal and Soc. Psych.,* 1957, *54,* 331–34.

Banks, W. P. Reaction time as a measure of summation of warmth. *Perception and Psychophysics,* 1973, *13,* 321–27.

Barlow, H. B., and Levick, J. M. The mechanism of directionally sensitive units in the rabbit's retina. *J. Physiol.* (London), 1965, *178,* 477–504.

Bartoshuk, L. M. Taste mixtures: Is mixture suppression related to compression? *Physiology and Behavior,* 1975, *14,* 643–49.

Bartoshuk, L. M., Harned, M. A., and Parks, L. H. Taste of water in the cat: Effects on sucrose preference. *Science,* 1971, *171,* 699–701.

Bartoshuk, L. M., Lee, C.-H., and Scarpellino, R. Sweet taste of water induced by artichoke (Cynara scolymus). *Science,* 1972, *178,* 988–90.

Bartoshuk, L. M., McBurney, D. H., and Pfaffmann, C. Taste of sodium chloride solutions after adaptation to sodium chloride: Implications for the "Water taste." *Science,* 1964, *143,* 967–68.

271

Beidler, L. M. Innervation of rat fungiform papilla. In C. Pfaffmann (ed.), *Olfaction and taste (III)*. New York: Rockefeller University Press, 1969, pp. 352–69.

Békésy, G. von. The variation of phase along the basilar membrane with sinusoidal vibration. *J. Acoust. Soc. America*, 1947, *19*, 452–60.

Békésy, G. von. The ear. *Scientific American*, 1957, *197* (2), 66–78.

Békésy, G. von. Taste theories and the chemical stimulation of single papillae. *J. Appl. Physiol.*, 1966, *21*, 1–9.

Békésy, G. von. *Sensory inhibition.* Princeton, N.J.: Princeton University Press, 1967.

Berglund, B., Berglund, U., Lindvall, T., and Svensson, L. T. A quantitative principle of perceived intensity summation in odor mixtures. *J. Exp. Psych.*, 1973, *100*, 29–38.

Binns, H. Visual and tactual judgment as illustrated in a practical experiment. *Brit. J. Psych.*, 1937, *27*, 404–10.

Bishop, H. E. Innateness and learning in the visual perception of direction. (Doctoral dissertation, University of Chicago, 1959). Ann Arbor, Michigan: University Microfilms, 1959, No. 4924.

Blakemore, C., and Cooper, G. F. Development of the brain depends on the visual environment. *Nature*, 1970, *228*, 477–78.

Boring, E. G. A new ambiguous figure. *Am. J. Psych.*, 1930, *42*, 444–45.

Boring, E. G. The moon illusion. *Am. J. Physics*, 1943, *11*, 55–60.

Boring, E. G. *A history of experimental psychology.* New York: Appleton-Century-Crofts, 1957.

Boring, L. D., and Boring, E. G. Temporal judgments after sleep. In *Studies in psychology (E. B. Titchener commemorative volume)*. Worcester, Mass.: L. N. Wilson, 1917.

Bornstein, M. H. Color vision and color naming: A psychophysical hypothesis of cultural difference. *Psych. Bull.*, 1973, *80*, 257–85.

Bossom, J., and Hamilton, C. R. Interocular transfer of prism-altered coordinations in split-brain monkeys. *J. Comp. Physiol. Psych.*, 1963, *56*, 769–74.

Bower, T. G. R. The object in the world of the infant. *Scientific American*, 1971, *225* (4), 30–38.

Bower, T. G. R. Stimulus variables determining space perception in infants. *Science*, 1965, *149*, 88–89.

Bower, T. G. R., Broughton, J. M., and Moore, M. K. The coordination of visual and tactual input in infants. *Perception and Psychophysics*, 1970, *8*, 51–53.

Brattgard, S. The importance of adequate stimulation for the chemical composition of retinal ganglion cells during early postnatal development. *Acta Radiologica Supplement*, 1952, *96*.

Breitmeyer, B. G. and Ganz, L. Implications of sustained and transient channels for theories of visual pattern masking, saccadic suppression, and information processing. *Psych. Rev.* 1976, *83*, 1–36.

Broadbent, D. E. *Perception and communication.* London: Pergamon Press, 1958.

Broadbent, D. E. and Gregory, M. Perception of emotionally toned words. *Nature*, 1967, *215*, 581–84.

Brosgole, L. The autokinesis of an after-image. *Psychonomic Science*, 1968, *12*, 233–34.

Brown, K. T., Watanabe, K., and Murakami, M. Early and late receptor potentials of monkey cones and rods. *Cold Spring Harbor Symposia on Quantitative Biology*, 1965, *30*, 457–82.

Brown, P. K., and Wald, G. Visual pigments in single rods and cones of the human retina. *Science*, 1964, *144*, 45–52.

Brown, R. H. Velocity discrimination and the intensity-time relation. *J. Optical Soc. Am.*, 1955, *45*, 189–92.

Bujas, Z. Kontrast- und Hemmungserscheinungen bei disparaten simultanen Geschmacksreizen. *Acta Instituti Psychologica Universitatis Zagrebensis*, 1937, *2*, 3–12.

Bujas, Z. L'adaptation gustative et son mecanisme. *Acta Instituti Psychologici, Zagreb*, 1953, *17*, 1–11.

Bujas, Z., and Ostojcic, A. La sensibilité gustative en fonction de la surface excitée. *Acta Instituti Psychologica Universitatis Zagrebensis*, 1941, *13*, 1–20.

Cain, W. S. Spatial discrimination of cutaneous warmth. *Am. J. Psych.*, 1973, *86*, 169–81.

Cain, W. S. Perception of odor intensity and the time course of olfactory adaptation. *ASHRAE Transactions*, 1974, *80*, 53–75.

Campos, J. J., Langer, A., and Krowitz, A. Cardiac responses on the visual cliff in prelocomotor human infants. *Science*, 1970, *170*, 196–97.

Chow, K. L., Riesen, A. H., and Newell, F. W. Degeneration of retinal ganglion cells in infant chimpanzees reared in darkness. *J. Comp. Neurol.*, 1957, *107*, 27–42.

Collings, V. B. Human taste response as a function of locus of stimulation on the tongue and soft palate. *Perception and Psychophysics*, 1974, *16*, 169–74.

Collins, W. E. Vestibular responses from figure skaters. *Aerospace Medicine*, 1966, *37*, 1098–1104.

Cone, R. A. Early receptor potential of the vertebrate eye. *Cold Spring Harbor Symposia on Quantitative Biology*, 1965, *30*, 483–93.

Cornsweet, T. N. The staircase method in psychophysics. *Am. J. Psych.*, 1962, *75*, 485–91.

Cornsweet, T. N. *Visual perception*. New York: Academic Press, 1970.

Davis, H. Some principles of sensory receptor action. *Physiol. Rev.*, 1961, *41*, 391–416.

Davis, H., Benson, R. W., Covell, W. P., Fernandez, C., Goldstein, R., Katsuki, Y., Legouix, J.-P., McAuliffe, D. R., and Tasaki, I. Acoustic trauma in the guinea pig. *J. Acoust. Soc. America*, 1953, *25*, 1180–89.

Davis, H., and Silverman, S. R. *Hearing and deafness*. New York: Holt, Rinehart & Winston, 1960.

Day, R. H. Visual spatial illusions: A general explanation. *Science*, 1972, *175*, 1335–40.

Deich, R. F. Children's perception of differently oriented shapes: Word recognition. *Perceptual and Motor Skills*, 1971, *32*, 695–700.

Denes, P. B., and Pinson, E. N. *The speech chain*. Bell Telephone Laboratories, 1963.

Deregowski, J. B. A pictorial paradox. *Acta Psychologica*, 1969, *31*, 365–74.

Deregowski, J. B. Pictorial perception and culture. *Scientific American*, 1972, *227* (5), 82–88.

Deutsch, J. A. *The structural basis of behavior*. Chicago: University of Chicago Press, 1960.

DeValois, R. L. Behavioral and electrophysiological studies of primate vision. In W. D. Neff (ed.), *Contributions to sensory physiology* (Vol. 1). New York: Academic Press, 1965, pp. 137–78.

Ditchburn, R. N., and Ginsborg, B. L. Vision with a stabilized retinal image. *Nature*, 1952, *170*, 36–37.

Doane, B. K., Mahatoo, W., Heron, W., and Scott, T. H. Changes in perceptual function after isolation. *Canad. J. Psych.*, 1959, *13*, 210–19.

Dowling, J. E., and Boycott, B. B. Organization of the primate retina: Electron microscopy. *Proceedings of Royal Society* (London), Ser. B 1966, *166*, 80–111.

Duncker, K. Über induzierte Bewegung. *Psychologische Forschung*, 1929, *12*, 180–259.

Ekman, G., Berglund, B., Berglund, U., and Lindvall, T. Perceived intensity of odor as a function of time of adaptation. *Scand. J. Psych.*, 1967, *8*, 177–86.

Elkind, D., Koegler, R. R., and Koegler, G. E. Studies in perceptual development: II. Part-whole perception. *Child Development*, 1964, *35*, 81–90.

Elliott, L. L. Backward masking: Monotic and dichotic conditions. *J. Acoust. Soc. America*, 1962, *34*, 1108–15.

Encyclopedia of World Art. Perspective (Vol. 11). New York: McGraw-Hill, 1966, pp. 183–221.

Engen, T., and McBurney, D. H. Magnitude and category scales of the pleasantness of odors. *J. Exp. Psych.*, 1964, *68*, 435–40.

Enright, J. T. Distortions of apparent velocity: A new optical illusion. *Science*, 1970, *168*, 464–67.

Erdelyi, M. H. A new look at the New Look: Perceptual defense and vigilance. *Psych. Rev.*, 1974, *81*, 1–25.

Eriksen, C. W. Discrimination and learning without awareness: A methodological survey and evaluation. *Psych. Rev.*, 1960, *67*, 279–300.

Eriksen, C. W. Perception and personality. In J. W. Wepman and R. W. Heine (eds.), *Concepts of personality*. Chicago: Aldine, 1963, pp. 31–62.

Fantz, R. L. The origin of form perception. *Scientific American*, 1961, *204* (5), 66–72.

Fantz, R. L. Ontogeny of perception. In A. M. Schrier, H. F. Harlow, and F. Stollnitz (eds.), *Behavior of nonhuman primates: Modern research trends* (Vol. 2). New York: Academic Press, 1965, pp. 365–403.

Foley, J. P., Jr. An experimental investigation of the effect of prolonged inversion of the visual field in the rhesus monkey. *J. Genetic Psych.*, 1940, *56*, 21–51.

Foulke, E., and Sticht, T. G. Review of research on the intelligibility and comprehension of accelerated speech. *Psych. Bull.*, 1969, *72*, 50–62.

Fox, R., Lehmkuhle, S. W., and Westendorf, D. H. Falcon visual acuity. *Science*, 1976, *192*, 263–64.

Fredericks, R. S., and Groves, M. Pupil change and stimulus pleasantness. *Proceedings of the 79th Annual Convention of the American Psychological Association*, 1971, *6*, 371–72.

Freedman, S. J., Wilson, L., and Rekosh, J. H. Compensation for auditory rearrangement in hand-ear coordination. *Perceptual and Motor Skills*, 1967, *24*, 1207–10.

Frisby, J. P. Real and apparent movement—same or different mechanisms? *Vision Research*, 1972, *12*, 1051–56.

Galambos, R. Suppression of auditory nerve activity by stimulation of efferent fibers to cochlea. *J. Neurophysiol.*, 1956, *19*, 424–37.

Galambos, R., Schwartzkopff, J., and Rupert, A. Microelectrode study of superior olivary nuclei. *Am. J. Physiol.*, 1959, *197*, 527–36.

Galanter, E. Contemporary psychophysics. In R. Brown et al. (eds.), *New directions in psychology*. New York: Holt, Rinehart & Winston, 1962, 89–156.

Gardner, M. Dermo-optical perception: A peek down the nose. *Science*, 1966, *151*, 654–57.

Garner, W. R. The effect of frequency spectrum on temporal integration of energy in the ear. *J. Acoust. Soc. America*, 1947, *19*, 808–15.

Gazzaniga, M. S. The split brain in man. *Scientific American*, 1967, *217* (2), 24–29.

Geldard, F. A. Vision, audition and beyond. In W. D. Neff (ed.), *Contributions to sensory physiology, 4*, 1970. New York: Academic Press, 1–17.

Geldard, F. A. *The human senses* (2nd Ed.). New York: Wiley, 1972.

Gibson, E. J. Improvement in perceptual judgments as a function of controlled practice or training. *Psych. Bull.*, 1953, *50*, 401–31.

Gibson, E. J. *Principles of perceptual learning and development*. New York: Appleton-Century-Crofts, 1969.

Gibson, E. J., and Walk, R. D. The visual cliff. *Scientific American*, 1960, *202* (4), 64–71.

Gibson, J. J. The perception of visual surfaces. *Am. J. Psych.*, 1950a, *63*, 367–384.

Gibson, J. J. The perception of the visual world. Boston: Houghton Mifflin, 1950b.

Gibson, J. J. Observations on active touch. *Psych. Rev.*, 1962, *69*, 477–91.

Gibson, J. J. *The senses considered as perceptual systems*. Boston: Houghton Mifflin, 1966.

Gibson, J. J., and Gibson, E. J. Perceptual learning: Differentiation or enrichment? *Psych. Rev.*, 1955, *62*, 32–41.

Goss, C. M. (ed.) *Gray's anatomy of the human body* (29th Ed.). Philadelphia: Lea & Febiger, 1973.

Graham, C. H. (ed.), *Vision and visual perception*. New York: Wiley, 1965.

Graham, C. H., and Cook, C. Visual acuity as a function of intensity and exposure-time. *Am. J. Psych.*, 1937, *49*, 654–61.

Graham, C. H., and Margaria, R. Area and the intensity-time relation in the peripheral retina. *Am. J. Physiol.*, 1935, *113*, 299–305.

Graybiel, A., Clark, B., MacCorquodale, K., and Hupp, D. I. Role of vestibular nystagmus in visual perception of moving target in dark. *Am. J. Psych.*, 1946, *59*, 259–66.

Green, D. M., and Swets, J. A. *Signal detection theory and psychophysics*. New York: Wiley, 1966.

Gregory, R. L. *Eye and brain: The psychology of seeing*. New York: McGraw-Hill, 1973.

Gregory, R. L., and Wallace, J. G. Recovery from early blindness. *Experimental Psychology Society Monograph 2*. Cambridge: Heffer, 1963.

Gregory, R. L., and Zangwill, O. L. The origin of the autokinetic effect. *Quart. J. Exp. Psych.*, 1963, *15*, 255–61.

Guilford, J. P., and Dallenbach, K. M. A study of the autokinetic sensation. *Am. J. Psych.*, 1928, *40*, 83–91.

Gulliksen, H. Louis Leon Thurstone, experimental and mathematical psychologist. *American Psychologist,* 1968, *23,* 786–802.

Hahn, H. Die adaptation des geschmacksinnes. *Zeitschrift für Sinnesphysiologie,* 1934, *65,* 105–45.

Hall, J. L., II. Binaural interaction in the accessory superior-olivary nucleus of the cat. *J. Acoust. Soc. America,* 1965, *37,* 814–23.

Hardy, M. Observations on the innervation of the macula sacula in man. *Anatom. Rec.,* 1934, *59,* 403–18.

Harmon, L. D., and Julesz, B. Masking in visual recognition: Effects of two-dimensional filtered noise. *Science,* 1973, *180,* 1194–97.

Harper, H. W., Jay, J. R., and Erickson, R. P. Chemically evoked sensations from single human taste papillae. *Physiology and Behavior,* 1966, *1,* 319–25.

Harris, C. S. Adaptation to displaced vision: Visual, motor or proprioceptive change? *Science,* 1963, *140,* 812–13.

Harris, C. S. Perceptual adaptation to inverted, reversed and displaced vision. *Psych. Rev.,* 1965, *72,* 419–44.

Harris, C. S., and Gibson, A. R. Is orientation-specific color adaptation due to edge detectors, afterimages, or "dipoles"? *Science,* 1968, *162,* 1506–7.

Hastorf, A. H., and Cantril, H. They saw a game: A case study. *J. Abnormal Soc. Psych.,* 1954, *49,* 129–34.

Hebb, D. O. The innate organization of visual activity, I. Perception of figure by rats raised in total darkness. *J. Genetic Psych.,* 1937, *51,* 101–26.

Hecht, S. Vision: II. The nature of the photoreceptor process. In C. Murchison (ed.), *A handbook of general experimental psychology.* Worcester, Mass.: Clark University Press, 1934, pp. 704–828.

Hecht, S., and Shlaer, S. Intermittent stimulation by light. V. The relation between intensity and critical frequency for different parts of the spectrum. *J. Gen. Physiol.,* 1936, *19,* 965–79.

Hecht, S., Shlaer, S., and Pirenne, M. H. Energy, quanta, and vision. *J. Gen. Physiol.,* 1942, *25,* 819–40.

Hein, A., and Diamond, R. M. Contrasting development of visually triggered and guided movements in kittens with respect to interocular interlimb equivalence. *J. Comp. Physiol. Psych.,* 1971, *76,* 219–24.

Hein, A., Held, R., and Gower, E. C. Development and segmentation of visually controlled movement by selective exposure during rearing. *J. Comp. Physiol. Psych.,* 1970, *73,* 181–87.

Held, R. Plasticity in sensory-motor systems. *Scientific American,* 1965, *213* (5), 84–94.

Held, R., and Bossom, J. Neonatal deprivation and adult rearrangement: Complementary techniques for analyzing plastic sensory-motor coordinations. *J. Comp. Physiol. Psych.,* 1961, *54,* 33–37.

Held, R., and Hein, A. V. Adaptation of disarranged hand-eye coordination contingent upon re-afferent stimulation. *Perceptual and Motor Skills,* 1958, *8,* 87–90.

Held, R., and Hein, A. V. Movement produced stimulation in the development of visually-guided behavior. *J. Comp. Physiol. Psych.,* 1963, *56,* 872–76.

Hellman, R. P., and Zwislocki, J. J. Monaural loudness function at 1000 cps and interaural summation. *J. Acoust. Soc. America,* 1963, *35,* 856–65.

Helson, H. *Adaptation level theory.* New York: Harper & Row, 1964.

Henderson, D. C. The relationships among time, distance, and intensity as determinants of motion discrimination. *Perception and Psychophysics,* 1971, *10,* 313–20.

Hernandez-Peón, R., Scherrer, H., and Jouvet, M. Modification of electrical activity in cochlear nucleus during "attention" in unanesthetized cats. *Science,* 1956, *123,* 331–32.

Heron, W., Doane, B. K., and Scott, T. H. Visual disturbances after prolonged perceptual isolation. *Canad. J. Psych.,* 1956, *10,* 13–18.

Hess, E. H. Space perception in the chick. *Scientific American,* 1956, *195* (1), 71–80.

Hess, E. H. Attitude and pupil size. *Scientific American,* 1965, *212* (4), 46–54.

Hochberg, J. Perception: 1. Color and shape. In J. W. Kling and L. A. Riggs (eds.), *Experimental psychology* (3rd Ed.), New York: Holt, Rinehart, & Winston, 1971, pp. 396–474.

von Holst, E., and Mittelstaedt, H. Das Reafferenz-prinzip. *Die Naturwissenschaften.* 1950. *20,* 464–67.

Hood, J. D. Studies in auditory fatigue and adaptation. *Acta Oto-Laryngologica,* Supplement, 1950, *92,* 1–57.

Howard, I. P., Craske, B., and Templeton, W. B. Visuomotor adaptation to discordant exafferent stimulation. *J. Exp. Psych.,* 1965, *70,* 189–91.

Howard, I. P., and Templeton, W. B. *Human spatial orientation.* New York: Wiley, 1966.

Howes, D., and Solomon, R. L. A note on McGuinnies' emotionality and perceptual defense. *Psych. Rev.,* 1950, *57,* 229–34.

Howes, D., and Solomon, R. L. Visual duration threshold as a function of word probability. *J. Exp. Psych.,* 1951, 401–10.

Hubel, D. H., and Wiesel, T. N. Receptive fields of single neurons in the cat's striate cortex. *J. Physiol.,* 1959, *148,* 574–91.

Hubel, D. H., and Wiesel, T. N. Receptive fields, binocular interaction and functional architecture in the cat's visual cortex. *J. Physiol.,* 1962, *160,* 106–54.

Hubel, D. H., and Wiesel, T. N. The period of susceptibility to the physiological effects of unilateral eye closure in kittens. *J. Physiol.,* 1970, *206,* 419–36.

Hunt, C. C., and McIntyre, A. K. Properties of cutaneous touch receptors in cat. *J. Physiol.,* 1960, *153,* 99–112.

Hunter, W. S., and Sigler, M. The span of visual discrimination as a function of time and intensity of stimulation. *J. Exp. Psych.,* 1940, *26,* 160–79.

Hurvich, L. M., and Jameson, D. Opponent processes as a model of neural organization. *Am. Psychologist,* 1974, *29,* 88–102.

Inhelder, B., and Piaget, J. *The growth of logical thinking from childhood through adolescence.* New York: Basic Books, 1958.

Inhelder, B., and Piaget, J. *The early growth of logic in the child.* New York: Harper & Row, 1959.

James, W. *The principles of psychology.* New York: Henry Holt, 1890 (Dover, 1950).

Johnson, B., and Beck, F. L. The development of space perception: I. Stereoscopic vision in preschool children. *J. Genetic Psych.,* 1941, *58,* 247–54.

Julesz, B. Binocular depth perception without familiarity cues. *Science,* 1964, *145,* 356–62.

Kagan, J. The growth of the "face" schema: Theoretical significance and methodological issues. In J. Hellmuth (ed.), *Exceptional infant.* Vol. 1. *The normal infant.* Seattle: Special Child Publications, 1967.

Kalil, R., and Freedman, S. J. Compensation for auditory re-arrangement in the absence of observer movement. *Perceptual and Motor Skills,* 1967, *24,* 475–78.

Kaufman, J., Belmont, I., Birch, H. G., and Zach, L. J. Tactile and visual sense system interaction: A developmental study using reaction time models. *Develop. Psychobiol.,* 1973, *6,* 165–76.

Kaufman, L. *Sight and mind.* New York: Oxford University Press, 1974.

Kaufman, L., and Rock, I. The moon illusion. *Scientific American,* 1962, *207* (1), 120–32.

Kellogg, W. N. Sonar system of the blind. *Science,* 1962, *137,* 399–404.

Kelly, D. H. Theory of flicker and transient responses, I. Uniform fields. *J. Optical Soc. America,* 1971, *61,* 537–46.

Kenshalo, D. R., Decker, T., and Hamilton, A. Spatial summation on the forehead, forearm, and back produced by radiant and conducted heat. *J. Comp. Physiol. Psych.,* 1967, *63,* 510–15.

Kenshalo, D. R., and Scott, H. H., Jr. Temporal course of thermal adaptation. *Science,* 1966, *151,* 1095–96.

Kiesow, F. Beiträge zur physiologischen psychologie des geschmacksinnes. *Philosophische Studien,* 1894, *10,* 523–61.

Klein, G. S. Semantic power of words measured through the interference with color naming. *Am. J. Psych.,* 1964, *77,* 576–88.

Kohler, I. Experiments with goggles. *Scientific American,* 1962, *206* (5), 62–72.

Kravitz, J. H., and Wallach, H. Adaptation to displaced vision contingent upon vibrating stimulation. *Psychonomic Science,* 1966, *6,* 465–66.

Krueger, L. E. David Katz's Der aufbau der tastwelt [The world of touch]: A synopsis. *Perception and Psychophysics,* 1970, *7,* 337–41.

Kuffler, S. W. Discharge patterns and functional organization of mammalian retina. *J. Neurophysiol.,* 1953, *16,* 37–68.

Leibowitz, H. W. The relation between the rate threshold for the perception of movement and luminance for various durations of exposure. *J. Exp. Psych.,* 1955, *49,* 209–14.

Leibowitz, H. W., Brislin, R., Perlmutter, L., and Hennessy, R. Ponzo perspective illusion as a manifestation of space perception. *Science,* 1969, *166,* 1174–76.

Lettvin, J. Y., Maturana, H. R., McCulloch, W. S., and Pitts, W. H. What the frog's eye tells the frog's brain. *Proceedings of the Institute of Radio Engineering,* 1959, *47,* 1940–51.

Libby, W. L., Lacy, B. C., and Lacey, J. I. Pupillary and cardiac activity during visual attention. *Psychophysiology,* 1973, *10,* 270–94.

Liberman, A. M. Some results of research on speech perception. *J. Acoust. Soc. America,* 1957, *29,* 117–23.

Lindsay, P. H., and Norman, D. A. *Human information processing.* New York: Academic Press, 1972.

Lindsley, D. B., Schreiner, L. H., Knowles, W. B., and Magoun, H. W. Behavioral and EEG changes following chronic brain stem lesions in the cat. *Electroencephal. and Clin. Neurophysiol.,* 1950, *2,* 483–98.

Lissmann, H. W. Electric location by fishes. *Scientific American,* 1963, *208* (3), 50–59.

London, I. D. A Russian report on the postoperative newly seeing. *Am. J. Psych.,* 1960, *73,* 478–82.

Ludvigh, E. J. Visual and stereoscopic activity for moving objects. In Spigel,

I. M. (ed.), *Readings in the study of visually perceived movement.* New York: Harper & Row, 1965.

Mach, E. *The analysis of sensation.* New York: Dover, 1959 (Reprint).

MacNichol, E. F., Jr. Retinal mechanisms of color vision. *Vision Research,* 1964, *4,* 119–33.

MacNichol, E. F., Jr., and Svaetichin, G. Electric responses from the isolated retinas of fishes. *Am. J. Ophthalmol.,* 1958, *46,* 26–40.

Mackworth, N. H., and Bruner, J. S. How adults and children search and recognize pictures. *Human Development,* 1970, *13,* 149–77.

Makous, W. L. Cutaneous color sensitivity: Explanation and demonstration. *Psych. Rev.,* 1966, *73,* 280–94.

Malott, R. W., Malott, M. K., and Pokrzywinski, J. The effects of outward pointing arrowheads on the Müeller-Lyer illusion in pigeons. *Psychonomic Science,* 1967, *9,* 55–56.

Marks, L. E. *Sensory processes: The new psychophysics.* New York: Academic Press, 1974.

Marks, L. E., and Stevens, J. C. The form of the psychophysical function near threshold. *Perception and Psychophysics,* 1968a, *4,* 315–18.

Marks, L. E., and Stevens, J. C. Perceived warmth and skin temperature as functions of the duration and level of thermal irradiation. *Perception and Psychophysics,* 1968b, *4,* 220–28.

Marks, L. E., and Stevens, J. C. Perceived cold and skin temperature as functions of stimulation level and duration. *Am. J. Psych.,* 1972, *85,* 407–19.

Marks, L. E., and Stevens, J. C. Temporal summation related to the nature of the proximal stimulus for the warmth sense. *Perception and Psychophysics,* 1973, *14,* 570–76.

Marks, W. B., Dobelle, W. H., and MacNichol, E. F., Jr. Visual pigments of single primate cones. *Science,* 1964, *143,* 1181–83.

Marler, P. Developments in the study of animal communication. In P. R. Bell (ed.) *Darwin's biological work.* London: Cambridge University Press, 1959, 150–206.

Masterton, B., and Diamond, I. T. Hearing: Central neural mechanisms. In E. C. Carterette and M. P. Friedman (eds.), *Handbook of perception* (Vol. III). New York: Academic Press, 1974, pp. 407–48.

Matin, L., and MacKinnon, G. E. Autokinetic movement: Selective manipulation of directional components by image stabilization. *Science,* 1964, *143,* 147–48.

McBurney, D. H. Effects of adaptation on human taste function. In C. Pfaffmann (ed.), *Third international symposium on olfaction and taste.* New York: Rockefeller University Press, 1969, 407–19.

McBurney, D. H., and Bartoshuk, L. M. Water taste in mammals. In D. Schneider (ed.), *Olfaction and Taste* IV. Stuttgart: Wissenschaftliche Verlagsgesellschaft, 1972, pp. 329–35.

McBurney, D. H., Collings, V. B., and Glanz, L. M. Temperature dependence of human taste responses. *Physiology and Behavior,* 1973, *11,* 89–94.

McBurney, D. H., Kasschau, R. A., and Bogart, L. M. The effect of adaptation on taste jnds. *Perception and Psychophysics,* 1967, *2,* 175–78.

McBurney, D. H., and Pfaffmann, C. Gustatory adaptation to saliva and sodium chloride. *J. Exp. Psych.,* 1963, *65,* 523–29.

McCollough, C. Color adaptation of edge-detectors in the human visual system. *Science,* 1965, *149,* 1115–16.

McCutcheon, N. B., and Saunders, J. Human taste papilla stimulation: Stability of quality judgments over time. *Science*, 1972, *175*, 214–16.

McGinnies, E. Emotionality and perceptual defense. *Psych. Rev.*, 1949, *39*, 242–55.

Meiselman, H. L. Does the sense of taste adapt completely? Paper presented at Eastern Psychological Association, 1974.

Melzack, R., and Wall, P. D. On the nature of cutaneous sensory mechanisms. *Brain*, 1962, *85*, 331–56.

Melzack, R., and Wall, P. D. Pain mechanisms: A new theory. *Science*, 1965, *150*, 971–79.

Meyer, M. E. Discrimination learning under various combinations of discrimination. *J. Comp. Physiol. Psych.*, 1964, *58*, 146–47.

Miller, R. J. Cross-cultural research in the perception of pictorial materials. *Psych. Bull.*, 1973, *80*, 135–50.

Mitchell, D. E., Freeman, R. D., Millodot, M., and Haegerstrom, G. Meridional amblyopia: Evidence for modification of the human visual system by early visual experience. *Vision Research.* 1973, *13*, 535–58.

Money, K. E. Motion sickness. *Physiol. Rev.*, 1970, *50*, 1–39.

Money, K. E., and Myles, W. S. Motion sickness and other vestibulo-gastric illnesses. In R. F. Naunton (Ed.) *The vestibular system.* New York: Academic Press, 1975, 371–77.

Moray, N. *Attention: Selective processes in vision and hearing.* London: Hutchenson Educational Ltd., 1969.

Moruzzi, G., and Magoun, H. W. Brain stem reticular formation and activation of the EEG. *Electroencephal. and Clin. Neurophysiol.*, 1949, *1*, 455–73.

Moulden, B. Adaptation to displaced vision: Reafference is a special case of the cue-discrepancy hypothesis. *Quart. J. Exp. Psych.*, 1971, *23*, 113–17.

Moulton, D. G., and Beidler, L. M. Structure and function in the peripheral olfactory system. *Physiol. Rev.*, 1967, *47*, 1–52.

Mozell, M. M. The spatiotemporal analysis of odorants at the level of the olfactory receptor sheet. *J. Gen. Physiol.*, 1966, *50*, 25–41.

Mozell, M. M. The chemical senses II. Olfaction. In J. W. Kling and L. R. Riggs (eds.), Woodworth and Schlosberg's *Experimental Psychology* (3rd Ed.). New York: Holt, Rinehart & Winston, 1971, pp. 193–222.

Murch, G. M. *Visual and auditory perception.* Indianapolis: Bobbs-Merrill, 1973.

Nafe, J. P., and Wagoner, K. S. The nature of pressure adaptation. *J. Gen. Psych.*, 1941, *25*, 323–51.

Orne, M. T. Hypnosis, motivation and the ecological validity of the psychological experiment. In W. J. Arnold and W. M. Page (eds.), *Nebraska Symposium on Motivation.* Lincoln: University of Nebraska Press, 1970, pp. 187–265.

Parrish, M., Lundy, R. M., and Leibowitz, H. W. Hypnotic age-regression and magnitudes of the Ponzo and Poggendorff illusions. *Science*, 1968, *159*, 1375–76.

Perkel, D. H., and Bullock, T. H. Neural coding. *Neurosciences Research Progress Bulletin*, 1968, *6*, entire 3rd issue.

Pettigrew, J. D., and Freeman, R. D. Visual experience without lines: Effect on developing cortical neurons. *Science*, 1973, *182*, 599–601.

Pfaffmann, C. Gustatory afferent impulses. *J. Cellular and Comp. Physiol.*, 1941, *17*, 243–58.

Pfaffmann, C. The sense of taste. In J. Field, H. W. Magoun and V. E. Hall (eds.) *Handbook of Physiology*, Vol. 1. Washington, D. C.: American Physiological Society, 1959, pp. 507–33.

Pfister, M. H. Über das Verhalten der Hühner beim Tragen von Prismen. Doctoral dissertation, University of Innsbruck, 1955. Cited by R. L. Gregory, *Eye and brain* (2nd Ed.). New York: McGraw-Hill, 1973.

Piaget, J. *The origins of intelligence in children.* New York: International Universities Press, 1952.

Picton, T. W., Hillyard, S. A., Galambos, R., and Schiff, M. Human auditory attention: A central or peripheral process? *Science*, 1971, *173*, 351–53.

Postman, L., Bruner, J. S., and McGinnies, E. Personal values as selective factors in perception, *J. Abnormal and Soc. Psych.*, 1948, *43*, 142–54.

Pritchard, R. M. Stabilized images on the retina. *Scientific American*, 1961, *204* (6), 72–78.

Ratliff, F. *Mach bands: Quantitative studies on neural networks in the retina.* San Francisco: Holden-Day, 1965.

Rechtschaffen, A., and Mednich, S. A. The autokinetic word technique. *J. Abnormal and Soc. Psych.*, 1955, *51*, 346.

Reynolds, G. S., and Stevens, S. S. Binaural summation of loudness. *J. Acoust. Soc. America*, 1960, *32*, 1337–44.

Riesen, A. H. The development of visual perception in man and chimpanzee. *Science*, 1947, *106*, 107–8.

Riesen, A. H. Arrested vision. *Scientific American*, 1950, *183* (1), 16–19.

Riesen, A. H. Sensory deprivation. In E. Steller and J. M. Sprague (eds.), *Progress in physiological psychology*. New York: Academic Press, 1966, pp. 117–47.

Riesen, A. H., and Aarons, L. Visual movement and intensity discrimination in cats after early deprivation of pattern vision. *J. Comp. and Physiol. Psych.*, 1959, *52*, 142–49.

Riggs, L. A., Ratliff, F., Cornsweet, J.C., and Cornsweet, T. N. The disappearance of steadily fixated test objects. *J. Optical Soc. America*, 1953, *43*, 495–501.

Robinson, J. O. *The psychology of visual illusion.* London: Hutchinson and Co., Ltd., 1972.

Rock, I. *The nature of perceptual adaptation.* New York: Basic Books, 1966.

Rock, I. *An introduction to perception.* New York: Macmillan, 1975.

Rock, I., and Kaufman, L. The moon illusion. II. *Science*, 1962, *136*, 1023–31.

Rose, J. E., Gross, N. B., Geisler, C. D., and Hind, J. E. Some effects of binaural stimulation on the activity of single neurons in the inferior colliculus of the cat. *J. Neurophysiol.*, 1966, *29*, 288–314.

Rossi, P. J. Adaptation and negative aftereffect to lateral optical displacement in newly hatched chicks. *Science*, 1968, *160*, 430–32.

Rushton, W. A. H. Peripheral coding in the nervous system. In W. A. Rosenblith (ed.), *Sensory communication*. Cambridge, Mass.: M. I. T. Press, 1961, pp. 169–81.

Rushton, W. A. H. Visual adaptation. *Proceedings of the Royal Society of London*, B., 1965, *162*, 20–46.

Schlosberg, H. Stereoscopic depth from single pictures. *Am. J. Psych.*, 1941, *54*, 601–5.

Segall, M. H., Campbell, D. T., and Herskovits, M. J. *The influence of culture on visual perception.* Indianapolis: Bobbs-Merrill, 1966.

Sekuler, R. W., and Ganz, L. Aftereffect of seen motion with a stabilized retinal image. *Science,* 1963, *139,* 419–20.

Sekuler, R. W., and Pantle, A. A model for aftereffects of seen movement. *Vision Research,* 1967, *7,* 427–39.

Senden, M. von. Raum- und Gestaltauffassung bei operierten Blindgeborenen vor und nach der Operation. Leipzig: Barth, 1932. English translation by P. Heath, *Space and sight.* Glencoe, Ill.: Free Press, 1960.

Sherif, M. A study of some social factors in perception. *Archives of Psychology,* 1935, *187,* 60 pp.

Sherif, M. An experimental approach to the study of attitudes. *Sociometry,* 1937, *1,* 90–98.

Shlaer, R. An Eagle's eye: Quality of the retinal image. *Science,* 1972, *176,* 920–22.

Smith, D. V. Taste intensity as a function of area and concentration: Differentiation between compounds. *J. Exp. Psych.,* 1971, *87,* 163–71.

Smith, D. V., and McBurney, D. H. Gustatory cross-adaptation: Does a single mechanism code the salty taste? *J. Exp. Psych.,* 1969, *80,* 101–5.

Smith, K. U. *Delayed sensory feedback and behavior.* Philadelphia: W. B. Saunders Co., 1962.

Sokolov, E. N. *Perception and the conditioned reflex.* New York: Macmillan, 1963.

Sperry, R. W. Effect of 180 degree rotation of the retinal field on visuomotor coordination. *J. Exp. Zool.,* 1943, *92,* 263–79.

Sperry, R. W. Mechanism of neural maturation. In S. S. Stevens (ed.), *Handbook of experimental psychology.* New York: Wiley, 1951, pp. 236–80.

Sperry, R. W. The eye and the brain. *Scientific American,* 1956, *194* (5), 48–52.

Spitz, H. H., and Borland, M. D. Redundancy in line drawings of familiar objects: Effects of age and intelligence. *Cognitive Psychology,* 1971, *2,* 196–205.

Steinberg, J. C., and Gardner, M. B. The dependence of hearing impairment on sound intensity. *J. Acoust. Soc. America,* 1937, *9,* 11–23.

Stevens, J. C., and Cain, W. S. Effort in isometric muscular contractions related to force level and duration. *Perception and Psychophysics,* 1970, *8,* 240–44.

Stevens, J. C., and Rubin, L. L. Psychophysical scales of apparent heaviness and the size weight illusion. *Perception and Psychophysics,* 1970, *8,* 225–30.

Stevens, J. C., and Stevens, S. S. Brightness function: Effects of adaptation. *J. Optical Soc. America,* 1963, *53,* 375–85.

Stevens, S. S. On the psychophysical law. *Psych. Rev.,* 1957, *64,* 153–81.

Stevens, S. S. Adaptation-level vs. the relativity of judgment. *Am. J. Psych.,* 1958, *71,* 633–46.

Stevens, S. S. Sensation and psychological measurement. In E. G. Boring, H. S. Langfeld, and H. P. Weld (eds.), *Foundations of psychology.* New York: Wiley, 1948, pp. 250–68.

Stevens, S. S. Mathematics, measurement, and psychophysics. In S. S. Stevens (ed.), *Handbook of experimental psychology.* New York: Wiley, 1951, pp. 1–49.

Stevens, S. S., and Davis, H. *Hearing.* New York: Wiley, 1938.

Stevens, S. S., and Guirao, M. Loudness functions under inhibition. *Perception and Psychophysics,* 1967, *2,* 459–65.

Stratton, G. M. Some preliminary experiments on vision without inversion of the retinal image. *Psych. Rev.,* 1896, *3,* 611–17.

Stratton, G. M. Vision without inversion of the retinal image. *Psych. Rev.,* 1897a, *4,* 341–60.

Stratton, G. M. Vision without inversion of the retinal image. *Psych. Rev.,* 1897b, *4,* 463–81.

Stroop, J. R. Studies of interference in serial verbal reactions. *J. Exp. Psych.,* 1935, *18,* 643–62.

Supa, M., Cotzin, M., and Dallenbach, K. M. "Facial vision": The perception of obstacles by the blind. *Am. J. Psych.,* 1944, *57,* 133–83.

Svaetichin, G. The cone action potential. *Acta Physiologica Scandinavica,* 1956, *39,* 17–46.

Svaetichin, G., and MacNichol, E. F., Jr. Retinal mechanisms for chromatic and achromatic vision. *Annals of the New York Academy of Science,* 1958, *74,* 385–404.

Tasaki, I. Nerve impulses in individual auditory nerve fibers of guinea pig. *J. Neurophysiol.,* 1954, *17,* 97–122.

Taub, E. Prism compensation as a learning phenomenon: A phylogenetic perspective. In S. J. Freedman (ed.), *The neuropsychology of spatially orient ed behavior.* Homewood, Ill.: Dorsey Press, 1968, pp. 77–106.

Taub, E., and Goldberg, I. A. Prism adaptation: Control of intermanual transfer by distribution of practice. *Science,* 1973, *180,* 755–57.

Taylor, A. C. Selectivity of nerve fibers from the dorsal and ventral roots in the development of the frog limb. *J. Exp. Zool.,* 1944, *96,* 159–85.

Taylor, M. M., and Creelman, C. D. PEST: Efficient estimates on probability functions. *J. Acoust. Soc. America,* 1967, *41,* 782–87.

Teghtsoonian, R. On the exponent in Stevens' Law and the constant in Ekman's Law. *Psych. Rev.,* 1971, *78,* 71–80.

Toch, H. H. The effect of 'meaning' on the autokinetic illusion. *Am. J. Psych.,* 1962, *75,* 605–11.

Toch, H., and Schulte, R. Readiness to perceive violence as a result of police training. *Brit. J. Psych.,* 1961, *52,* 389–93.

Treisman, A. M. Strategies and models of selective attention. *Psych. Rev.,* 1969, *76,* 282–99.

Treisman, A. M., and Geffen, G. Selective attention: Perception or response? *Quart. J. Exp. Psych.,* 1967, *19,* 1–17.

Uexkull, J. von. *Streifzüge durch die Umwelten von Tieren and Menschen.* Berlin: Springer, 1934.

Wagner, H. G., MacNichol, E. F., Jr., and Wolbarsht, M. L. The response properties of single ganglion cells in the goldfish retina. *J. Gen. Physiol.,* 1960, *43,* Suppl. 2, 45–62.

Wald, G. Human vision and the spectrum. *Science,* 1945, *101,* 653–58.

Wald, G., and Brown, P. K. Human color vision and color blindness. *Cold Spring Harbor Symposia on Quantitative Biology,* 1965, *30,* 345–59.

Walk, R. D. Two types of depth discrimination by the human infant with five inches of visual depth. *Psychonomic Science,* 1969, *14,* 253–54.

Walk, R. D., and Gibson, E. J. A comparative and analytical study of visual depth perception. *Psychological Monographs,* 1961, *75* (519), entire issue.

Wallach, H. The perception of motion. *Scientific American,* 1959, *201* (1), 56–60.

Wallach, H., Kravitz, J. H., and Lindauer, J. A passive condition for rapid adaptation to displaced visual direction. *Am. J. Psych.,* 1963, *76,* 568–78.

Ward, W. D. Further observations on contralateral remote masking and related phenomena. *J. Acoust. Soc. America,* 1967, *42,* 593–600.

Wegel, R. L., and Lane, C. E. The auditory masking of one pure tone by another and its probable relation to the dynamics of the inner ear. *Physical Review*, 1924, *23*, 266–85.

Weinstein, S. Intensive and extensive aspects of tactile sensitivity as a function of body part, sex, and laterality. In D. R. Kenshalo (ed.), *The skin senses*. Springfield, Ill.: Charles C Thomas, 1968, 195–222.

Weiskrantz, L., Elliott, J., and Darlington, D. Preliminary observations on tickling oneself. *Nature*, 1971, *230*, 598–99.

Weiss, P. A. Further experimental investigations on the phenomenon of homologous response in transplanted amphibian limbs. IV. Reverse locomotion after the interchange of right and left limbs. *J. Comp. Neurol.*, 1937, *7*, 269–315.

Weisstein, N., and Bisaha, J. Gratings mask bars and bars mask gratings: Visual frequency response to aperiodic stimuli. *Science*, 1972, *176*, 1047–49.

Wetherill, G. B., and Levitt, H. Sequential estimation of points on a psychometric function. *Brit. J. Math. and Stat. Psych.*, 1965, *18*, 1–10.

White, B. L. An analysis of excellent early education practices: Preliminary report. *Interchange*, 1971, *2*, 71–88.

White, B. L., Castle, P., and Held, R. Observations on the development of visually-directed reaching. *Child Development*, 1964, *35*, 349–64.

White, B. L., and Held, R. Plasticity of sensorimotor development in the human infant. In J. F. Rosenblith and W. Allinsmith (eds.), *Causes of behavior*. Boston: Allyn & Bacon, 1966.

Witkin, H. A. The perception of the upright. *Scientific American*, 1959, *200* (2), 50–56.

Witkin, H. A., and Asch, S. E. Studies in space orientation. IV. *J. Exp. Psych.*, 1948, *38*, 762–82.

Witkin, H. A., Dyk, R. B., Fattuson, H. F., Goodenough, D. R., and Karp, S. A. *Psychological differentiation*. New York: Wiley, 1962.

Witkin, H. A., Lewis, H. B., Hertzman, M., Machover, K., Meissner, P. B. and Wapner, S. *Personality through perception*. New York: Harper & Row, 1954.

Wohlwill, J. F. Developmental studies of perception. *Psych. Bull.*, 1960, *57*, 249–88.

Wohlwill, J. F. Texture of the stimulus field and age as variables in the perception of relative distance in photographic slides. *J. Exp. Child Psych.*, 1965, *2*, 163–77.

Woodworth, R. S. The puzzle of color vocabularies. *Psych. Bull.*, 1910, *7*, 325–34.

Worden, F. G. Attention and auditory physiology. In E. Stellar and J. M. Sprague (eds.), *Progress in physiological psychology*, 1. New York: Academic Press, 1966, pp. 45–116.

Wright, W. D. A re-determination of the trichromatic coefficients of the spectral colours. *Transactions of the Optical Society* (London), 1928–29, *30*, 141–64.

Wright, W. D. *Researches on normal and defective colour vision*. St. Louis: Mosby, 1947.

Zajonc, R. B. Response suppression in perceptual defense. *J. Exp. Psych.*, 1962, *64*, 206–14.

Zimbardo, P. B., Marshall, G., and Maslach, C. Liberating behavior from time-bound control: Expanding the present through hypnosis. *J. App. Soc. Psych.*, 1971, *1*, 305–23.

Zubek, J. P., Pushkar, D., Sansom, W., and Gowing, J. Perceptual changes after prolonged sensory isolation (darkness and silence). *Canad. J. Psych.*, 1961, *15*, 83–100.

Index